HISTORY, ...EDOM

HISTORY, LABOUR, AND FREEDOM

Themes from Marx

G. A. COHEN

CLARENDON PRESS · OXFORD

1988

Oxford University Press, Walton Street, Oxford OX2 6DP
Oxford New York Toronto
Delhi Bombay Calcutta Madras Karachi
Petaling Jaya Singapore Hong Kong Tokyo
Nairobi Dar es Salaam Cape Town
Melbourne Auckland
associated companies in
Berlin Ibadan

Oxford is a trade mark of Oxford University Press

Published in the United States
by Oxford University Press, New York

British Library Cataloguing in Publication Data
Cohen, G. A.
History, labour and freedom : themes from Marx
1. Marxism. Historical materialism
I. Title
335.4'119
ISBN 0–19–824779–6
ISBN 0–19–824816–4 Pbk

Library of Congress Cataloging in Publication Data
Cohen: Gerald Allan, 1941–
History, labour, and freedom : themes from Marx / G. A. Cohen. p.cm.
Bibliography: p.
1. Marx, Karl, 1818–1883. 2. Historical materialism. 3. Labor and laboring
classes.
4. Liberty. I. Title.
HX39.55.C574 1988 335.4—dc19 88–19574
ISBN 0–19–824779–6 ISBN 0–19–824816–4 pbk.

Typeset by Pentacor Ltd, High Wycombe, Bucks
Printed and bound in Great Britain by
Biddles Ltd., Guildford and King's Lynn

*With gratitude and love
to Gideon, Miriam, and Sarah*

Preface

Marxism sees history as a protracted process of liberation—from the scarcity imposed on humanity by nature, and from the oppression imposed by some people on others. Members of ruling and subject classes share the cost of natural scarcity unequally, and Marxism predicts, and fights for, the disappearance of society's perennial class division.

The growth across the ages of the human power to produce defeats scarcity and thereby enables humanity to free itself from both material and social adversity. But the freedom to be had in the productive maturity of the species is necessarily lacking in the process which achieves that maturity. Unfreedom, exploitation, and indignity are the price which the mass of humanity must pay for the part they play in creating the material wherewithal of human liberation.

The book begins with an outline of the theory—historical materialism—which gives rigorous form to the Marxist vision. Historical materialism distinguishes sharply between fundamental and derivative elements in social existence, and Chapters 2 and 3 defend two of those sharp distinctions: between the economic base and the legal and political superstructure on the one hand, and between social being and personal consciousness on the other.

Jean-Paul Sartre said that, if human beings were not free, they would not need to be liberated. The aspiration to liberation presupposes an essential freedom of thought and action, which people display even under the least propitious conditions. Chapter 4 shows how individual freedom of choice is consistent with the historical materialist claim that the advent of socialism is inevitable. It is an attempt to reconcile confidence that a better society is bound to come with the imperatives of revolutionary activism.

Marxism represents social adversity as a consequence of material adversity. In my *Karl Marx's Theory of History* I defended the priority of the material side, and I argued that the succession of forms of society could be explained by an autonomous development of material power. Chapter 5 refutes a common and misplaced objection to that thesis, which was pressed with great sophistication by Joshua Cohen. The chapter vindicates the autonomous character of the material process of liberation against Cohen's counter-contention that social structures control that process and are therefore not explicable in terms of it.

While the first part of the book expounds historical materialism, and defends it against objections with which I disagree, in the second part I express some reservations of my own about the theory, and I offer reformulations of it which seek to accommodate them.

Chapter 6 exposes a serious ambiguity in the use of a key expression of the theory. I show that there are many ways in which relations of production, in the reactionary phase of the history of a social form, may be said to *fetter* the available productive forces, and I discuss the comparative merits of various proposals for removing unwanted ambiguity from the fettering concept.

Chapter 7 confronts a familiar argument which purports to prove the substantial truth of historical materialism, in advance of examination of the record of history. My refutation of the argument establishes that the question of the truth of historical materialism is far more open than many Marxists think it is.

One thing which makes that question open is the strength of non-material culture, much of which appears to lack grounding in material constraint. Chapter 7 is a somewhat unbuttoned meditation on that theme, and Chapter 8 is a reparative effort conducted in its light. I offer a revision of historical materialism, which, so I argue, preserves its spirit and import, and which renders it much less vulnerable to counter-example from the domain of non-material culture (for example, religion and nationalism).

The final part of the book studies the unfreedom and exploitation under which workers labour in contemporary class society, but its opening chapter describes a form of freedom which capitalist workers have and earlier exploited producers lacked. Chapter 11 is more about the injustice of the proletarian position than about its lack of freedom, but the latter theme is pursued in detail in the closing trio of chapters.

The book assembles previously published material, but I have done a lot of adding, subtracting, and revising, to eliminate repetition, to establish connections, and to bring the end-product closer to my present thinking than some of the original articles are. People contrast mere collections of essays with real books: in the terms of that distinction, this book is more real than some, but it is not completely real. It has a thematic unity which, I hope, compensates for occasional lapses of continuity in the passage from one chapter to another.

The articles on which I have drawn are listed on p. xvi below. I am grateful to the editors and publishers of the books and journals in which they appeared for permission to reprint material here.

Chapter 1 combines parts of 'Forces and Relations of Production' and 'A Reply to Four Critics', but its closing section is new.

Chapter 2 begins with new material, to which I have adjoined part of the response to criticisms of me by Steven Lukes which I gave in my 'Reply to Four Critics'.

Chapter 3 reproduces, with some modifications, a critique of the late John Plamenatz which was offered in the article from which the chapter takes its title.

Chapter 4 is a fresh go at a problem which I tried to solve in my article on 'Historical Inevitability and Human Agency in Marxism'. I rapidly became dissatisfied with the first six sections of that article, and they have been comprehensively rewritten for this book.

Chapter 5 replicates an article of the same name which I wrote together with Will Kymlicka, who was then at New College, Oxford, and who is now at Princeton. The joint authorship explains the chapter's use of 'we' instead of 'I', and its references to G. A. Cohen in the third person. I am grateful to Will for allowing me to reprint the article here.

Chapter 6 is substantially new: it is a five-fold expansion of one section of 'Forces and Relations of Production'.

Chapter 7 is a considerably extended version of a critique of Engels which appeared, in slightly different forms, in 'Being, Consciousness and Roles', and in 'Restricted and Inclusive Historical Materialism'.

Chapter 8 reproduces, with a few changes, the article which bears its name.

Chapter 9 is a revised and expanded version of the article of the same name.

Chapter 10 is a lightly revised reissue of 'Marx's Dialectic of Labour'.

Chapter 11 expands and revises the article from which it draws its title. It also incorporates a few pages of 'More on Exploitation and the Labour Theory of Value'.

Chapter 12 is a virtually unrevised reissue of a recently published article.

Chapter 13 is a somewhat revised version of the relevant article.

Chapter 14 is almost entirely unrevised. That is not because it represents, in every particular, my current view, but because I thought it inappropriate to alter the text of the lecture which it originally was.

The chapters of this book display different degrees of attachment to historical materialism, since a number of them derive from a period during which I was reconsidering my commitment to the theory. My initial ingestion of Marxism took place in a peculiar milieu, which I should here like to describe.

My parents were Jewish factory workers in Montreal who met in the course of struggles to build unionism in the garment trade, in the face of (literally) brutal boss and police repression. When I was four years old, they enrolled me in the Morris Winchewsky Yiddish School, which was run by a communist Jewish organization. It was the only school that I attended until I was eleven, when raids by the 'Red Squad' of the Province of Quebec police on the premises of the organization and on the school itself made it impossible for the school to continue. (This was in 1952, and the raids were part of the local contribution to the McCarthyite persecution then still proceeding in North America. The Quebecois version of McCarthyism was less insidious than the real article occurring south of the border, but it was also cruder and, especially for a child, more immediately frightening.)

That background caused me to be familiar with Marxist ideas pretty early on, and by the time I reached McGill University to embark on a BA I had read, with imperfect understanding, a number of what were called the 'classics' of Marxism. I was certain, at seventeen, that Engels's *Anti-Dühring* contained all the important philosophical truth that there was. I came to see its limitations as an undergraduate, and I concluded that its philosophical sections, by contrast with those on society and history, were naïve. But my commitment to historical materialism was more durable, and I long intended to expound and defend it as best I could, and eventually, in 1978, I published *Karl Marx's Theory of History: A Defence*, in fulfilment of that long-standing intention.

That book owed part of its character to the circumstance that I moved in 1961 from McGill to Oxford, where, under the benign guidance of Gilbert Ryle, I acquired the technique of analytical philosophy. Almost all politically committed students were, at that time, and throughout the sixties, hostile to Oxford philosophy. They regarded it as bourgeois, or trivial, or both. I saw that it was bourgeois, or, anyway, certainly not anti-bourgeois, but I experienced no antipathy to it. If you are young and left-wing, and you come to university with a thirst for relevant ideas, and academic philosophy of the Oxford kind is the first system of thought which you encounter, then it will be hard for you not to feel disappointed or even cheated by it, and it will be natural for you to think of Marxism as a powerful alternative and antidote to it. But if, as I did, you start with Marxism, then it is not difficult to take analytical philosophy on board. I came to Oxford already steeped in Marxism, and so, unlike most of my politically congenial contemporaries, I did not look to university philosophy to furnish me with ideas that mattered: I did not expect it to address itself to the questions agitating the real world. Hence Oxford philosophy did not disappoint me, in the way that it did so many of my contemporaries, and I used it with enthusiasm to clarify, as best I could, the central claims of historical materialism.

Karl Marx's Theory of History was a strenuous undertaking, since it was written, so to speak, in double harness: because it was a defence, and a defence of Marx, virtually every contention in it had to be both plausibly attributable to Marx and reasonable in its own right.

When I had finished the book, an unexpected thing happened. I came to feel, what I had not consciously anticipated when planning or writing it, that I had written the book in repayment for what I had received. It reflected gratitude to my parents, to the school which had taught me, to the political community in which I was raised. It was my homage to the milieu in which I learned the plain Marxism which the book defended. But, now that the book was written, the debt was paid, and I no longer felt obliged to adjust my thinking to that of Marx. I felt, for the first time, that I could think entirely for myself. I certainly did not forthwith stop believing what I had believed when I embarked upon the book, but I no longer experienced my commitment to those beliefs as an existential necessity.

In the aftermath of that loosening of the original attachment, I have thought more critically about historical materialism. But I have also shifted my attention to other topics, some of which are addressed in a rough-and-ready way in the final chapter of this book, and pursued with greater care in later work which it would have been inappropriate to reprint here. I think that three questions should command the attention of those of us who work within the Marxist tradition today. They are the questions of design, justification, and strategy, in relation to the project of opposing and overcoming capitalism. The first question is, What do we want? What, in general, and even not so general terms, is the form of the socialist society that we seek? The second question is, Why do we want it? What exactly is wrong with capitalism, and what is right about socialism? And the third question is, How can we achieve it? What are the implications for practice of the fact that the working class in advanced capitalist society is not now what it was, or what it was once thought to be?

In my work on those questions, and on many of the chapters in this book, I have had the inestimable benefit of membership in a small group of (sufficiently) like-minded investigators which was formed, through the initiative of Jon Elster, in 1979. We meet annually for a few days, and I should like to thank the group's members (Pranab Bardhan, Bob Brenner, Jon Elster, Adam Przeworski, John Roemer, Hillel Steiner, Robert Van der Veen, Philippe Van Parijs, and Erik Wright) for the stimulation they have given me and for their severe scrutiny of my efforts. There are also dozens of other people who made valuable criticisms of the drafts of the articles from which these chapters have been drawn, and in later exchanges. Because there have been so many of them, and because I have only an incomplete record and recall of their contributions, I hope that they will forgive me for not naming them. But I do have to name three people. The first is my friend Arnold Zuboff, whose fertile and razor-sharp mind is always at my disposal, and who has had a strongly improving influence on every part of this book. The second is Jo Wolff, who kindly agreed to read through the final manuscript, and who made many excellent criticisms and suggestions. And the third is John Roemer who suggested the book's title.

I thank my family for their forbearance when I was hard to live with because Marxist problems were persecuting me, and especially my wife Maggie, who not only offered her solidarity and support but also clarified difficult ideas for me. My gratitude to Michèle Jacottet, who processed the words and gave advice of several kinds, is also very great. Finally, I thank the members and staff of All Souls College for the generous manner in which they have received and encouraged me, during the opening years of my professorship here, when this book was completed.

G. A. Cohen

Oxford
Christmas 1987

Contents

Sources

Articles used in the Preparation of this Book:

'Marx's Dialectic of Labour', *Philosophy and Public Affairs* 3, no. 3 (Spring 1974), 235–61. © 1974 Princeton University Press.

'Being, Consciousness and Roles', in C. Abramsky (ed.), *Essays in Honour of E. H. Carr* (London, Macmillan, 1974), 82–97.

'The Labour Theory of Value and the Concept of Exploitation', *Philosophy and Public Affairs*, 8, no. 4 (Summer 1979), 338–60. © 1979 Princeton University Press.

'Freedom, Justice and Capitalism', *New Left Review*, 126 (1981), 3–16.

'The Structure of Proletarian Unfreedom', *Philosophy and Public Affairs*, 12, no. 1 (Winter 1983), 3–34. © 1983 Princeton University Press.

'Reconsidering Historical Materialism', in *Marxism: Nomos XXVI*: 227–52, edited by J. Roland Pennock and John W. Chapman. © 1983 New York University Press.

'Forces and Relations of Production', in B. Matthews (ed.), *A Hundred Years of Marxism* (London, Lawrence and Wishart, 1983), 111–35.

'More on Exploitation and the Labour Theory of Value', *Inquiry*, 26 (1983), 309–31.

'Reply to Four Critics', *Analyse und Kritik*, 5 (1983), 195-222.

'Restricted and Inclusive Historical Materialism', *Irish Philosophical Journal*, 1 (1984), 3–31.

'Historical Inevitability and Human Agency in Marxism', in Sir John Mason (ed.), *Predictability in Science and Society* (London, The Royal Society and the British Academy, 1986), 65–87.

'Are Disadvantaged Workers who Take Hazardous Jobs Forced to Take Hazardous Jobs?' in G. Ezorsky (ed.), *Moral Rights in the Workplace* (Albany, State University of New York Press 1987), 61–80.

'Human Nature and Social Change in the Marxist Conception of History', *Journal of Philosophy*, 85 (1988), 171–91.

A Note on References

Full titles of works cited, with place and date of publication, are given in the list at the end of the volume. Passages in italics are that way in the original, unless otherwise stated. With minor exceptions, the modern editions cited of works by Marx and Engels are English translations, but I have often modified the translation, drawing on other translations of the same works, and usually in order to produce a more literal translation.

I

*Historical Materialism—Exposition
and Defence*

I

FORCES AND RELATIONS OF PRODUCTION

1. In the first section of this chapter I present, in summary form, the interpretation of historical materialism which I offered in my book on *Karl Marx's Theory of History*.[1] I define and connect the concepts of forces and relations of production, and I maintain that the basic explanations of historical materialism are *functional* explanations. Section 2 places the idea that all history is the history of class struggle in the framework of the theory expounded in section 1. A central claim of that theory is the *Development Thesis*, which says that the productive forces tend to grow in power throughout history. In section 3 I try to dispel a widespread misconstrual of my argument for the Development Thesis, and in section 4 I explore ways of modifying both that argument and our understanding of what the Development Thesis implies.

KMTH says, and it says that Marx says, that history is, fundamentally, the growth of human productive power, and that forms of society (which are organized around economic structures) rise and fall according as they enable and promote, or prevent and discourage, that growth.

The canonical text for this interpretation of Marx is his famous 1859 Preface to *A Contribution to the Critique of Political Economy*, some sentences of which we shall look at shortly. I argue (in section 3 of chapter 6 of *KMTH*) that the Preface makes explicit the standpoint on society and history which Marx occupied throughout his mature writings, on any reasonable view of the date at which he reached theoretical maturity. In attending to the Preface, we are not looking at just one text among many, but at that text which gives the clearest statement of the theory of historical materialism.

The presentation of the theory in the Preface begins as follows:

In the social production of their life men enter into definite relations that are indispensable and independent of their will, relations of production which *correspond* to a definite stage of development of their material productive forces. The sum total of these relations constitutes the economic

---

[1] This work is referred to hereafter as *KMTH*.

structure of society, the real *basis, on which arises* a legal and political superstructure . . . [2]

These sentences mention three ensembles, the productive forces, the relations of production, and the superstructure, among which certain explanatory connections (here indicated by italics) are asserted. I shall first say what I think the ensembles are, and I shall then describe the explanatory connections among them. (All of what follows is argued for in *KMTH*, but not all of the argument is given in what follows, which may therefore wrongly impress the reader as dogmatic.)

The productive forces are those facilities and devices which are used to productive effect in the process of production: means of production on the one hand, and labour power on the other. Means of production are physical productive resources: tools, machinery, raw materials, premises, and so forth. Labour power includes not only the strength of producers, but also their skills, and the technical knowledge (which they need not understand) they apply when labouring. Marx says, and I agree, that this subjective dimension of the productive forces is more important than the objective or means of production dimension; and within the more important dimension the part most capable of development is knowledge. Hence, in its later stages, the development of the productive forces is largely a function of the development of productively useful science. If you want to turn a productively advanced society into a backward one, you will not achieve much by destroying its physical instruments of production. As long as its productive know-how remains intact, the society will before long restore itself, as Germany did when, according to a once prevalent view, its industry had been devasted by the Second World War. Some think that Germany suffered less material destruction than the word 'devastated' suggests, and perhaps they are right. But the old view about the German recovery was not a ridiculous one, and the reason why it was not ridiculous is because there is, as I am here maintaining, no inherent barrier to reconstituting the physical side of productive power, as long as its cognitive side is undamaged. If, by contrast, you somehow remove productive know-how from the heads of producers, but spare their material facilities, then, unless they import knowledge afresh from abroad, their advanced facilities will decay and they will need centuries to recoup.

---

[2] *Critique of Political Economy*, 20 (my emphases).

Note that Marx takes for granted in the Preface, what elsewhere he asserts outright, that 'there is a continual movement of growth in productive forces'.[3] I argue (in section 6 of chapter 2 of *KMTH*) that the right standard for measuring that growth in power is how much (or, rather, how little) labour must be spent with given forces to produce what is required to satisfy the inescapable physical needs of the immediate producers.[4] This criterion of social productivity is less equivocal than others which may come to mind, but the decisive reason for choosing it is not its relative clarity but its theoretical appropriateness: if relations of production correspond, as the theory says they do, to levels of development of productive power, then this way of measuring productive power makes the theory's correspondence thesis more plausible.[5]

I do not say that the only explanatory feature of productive power is how much there is of it: qualitative features of productive forces also help to explain the character of relations of production. My claim is that in so far as quantity of productive power is what matters, the key quantity is how much time it takes to (re)produce the producers, that is to say, to produce what they must consume to be able to continue working (as opposed to what they actually consume, which generally, and in contemporary capitalist society considerably, exceeds what they must consume). It is the amount of time available beyond, or surplus[6] to, that historically dwindling requirement that is so fateful for the form of the second ensemble we need to describe, the relations of production.

Relations of production are relations of economic power, of the economic power[7] people enjoy or lack over labour power and means of production. In a capitalist society relations of production include the economic power capitalists have over means of production, the economic power workers (unlike slaves) have over

---

[3] *The Poverty of Philosophy*, 166.

[4] As opposed, for example, to their socially developed needs, reference to which would be inappropriate here (though not, of course, everywhere).

[5] For a set of correspondences of relations to forces of production, see *KMTH* 198, and pp. 155–6 below.

[6] This is not the only important concept of surplus in Marxism, but I invoke it here because it is a concept of something purely material, and I conceive historical materialism as an attempt to explain the social by reference to the material: see *KMTH* 61, 98, and ch. 4 *passim* for defence of the distinction between material and social properties of society.

[7] I call such power 'economic' in virtue of what it is power over, and irrespective of the means of gaining, sustaining, or exercising the power, which need not be economic. See *KMTH* 223–4 and ch. 2 below *passim*.

their own labour power, and the lack of economic power workers have over means of production. Immediate producers may have no economic power, some economic power, or total economic power over their own labour power and over the means of production they use. If we permit ourselves a measure of idealization, we can construct table 1, which rather neatly distinguishes the relations of production of historically important immediate producers.

TABLE I

	Amount of economic power over	
	His labour power	The means of production he uses
Slave	None	None
Serf	Some	Some
Proletarian	All	None
Independent	All	All

The table names three subordinate producers, and one independent. Since one may have no, some, or total economic power over one's labour power and over the means of production one uses, there are nine cases to consider. I think it is diagnostically valuable to inquire which of the remaining five cases are logically or otherwise possible, and which in turn of those are actual, but I shall not enter on that discussion here.[8]

Now the sum total of relations of production in a given society is said to constitute the economic structure of that society, which is also called—in relation to the superstructure—the basis, or base, or foundation. The economic structure or base therefore consists of relations of production only: it does not include the productive forces. It is true that to exclude the productive forces from the economic structure runs against the usual construal of Marx,[9] but he actually said that the economic structure is constituted of relations of production, and he had systematic reasons for saying so.[10] People mistakenly suppose that the productive forces belong to the economic base because they wrongly think that the

---

[8] The discussion is pursued at *KMTH* 66–9.

[9] See *KMTH* 29 n.2 for a list of authors who take for granted that productive forces belong to the economic structure.

[10] See *KMTH* 28–9. I have now, alas, noticed a passage which seems to locate the forces within the economic base, but I shall continue to situate them outside it, since

explanatory importance of the forces ensures their membership in it. But while the forces indeed possess that importance, they are not part of the economic base.[11] To stay with the spatial metaphor, they are below the economic foundation, the ground on which it rests.[12] (Since it consists of relations of economic power, the economic base would be obliterated by a fever of social disobedience in which all economic power melted away, yet means of production and technical knowledge, and, therefore, the productive forces, remain intact in that fantasy. Total social disarray eliminates economic structure while leaving the productive forces entirely unchanged.)

The Preface describes the superstructure as legal and political. So it at any rate includes the legal and state institutions of society, or at least some of them. It is customary to locate other institutions within it too, and it is controversial what its correct demarcation is: my own view is that there are strong textual and systematic reasons for supposing that the superstructure is a lot smaller than many commentators think it is.[13] It is certainly false that every non-economic social phenomenon is superstructural: artistic creation, for example, is demonstrably not, just as such, superstructural for Marx. In this exposition I shall discuss property law only, which is uncontroversially a part of the superstructure.

So much for the identity of the three ensembles mentioned in the Preface. Now relations of production are said to *correspond* to the level of development of the productive forces, and in turn to be a *foundation* on which a superstructure rises. I think these are ways of saying that the level of development of the productive forces explains the nature of the production relations, and that they in turn explain the character of the superstructure co-present with them. But what kind of explanation is ventured here? I argue that in each case what we have is a species of functional explanation.

the theoretical reasons for doing so strike me as overwhelming. (The recalcitrant passage is at the foot of *Capital* i, 175).

[11] And, in my view, they are not *economic* phenomena of any kind: my reasons for denying that they are will be found in *KMTH*, ch. 4, sect. 1.

[12] See *KMTH* 30 for a distinction between the material and the economic bases of society: the productive forces belong to the former and are therefore not part of the latter.

[13] I criticize the common practice of overpopulating the superstructure in my review of Melvin Rader's *Marx's Interpretation of History*. For a systematic way of confining the superstructure, see ch. 9 sects. 6, 8 below.

What is functional explanation? Here are two examples of it: 'Birds have hollow bones because hollow bones facilitate flight', 'Shoe factories operate on a large scale because of the economies large scale brings'. In each case something (birds having hollow bones, shoe factories operating on a large scale) which has a certain effect (flight facilitation, economies of scale) is explained by the fact that it has that effect.

But now let me be somewhat more precise.[14] Suppose that e is a cause and f is its effect, and that we are offered a functional explanation of e in terms of its possession of that effect. Note first that the form of the explanation is not: e occurred because f occurred. If that were its form, functional explanation would be the exact opposite of ordinary causal explanation, and it would have the fatal defect that it represented a later occurrence as explaining an earlier one. Nor may we say that the form of the explanation is 'e occurred because it caused f'. Similar constraints on explanation and time order rule that candidate out: by the time e has caused f, e has occurred, so that the fact that it caused f could not explain its occurrence. The only remaining candidate, which I therefore elect, is: e occurred because it would cause f, or, less tersely but more properly: e occurred because the situation was such that an event like e would cause an event like f.

Now if this account of what functional explanations are is correct, then the main explanatory theses of historical materialism are functional explanations, for the following reasons: Marx never denied, and he sometimes asserted, and it is, moreover, manifestly true, that superstructures hold foundations together, and that relations of production control the development of the productive forces. Yet Marx also held that the character of the superstructure is explained by the nature of the base, and that the latter is explained by the nature of the productive forces. If the intended explanations are functional ones, we have consistency between the effect of A on B and the explanation of A by B, *and I do not know any other way of rendering historical materialism consistent.*[15]

---

[14] But not as precise as in *KMTH*, ch. 9 sects. 4, 7, and ch. 10, where the structure of functional explanation is described in greater detail.

[15] The only author who, to my knowledge, shows a complete understanding of the problem but attempts a different solution to it is Philippe Van Parijs, whose solution to the problem I do not understand. See his 'Marxism's Central Puzzle', and my comments in 'Reply to Four Critics', 204–6.

I shall now expound in greater detail one of the two functional explanatory theses, that which concerns base and superstructure.

The base, it will be recalled, is the sum total of production relations, these being relations of power over labour capacity and means of production. The capitalist's control of means of production is an illustration. And the superstructure, we saw, has more than one part, exactly what its parts are being somewhat uncertain, but certainly one *bona fide* part of it is the legal system, which will occupy us here.

In a capitalist society capitalists have effective power over means of production. What confers that power on a given capitalist, say an owner of a factory? On what can he rely if others attempt to take control of the factory away from him? An important part of the answer is this: he can rely on the law of the land, which is enforced by the might of the state. It is no great oversimplification to say that it is his legal right which causes him to have his economic power, since what he is effectively able to do depends on what he is legally entitled to do. And this is in general true in law-abiding society with respect to all economic powers and all economic agents. We can therefore say: in law-abiding society people have the economic powers they do because they have the legal rights they do.

That seems to refute the doctrine of base and superstructure, since here superstructural conditions—what legal rights people have—determine basic ones—what their economic powers are. Yet although it seems to refute the doctrine of base and superstructure, it cannot be denied. And it would not only seem to refute it, but actually would refute it, were it not possible, *and therefore mandatory* (for historical materialists), to present the doctrine of base and superstructure as an instance of functional explanation. For we can add, to the undeniable truth emphasized above, the further thesis that the given capitalist enjoys the stated right because it belongs to a structure of rights, a structure which obtains because it sustains an analogous structure of economic power. The content of the legal system is explained by its function, which is to help sustain an economy of a particular kind. People do usually get their powers from their rights, but in a manner which is not only allowed but demanded by the way historical materialism explains superstructural rights by reference to basic powers. Hence the effect of the law of property on the economy is not, as is often supposed, an embarrassment to historical materialism. It is something which historical materialism is committed to emphasizing, because of the particular way in which it explains law in terms of economic conditions.

Legal structures rise and fall when and because they sustain and frustrate forms of economy which, I now add, advance the development of the productive forces. The addition implies an explanation why whatever economic structure obtains at a given time does obtain at that time. Once more the explanation is a functional one: the prevailing production relations prevail *because* they are relations which advance the development of the productive forces. The existing level of productive power determines what relations of production would raise its level, and relations of that type consequently obtain. In other words: if production relations of kind *k* obtain, then that is because *k*-type relations are suitable to the development of the forces, in virtue of their existing level of development: that is the canonical form of the explanation in the standard case. But I should also mention the transitional case, in which the relations are not suitable to the development of the forces but, on the contrary, fetter them. In transitional cases the prevailing relations obtain because they recently *were* suitable to the development of the forces, and the class they empower has managed to maintain control despite their no longer being so: it is because ruling classes have an interest in the maintenance of obsolete relations that their *immediate* replacement by freshly suitable relations is not to be expected. People do not rush towards the dustbin of history just as soon as they have played out their historical role.

Now since

1. the level of development of productive power explains why certain relations, and not others, would advance productive power,

and

2. relations which advance productive power obtain because they advance productive power,

it follows that

3. the level of development of productive power explains the nature of the economic structure (of, that is, the sum total of production relations).

Proposition (3) assigns explanatory primacy to the productive forces. Note that neither (1) nor (2), taken separately from the other, establishes that (3), the Primacy Thesis, is true. It should be evident that (1) does not assign explanatory primacy over the production relations to the productive forces, since (1) says nothing about what sort of economic structure will in fact obtain. And, although it is less evident, it is also true that (2) does not confer explanatory primacy on the level of development of the forces. The reason why (2) does not do so—the reason, that is, why (2) is insufficient to establish (3)—is that (2) is consistent with (3)-defeating non-(1) explanations of the character relations must possess to advance productive power. One such non-(1) explanation would be:

4. The dominant ideology, which is not explained by the level of development of the productive forces, determines what relations would advance that development further.

Figure 1[16] shows how (3) is derived from (1) and (2): (1) says that the level of development of the productive forces explains why relations of kind k would now raise that level, and (2) says that the fact that relations of that kind are apt to raise the level of development of the forces explains why just such relations obtain. Proposition (3) is derived through deletion of the middle portion of the schema, and it is justified, given (1) and (2), by the transitivity of explanation.

Now to say that A explains B is not necessarily to indicate *how A* explains B. The child who knows that the match burst into flame because it was struck may not know how the latter event explains the former, because he is ignorant of the relationship between friction and heat, the contribution of oxygen to combustion, and so on. In a widely favoured idiom, he may not know the *mechanism* linking cause and effect, or, as I prefer to say, he may be unable to *elaborate* the explanation. In the relevant sense of 'how', we require

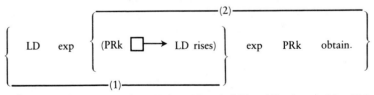

---

16 It comes from p. 220 of my 'Walt on Historical Materialism', an article which provides further clarification of the *KMTH* claims about the relationship between forces and relations of production.

an answer to the questions: *How does the fact that the economic structure promotes the development of the productive forces explain the character of the economic structure?* and *How does the fact that the superstructure protects the base explain the character of the superstructure?* Recall the functional explanation of the hollow bones of birds: to say, correctly, that birds have hollow bones because the feature is useful for flight is not to say how its usefulness accounts for its emergence and/or persistence. To that question Lamarck gave an unacceptable answer and Darwin an excellent one, which was later rendered even better, through developments in genetic theory. To corresponding questions about explanations of large scale in terms of economies of scale one may answer by referring to conscious human purposes, or to an economic analogue of chance variation and natural selection, or to some mix of the two.[17] But no one has given good answers to the similar questions (italicized above) about historical materialism. I offer some not very satisfactory answers in chapter 10 of *KMTH*. This seems to me an important area of future research for historical materialists, since the functional construal of their doctrine is hard to avoid.[18]

Let me now summarize my argument for the thesis that the chief explanatory claims of historical materialism are functional in form. Those claims are that

  3. the level of development of productive power explains the nature of the economic structure

and

  5. the economic structure explains the nature of the superstructure.

I take (3) and (5) to be functional explanations because I cannot otherwise reconcile them with two further Marxian theses, namely that

  6. the economic structure promotes the development of the productive forces

and

  7. the superstructure stabilizes the economic structure.

(6) and (7) entail that the economic structure is functional for the

[17] See *KMTH* 287–9.
[18] For valuable work on the problem of the mechanism in functional explanation, see Van Parijs, *Evolutionary Explanation in the Social Sciences*.

development of the productive forces, and that the superstructure is functional for the stability of the economic structure. These claims do not by themselves entail that economic structures and super-structures are *explained* by the stated functions: A may be functional for B even though it is false that A exists *because* it is functional for B. (The bridge of my nose is functional for my vision, since it helps to support my spectacles, but, unlike my right eye, it does not exist *because* it is functional for vision.) But (6) and (7), *in conjunction with* (3) *and* (5), do force us to treat historical materialist explanation as functional. No other treatment preserves consistency between the explanatory primacy of the productive forces over the economic structure and the massive control of the latter over the former, or between the explanatory primacy of the economic structure over the superstructure and the latter's regu-lation of the former.

I hold that the central explanations of historical materialism are functional explanations, and I defend functional explanation as an explanatory device, but I do not defend the sloppy functional explanatory theorizing in which so many Marxists engage.[19]

Many Marxist exercises in functional explanation fail to satisfy even the preliminary requirement of showing that A is functional for B (whether or not it is also *explained* by its function(s)). Take, for example, the claim that the contemporary capitalist state functions to protect and sustain the capitalist system. Legislation and policy in the direct interest of the capitalist class can reasonably be regarded as confirming it. But what about putative counter-examples, such as social welfare provision and legal immunities enjoyed by trade unions? These too might be functional for capitalism, in an indirect way, but that is something which needs to be argued with care, not just asserted. But those who propound the general claim about the state rarely trouble to say what sort of evidence would falsify or weaken it, and therefore every action of the state is treated as confirmatory, since there is always some way, legitimate or spurious, in which the action can be made to look functional.

Methodological indiscipline is then compounded when, having satisfied himself that state policy is functional, the theorist treats it, without further argument, as also functionally explained. He proceeds from 'A is functional for B' to 'B functionally explains A'

---

[19] For an impressive catalogue of methodologically lax uses of functional explanation, see Jon Elster's 'Marxism, Functionalism and Game Theory'.

without experiencing any need to justify the step, if, indeed, he notices that he has taken a step from one position to a distinct and stronger one.

2. 'The history of all hitherto existing society,' says *The Communist Manifesto*, 'is the history of class struggles.'[20] Yet class struggle was hardly mentioned in the foregoing outline of historical materialism. Therefore, a critic might say, either Marx had more than one theory of history, or that outline misrepresents his views.

One response would be to deflate the theoretical value of the quoted remark by emphasizing its political role as the first sentence of the main body of an insurrectionary text. But I prefer to leave the sentence intact and accommodate it. I do not want to deny that all history is the history of class struggle.

Why, then, did class struggle receive so little attention in section 1? Because that section was devoted to the fundamental explanations of the course of history and the structure of society, not to the main events of that course and the surface relief of society, where class struggle looms large.

There are two ways of accepting the *Manifesto* sentence without sacrificing the theory of section 1. The first, and less interesting, way is to take it as saying that *there is always a class struggle going on*. One may claim, in that spirit, that all history is the history of class struggle, without implying that that is all that history is, or even that that is what history most fundamentally is.

In the second way of taking the sentence, all history is the history of class struggle in the more important sense that *major historical changes are brought about by class struggle*. Yet that is consistent with the doctrine of section 1, since (so historical materialism says) if we want to know why class struggle effects this change rather than that, we must turn to the dialectic of forces and relations of production which governs class behaviour and is not explicable in terms of it, and which determines what the long-term outcome of class struggle will be.

Things other than forces and relations of production, such as the interactional structures studied by game theory,[21] help to explain

[20] *The Communist Manifesto*, 482.
[21] Jon Elster has persuaded me that game theory is supremely relevant to certain Marxist concerns, but I deny that it can replace, or even supplement, functional explanation at the very heart of historical materialism.

the vicissitudes of class struggle and the strategies pursued in it, but they cannot give a Marxist answer to the question why class wars (as opposed to battles) are settled one way rather than another. *Marx finds the answer in the character of the productive forces*: 'The conditions under which definite productive forces can be applied are the conditions of the rule of a definite class of society.'[22] The class which rules through a period, or emerges triumphant from epochal conflict does so because it is best suited, most able and disposed, to preside over the development of the productive forces at the given time. That answer may be untenable, but I cannot envisage an alternative to it which would qualify as historical materialist. It is, moreover, an answer which Marx did not merely give when generalizing about history, but which he applied to cases, as, for example, when he said that

If the proletariat overthrows the political rule of the bourgeoisie, its victory will only be temporary . . . as long as the material conditions have not yet been created which make necessary the abolition of the bourgeois mode of production.[23]

Note that Marx writes not 'make possible' but 'make necessary', a phrase which limits what can be independently decided by class struggle more than the former one would. *The Communist Manifesto* contains similar phrases,[24] and therefore cannot be recruited to the non-Marxist view that all history is, in the final analysis, *explained* by class struggle.

Prosecuting his contention that Marxism should abandon functional explanation and contract a liaison with game theory, Jon Elster remarks that 'game theory is invaluable to any analysis of the historical process that centres on exploitation, struggle, alliances and revolution.'[25] But for Marxian analysis those phenomena are not primary but, as it were, immediately secondary, on the periphery of the centre: they are among the 'forms in which men become conscious of the conflict [between forces and relations of production] and fight it out.[26] To put the point differently, we may

[22] *The German Ideology*, 52.
[23] *Moralising Criticism and Critical Morality*, 319; see Allen Wood, *Karl Marx*, 250 n. 41 for a list of texts which carry a similar message.
[24] According to the *Manifesto*, the 'economic and political dominion of the bourgeois class' was an outcome of the fact that feudal relations of production had become fetters on productive progress and therefore '*had* to be burst asunder' (p. 489).
[25] Elster, 'Marxism, Funtionalism and Game Theory', 453.
[26] Preface to *Critique of Political Economy*, 21.

say that the items of Elster's list are the actions at the centre of the historical process, but for Marxism there are also items more basic than actions at its centre.

By 'revolution' Elster must mean the political phenomenon of transfer of state power, as opposed to the transformation of economic structure political revolution initiates or reflects.[27] Many facts about political revolutions are accessible to game theoretical explanation, but not the world-historical facts that there was a bourgeois revolution and that there will be a proletarian one (if there will be a proletarian one).

While realizing that I insist on a 'fundamentalist' reading of historical materialism, Richard Miller notes that 'Cohen . . . allows that political and ideological struggle may be essential to the destruction of the old social relations.'[28] Indeed, and I am prepared to go further. I do not wish to deny that class struggle is always essential for social transformation. My position does not prevent me from accepting Marx and Engels' statement that 'the class struggle is the immediate driving power of history'.[29] On the contrary: it is the doctrine expounded in section 1 of this chapter which illuminates the otherwise puzzling occurrence of the word 'immediate' in this important sentence. 'Immediate' is opposed to 'underlying'.

The reader might now agree that the following characterization of my views distorts them:

Cohen . . . seems committed to the view that the kind of human activity capable of effecting social change would have to be not consciously political activity but technical and scientific activity: the invention of new technology, having as its unconscious byproduct the emergence of new social relations.[30]

[27] A clear distinction between transformation of economic structure and political revolution is made at ibid. 21.

[28] 'Productive Forces and the Forces of Change', 94. But Miller appears to think that this view of mine is an optional and rather arbitrarily added extra, 'readily detachable' from a theory assigning primacy to the development of the productive forces, since such a theory would 'suggest the effectiveness of an alternative to revolution, in which change is brought about by appeals to material desires common to all classes' ('Producing Change', 68). This rather astonishingly presupposes that the material interest of humanity could not conflict with the material interest of ruling class persons. For my part, I expect no one under socialism to be as rich as Rockefeller, and I therefore expect Rockefeller to be hostile to the idea of socialism.

[29] It comes from their letter of 17–18 Sept. 1879 to Bebel, Liebknecht, and Bracke: see *Selected Correspondence*, 307. (The word translated 'immediate' is *nächste*.)

[30] Richard Norman, review of *KMTH* 6.

I do not see how one can wring out of *KMTH* a denial that consciously political activity effects social change. How could an explanation why politics effects this social change rather than that one entail a denial that politics effects social change? Marx was not being untrue to what I claim was his theory when he called on workers, rather than scientists and technicians, to revolutionize society. In encouraging workers to bring about social change he was not asking them to bring about what would explain their doing so: the exhaustion of the progressive capacity of the capitalist order, and the availability of enough productive power to install a socialist one.

I admitted in section 1 that I do not have a good answer to the question how productive forces select economic structures which promote their development. To be sure, we can say that the adjustment of relations to forces occurs through class struggle. But that is not a fully satisfying answer to the stated question, since it does not specify the filiation, or filiations, from contradiction between forces and relations of production to the class struggle which is supposed to resolve it. What activates the prospective new class? What ensures its victory? These are the questions that need attention, and not only for the sake of good theory.[31]

I do not, then, 'downplay' 'the practical political significance', for Marxism, of class struggle.[32] In the Marxism I defend, class struggle has primary political significance, but the political dimension of society is not itself primary. The Marxist theory of history loses its coherence when it ceases to assign primacy to the development of the productive forces.

Milton Fisk would challenge this separation of politics from the development of the productive forces.[33] According to Fisk,

There is a political factor that enters into the development of the productive forces. The development of the productive forces within a set of

---

[31] For good criticisms of my failure to deal well with these questions see Elster, 'Cohen on Marx's Theory of History', 124; Levine and Wright, 'Rationality and Class Struggle' 58 ff.; Joshua Cohen, review of *KMTH*, 266 ff. In the rest of this section I deal with less good criticism, which is due to Milton Fisk. My reply to it is of rather secondary interest, and non-zealous readers may wish to move immediately to sect. 3.

[32] Suchting, '"Productive Forces" and "Relations of Production"', 174.

[33] He also disapproves, more generally, of my disposition to achieve clarity through recourse to 'sharp separations': I discuss that methodological question in ch. 3 sect. 3 below.

productive relations has limits set by the willingness of people to cooperate under those relations to develop the productive forces. It would be nice if we could say that their cooperation will be forthcoming when those relations have the potential for developing the forces. But the claim would be circular since the potential of the relations to develop the forces depends crucially on cooperation.[34]

But the stated claim is not, as Fisk contends, circular. For the fact that co-operation is a necessary condition of the relations *actually* developing the forces does not show that co-operation is a necessary condition of *their possessing the potential to do so*, in one pertinent reading of that phrase. Relations might possess the potential to develop the forces in the sense that if co-operation with them is forthcoming, they will do so: co-operation is evidently not necessary to their possessing *that* potential.

What is more, some relations would not develop the forces even if co-operation with them was assured. It follows that this hypothesis, of which the penultimate sentence in the above extract is an inexplicit formulation, is neither trivial nor circular: *co-operation is forthcoming just when, the relations being otherwise suitable, co-operation is crucial to the development of the forces.* (Consider the analogous hypothesis that pilots will man just those planes which are apt to fly when manned. The fact that these same planes would not fly unmanned does not make that plausible hypothesis circular.)

Now the non-circular and substantive claim italicized above is false for periods of transition from one social form to another, since, during such periods, more than one set of relations would, with co-operation, develop the forces, and it is logically impossible for more than one set to obtain. When 'the productive forces have been developed sufficiently under the existing productive relations to sustain a new social order'[35] both the old relations (at least for a time) and the prospective new ones would, with co-operation, develop the forces further, and in such a period which relations prevail indeed becomes what Fisk calls a political question, and one whose answer is not settled by the state of the productive forces. Those who falsely suppose that its answer is objectively available, and does not depend on class struggle, divide, as Fisk perceptively remarks, into 'adventurists [who] accuse opportunists of over-

[34] 'The Concept of Primacy', 192.
[35] Ibid.

estimating the ability of the ruling class to develop the productive forces, and opportunists [who] accuse adventurists of under-estimating that ability'[36] I agree with Fisk that both sides in that dispute suppose, wrongly, that there is a theoretical answer to a crucial question of practice.

But not all cases are transitional cases. Let us suppose, with Fisk,[37] that there was no objective answer to the question whether the Western ruling class could still develop the productive forces after 1945. Then either he thinks that there is never such an answer, or he grants that there sometimes is. But if he thinks that there never is, he is no Marxist. No Marxist, indeed no one with a shred of sociological initiation, could think that the British capitalist class might have been overthrown in 1795. A Marxist may think that there are cases of Fisk-like indeterminancy, but not that they are the general case. And I wonder whether Fisk himself really thinks that they are the general case. He refers, as we saw, to a time when 'the productive forces have been developed sufficiently . . . to sustain a new social order'.[38] That reference implies that there are other times when a new social order is impossible because the forces are *not* developed enough to sustain it. But if a new order is impossible for that reason, then Fisk will surely agree that it is impossible for an objective reason, which is independent of human will—in which case his disagreement with me disappears. He can only continue to disagree on the bizarre alternative view that even then the new order is impossible *simply* because people are unprepared to co-operate with it. Such a view combines a Utopian belief that what sort of society we have depends entirely on human will, with an un-Utopian belief that, for no objective reason, the required human will is sometimes necessarily unforthcoming.

The vicissitudes of class struggle decide just *when* a ruling class is supplanted, once a superior social order is objectively possible. But if one goes beyond that and says that the vicissitudes of class struggle decide whether or not the ruling class is supplanted at all, so that there is no objectively grounded answer to the question whether it will, in the end, go, then one denies the parameters within which, for Marxism, class struggle operates.

In my view class war is like war, and in war there are three pertinent possibilities:

[36] Ibid. 194.
[37] Ibid. 193.   [38] Ibid. 192.

i. We know that if we engage with the enemy, we shall win.

ii. We know that if we engage with the enemy, we shall lose.

iii. We know neither of these things, either because it it too difficult to know which of them is true, or because neither is true.

It might be thought that (i) and (ii) are not historically important cases.[39] I disagree. To be sure, they are not the cases in which there is likely to be massive class struggle: we will not engage in case (ii), and presuming , as one can, that they know what we know they will not engage in case (i). To the extent that people are knowledgeable and rational, (iii) is the only case in which class struggle will rage. But it is a matter of great historical importance that (i) and (ii) are true, when they are, and that classs struggle is, accordingly, muted. It is absurd to deny the historical importance of non-transitional periods.

3. The second paragraph of section 1 above entails two theses about forces and relations of production, the second of which was designated '3' on p. 10 above and the first of which is here numbered for the first time:

3. The level of development of productive power explains the nature of the economic structure.

8. The productive forces tend to develop throughout history.

In *KMTH*[40] I called (8) the Development Thesis, and (3) the Primacy Thesis: (3) asserts the explanatory primacy of the productive forces over the relations of production. I showed, in chapter 6 of *KMTH*, that Marx advanced both theses, and I then proceeded to argue for them in their own right. In the latter exercise, I began by adducing considerations in support of (8), and then, taking (8) as established, I derived (3) using (8) as a premiss. So my argument for the primacy of the productive forces incorporated an initial argument for thesis (8), the claim that the productive forces tend, inherently, to develop.

Now there is an apparent inconsistency, which I wish here to

[39] So Fisk claimed in the course of a discussion of his article, which he read to the London University Philosophy Group.

[40] p. 134.

expose and resolve, between my *argument* for the primacy of the productive forces (in section 4 of chapter 6 of *KMTH*) and my exposition of the *nature* of that primacy (in sections 5–7)). Section 4 is supposed to argue for a view sections 5–7 expound, but there is an apparent mismatch between the argument and what it is an argument for, which has given rise to an understandable and widespread misinterpretation of my position. That the misinterpretation is natural is shown by the fact that some of my most sophisticated critics have adopted it.

To expose the apparent inconsistency, let us ask: why do the forces of production tend to develop? Why, that is, do existing forces tend to be replaced by better ones? According to *KMTH*, the tendency obtains because superior forces make possible a lightening of the burden of human labour. There is a propensity to progress in productive power because such progress attenuates the material scarcity whose consequence is that people 'cannot satisfy their wants unless they spend the better part of their time and energy doing what they would rather not do, engaged in labour which is not experienced as an end in itself'.[41] This is the reason *underlying* the tendency to advance in productive power, and, consequently, the actual advance in which that tendency is realized.

Now while the tendency to productive improvement is realized if and only if there are recurrent particular instances of improvement, it does not follow that the explanation of each instance must be the same as, or even similar to, the explanation of the general tendency to improvement. The underlying reason for the tendency can explain why there *are* so many instances of improvement without explaining each particular instance of it. This point being crucial, it requires a measure of elaboration.

Whatever may be the underlying reason for productive progress,[42] the immediate mechanism of that progress is the replacement of less good forces by better ones, by human beings who

---

[41] Ibid. 152.

[42] By 'productive progress' I here mean reduction in labour input per unit output, and, more particularly—see *KMTH* 61–2—per unit output of product required for subsistence. This excludes what has equal right, in general, to be called productive progress, namely, (constant) capital-saving innovations, which could be labour-dissaving. Capitalists will, of course, introduce labour-dissaving improvements where they are profit-enhancing, and will thereby bring about productive regress, in the present confined sense. The key claim, which is not subverted by the distinction just acknowledged, is that capitalism obtains when it does because at that period

favour that replacement. Now the crucial point is that, while the underlying reason for productive progress in general is labour reduction, it does not follow that the reason for a given instance of that progress, the reason operative in the mind of the person(s) who caused better forces to be adopted, is to reduce the labour of some person or group. If a self-employing peasant adopts a superior plough, his reason for thereby improving the forces is indeed similar in content to what I say is the underlying reason for their improvement in general: he does so in order to reduce the amount of labour he must put in per unit output. But if a capitalist adopts productively superior instruments or methods, then he does so to protect or increase his profit, and not at all in order to lighten anyone's labour. Yet the underlying reason for productive progress even here, in my view, retains its role, since, according to that view, capitalism prevails when it does because of the massive contribution it makes to the conquest of scarcity, however remote that end may be from the motivation of forces-improving capitalists.

In sum, the reason for a particular improvement of the forces need not resemble the underlying reason why, in general, they improve, but I am widely misinterpreted as thinking that there always is that resemblance. Attention to my exposition of the nature of the primacy of the forces in sections 5–7 of chapter 6 would dispel such a misinterpretation, but it is fed by a natural misreading of the argument for primacy presented in section 4, to which I now turn.

The argument contains qualifications and auxiliary developments which there is no need here to rehearse.[43] I here repeat only the heart of the argument, which is that the productive forces tend to develop because people

are disposed to reflect on what they are doing and to discern superior ways of doing it. Knowledge expands, and sometimes its extensions are open to productive use, and are seen to be so. Given their rationality, and their inclement situation, when knowledge provides the opportunity of expanding productive power, they will tend to take it, for not to do so would be irrational.[44]

capitalist relations are optimal for bringing about labour-saving productive progress, even though they also bring about episodes of what must here be called productive regress. What matters is that capitalism's net effect is labour-saving productive progress, and more of it than any other relations would then precipitate.

[43] I rehearse them briefly in ch. 5 sect. 2, and 10 below.
[44] *KMTH* 153.

In this argument, human beings are rational and innovative creatures who have a scarcity problem, which they contrive to solve by improving their forces of production. It is natural, but wrong, to interpret the argument as requiring that the agents who actually introduce better forces always do so in order that their own burden of labour will be lightened. The picture I regrettably encouraged is of individual producers, or co-operating groups of them, striving to upgrade their skills and means of production, so that labour will lie less heavily upon them, a picture in which global productive progress is explained merely as the aggregrate result of those several strivings. Following Andrew Levine and Erik Wright,[45] we can call this the Rational Adaptive Practices (or RAP) view of the development of the forces. It is not the view I held, but it emerges naturally from the quoted passage. I did not hold it because it excludes the important possibility that the underlying reason for advance in productive power may contrast with the reason for particular instances of it, as is plainly illustrated by the development of the forces under capitalism. The way the forces develop under capitalism contradicts the picture of their development conveyed by the paragraph quoted above when it is read in the most natural way.

How, then, did I intend my argument? In my own construal of it, it was, as I said,[46] 'an attempt to render explicit the premises' of utterances of Marx quoted at pages 159–60 of *KMTH*. Here is one of them, from his letter to Annenkov of 1846:

in order that they may not be deprived of the result attained, and forfeit the fruits of civilization, [people] are obliged from the moment when their mode of intercourse no longer corresponds to the productive forces acquired, to change all their traditional social forms.[47]

Texts like the Annenkov letter confer a Marxian pedigree on my use of human rationality as a basis for asserting the primacy of the productive forces, but here that rationality is not applied at the point where it is applied on the RAP view, which such texts do not support. The claim here is not that the producers themselves introduce superior forces to lighten their own labour: that this happens is not denied, but it is not put forward as the general case.

---

[45] 'Rationality and Class Struggle', 54. For a fuller presentation of the Levine and Wright view, see ch. 5 sect. 4 below.
[46] *KMTH* 159.
[47] *Selected Correspondence*, 31.

Instead, what is said is that, being rational, people retain or reject relations of production according as the latter do or do not allow productive improvement to continue. In Philippe Van Parijs's apt formulation,[48] I do not here posit a 'search-and-selection process which operates directly on the . . . productive forces', but 'one which operates on the relations of production, which in turn control the search-and-selection of productive forces'. This is a non-RAP reading of the argument for the Development Thesis. It is the reading I intended, and, unlike the RAP reading, it is consistent with the exposition of the nature of the primacy of the forces in sections 5–7 of chapter 6 of *KMTH*.

In that exposition relations of production can be what I shall call the *source* of the development of the forces. Relations are a source of development when it is their emplacement in relations of production, and not any interest in reducing labour, which induces agents to improve the forces.[49] That relations are sometimes in this sense the source of the forces' development is compatible with the thesis of the primacy of the forces over the relations, as I elaborate it: the primacy thesis implies that when relations are the source of the development of the forces they obtain precisely *because* they ensure that development. As I wrote:

> The bourgeoisie is a set of men defined as such by their emplacement in the economic structure. It is that emplacement which makes them revolutionize the productive forces: a policy of innovation is imposed by competition. Capitalist production relations are, consequently, a prodigious stimulus to the development of the productive forces. But this is more than compatible with the thesis of the primacy of the productive forces as we have articulated it. It is congenial to the thesis, for we assert that the function of capitalist relations is to promote growth in productive power—they arise and persist when (and because) they are apt to do so.[50]

This is an application to capitalism of the general thesis defended in sections 5–7, that given relations of production have the character they do because of the contribution they make, in virtue of that character, to the development of the productive forces. The

[48] See 'Marxism's Central Puzzle', 96.

[49] It is possible for agents to seek to improve the forces *both* because of their emplacement in relations of production *and* out of an interest in reducing labour, but relations count as a source of development in the present purely technical sense just when the first condition holds and the second does not.

[50] *KMTH* 169–70. I have here added the phrase 'and because' to improve the expression of what I had in mind.

problematic relations for that functional explanatory claim are not such as capitalist ones which, being a source of, evidently contribute to, productive development. The problematic relations for the thesis that relations are functionally explained are the pre-capitalist relations which Marx called 'conservative': not being a source of development, they appear not to contribute to it. I devoted section 7 of chapter 6 to the problem conservative relations pose, and I tried to solve it by arguing that conservative relations could be, at the time when they obtain, optimal for productive development, and in place for that reason, even if they are only forms within which development occurs, rather than, like capitalist ones, its very source.

Now, whether or not conservative relations pose a problem for the RAP view of the development of the forces, capitalist ones pose an insoluble problem for it. Accordingly, I held a non-RAP view when I propounded the argument which has been so widely RAP-interpreted. I have now made the non-RAP reading of it more explicit. If, however, that reading of it should turn out to be unsustainable, then I would give up the argument, rather than the non-RAP view of the development of the forces, which capitalism makes mandatory.

4. The Development Thesis says that the productive forces tend to develop throughout history. That could mean that they tend to develop throughout human history as a whole, or, more strongly, throughout the history of each discrete society (and, therefore, in addition, throughout human history as a whole). The Development Thesis asserted in *KMTH* must be taken in the stronger of the two ways just distinguished. It must, that is, apply to every society taken separately, or, more precisely, to every society which suffers from scarcity,[51] since the premises of the *KMTH* argument for the Development Thesis apply to all societies under the sway of scarcity. (There are different ways of individuating societies, and I have no particular favourite, but the claims of the present section do not depend for their plausibility on what way of individuating societies one favours.)

---

[51] It is not intended to apply to societies of the 'Arcadian' kind which are mentioned at *KMTH* 23–4. See, too, *ibid.* 152 n. 2, and, for more on Arcadian exceptionalism, ch. 7, sect. 2 below.

I now sketch an argument for the strong Development Thesis which is somewhat different from the argument provided for it in *KMTH*, and which is immune to some of the criticisms that have been levelled against the *KMTH* argument. The new argument for the strong Development Thesis will lead to a consideration of the weaker version of the Thesis itself.

In *KMTH* I suggested, rather rashly, that, as long as scarcity prevails, people will tend to take whatever opportunities there are for expanding productive power, since it would be irrational for them not to.[52] I now concede that, as many of my critics have urged,[53] rationality does not always favour productive innovation, even where it is possible to achieve it. A ruling class in secure control of the production process might sometimes have good reason not to allow productive innovation and to try to extract more from the immediate producers without improving existing techniques. More generally: since it takes time and energy to introduce innovations, and since the process of introducing them carries opportunity costs and sometimes has unwanted (e.g. cultural) effects, it will, in certain circumstances, be irrational to introduce them.

That being conceded, one might still insist, first, that innovation will sometimes be rational, and will therefore sometimes be introduced, and, secondly, that because of rationality and inertia, achieved innovations are very unlikely to disappear, except when they are replaced by still superior techniques. Although people are not so bent on productive improvement that they will seize every opportunity of effecting it, they will certainly not lightly abandon such improvements as they have in fact effected. The upshot will therefore be a long-run tendency in every society to productive improvement, even if the tendency does not express itself in each period of every society's history.

Consider the case of capitalism. Suppose that productive improvements are introduced under capitalism if and only if they suit the interest of capitalists, and that labour-reducing productive improvement is, for some reason, often against that interest. We may surely nevertheless safely insist that it also often *is* in the interests of capitalists, and that it will virtually never be lost once it

[52] *KMTH* 153: see the quotation at p. 22 above.
[53] See, for example, Joshua Cohen, review of *KMTH*, 268, and Kai Nielsen, 'On Taking Historical Materialism Seriously', 328. It was Nielsen's article which prompted me to write much of the present section.

has been gained. It would follow that capitalism systematically brings about productive progress, and that it might be in place for that very reason, even if it is not always inclined to bring it about.

Under this more restrained use of the rationality premiss, two objections which I myself raised against the *KMTH* argument for the Development Thesis lose some of their force.[54] The first objection was that people might care a great deal about things other than defeating scarcity. The second was that, however much they might care about it as individuals, that which is rational for individuals is not necessarily selected by society. These facts are easier to acknowledge when the Development Thesis is defended in the new way that I have sketched.

An even more restrained use of the rationality premiss leads us to the weaker Development Thesis. Again we concede that there is no universal imperative of rationality to innovate, while insisting that achieved innovations will be preserved. Now, though, we increase the scope of the concession. We allow that a whole society might, even under scarcity, lack an internally generated (that is, not induced by contact with other societies) tendency to productive improvement, because of standing (e.g. cultural) circumstances. As long as circumstances are not always unpropitious in all societies, progress will occur somewhere, and its fruits will be preserved. On this account, (at least) the weaker version of the Development Thesis will be true: there will be a tendency to global improvement, to an improvement in the world as a whole, even if not every society will possess such a tendency.

The improvements here argued for occur globally in the elementary sense that whatever happens in some one place in the world happens in the world taken as a (possibly quite unintegrated) whole, even when its happening where it does has no impact anywhere else. But improving societies are likely, through conquest and other forms of influence, to establish hegemony over laggards, and, when that leads to integration of the latter in the former, then we can predicate the improvement of a larger societal whole, even when it permeates only the advanced part of that whole. Finally, the improvement may indeed permeate the larger whole.[55] If that happens regularly, then one might contend, on a new basis, that

[54] *KMTH* 153.

[55] According to 'underdevelopment' theory (see, e.g., André G. Frank, *Capitalism and Underdevelopment*) this is not what happens, (or not, at any rate, at first) as capitalism spreads across the world.

there is a tendency for the productive forces to develop in every society, either for reasons internal to that society, or, when there are no such reasons, because the society will eventually be dragged into the channel of progress by societies which generate it endogenously.

In the global presentation of the Development Thesis, there need be no society (other than human society as such) which develops the forces from their initial rudiments to the consummation of abundance. There may, instead, be what Ernest Gellner has called a 'torch-relay' pattern of development: having brought the forces up to a certain level, an erstwhile pioneering society retires in favour of another one, *which it has influenced*,[56] and which takes the forces further. And, as Gellner argues,

> parallel replication of the same stages in diverse societies is not merely no longer required by the theory, but becomes positively implausible. The powerful *rayonnement* of the torch-carrying zone . . . changes the rules of the game so much that societies lagging behind will no longer pass through the same stages as the pioneers.[57]

Advanced torch-carriers are likely, in time, to yield pride of place to once backward societies, and those societies do not have to repeat all the stages which the societies they begin by emulating went through. The torch shifts to a new carrier partly because the once advanced country or region tends to lock itself into the once progressive economic structure, which has lost its leadership value. The United States cannot readily remake its relations of production in the image of those under which Japan is currently helping to carry the torch. Being a pioneer can bring (eventual) disadvantages, and late starters have a head start when a new start is needed.[58]

[56] I emphasize that the new torch-carrier is influenced by its predecessor to forestall a possible accusation of Hegelianism, of the sort which William Shaw rightly or wrongly directs against the similar theory expounded by Kai Nielsen: see Shaw, 'Historical Materialism and the Development Thesis', 207, which comments on the Nielson article cited in n. 53 above. (For an intriguing glimmering of the torch-relay theory in Marx, but in a form which indeed invites the Hegelianism charge, see his 'Draft of an article on Friedrich List', 281.)

[57] Ernest Gellner, 'A Russian Marxist Philosophy of History', 64. This superb article is a critical study of Yu. I. Semenov, 'The Theory of Socio-Economic Formations and World History', which is in the same volume, and Gellner attributes the torch-relay model to him. (Semenov and Gellner are principally concerned with the succession of types of relations of production, but I am applying the torch-relay model to stages of development of the productive forces.)

[58] This theme is brilliantly discussed by Jon Elster in 'Historical Materialism and Economic Backwardness', 39–41. The Elster article offers a superb typology of the historical possibilities under contemplation here.

Gellner offers a lucid formulation of the strategy which I have adopted in the present section, which is to argue for a tendency to progress not on the basis of a statement about what must always happen but on the weaker basis of a claim about what will (surely) sometimes happen:

The conditions of upward development are . . . complex, and require . . . propitious circumstances . . . *The theory would only require that this combination of circumstances is sufficiently probable to ensure that it should occur sooner or later.* Once it occurred, the processes of torch-of-leadership assumption and of diffusion . . . would ensure the perpetuation of the new stage. It would constitute no objection to such a theory that the initial endogenous transformation would only occur in a minority of . . . societies.[59]

The shift to a global understanding of the Development Thesis generates fresh theoretical problems, which I shall not try to deal with here. One of them is the potent role which it assigns to war, as a diffuser of innovation and as a torch-shifter: it is not clear that assigning such a role to war is consistent with the emphases of historical materialism.[60] Another problem is the impact of the global view on the relationship between forces and relations of production. One could not now require that relations always correspond to the forces they envelop. Capitalist relations could appear in a technically backward region because it is the periphery of a more advanced centre. Whether there would remain a general tendency for relations to correspond to forces—whether, that is, the Primacy Thesis would still hold—is a moot point, and at least one commentator is confident that a globally interpreted 'Development Thesis no longer performs the function of supporting the Primacy Thesis'.[61] I have not thought enough about that problem to have a definite opinion about whether or not he is right.

---

[59] Gellner, 'A Russian Marxist Philosophy of History', 71 (my emphases). By omitting some of his words I have put Gellner's point in a more general form.

[60] See the discussion of conquest at *The German Ideology*, 84–5, which *might* be regarded as an obstacle to global construal of the Development Thesis.

[61] Shaw, 'Historical Materialism and the Development Thesis', 207.

2

BASE AND SUPERSTRUCTURE

1. The Marxian claim that the economic structure of society constitutes its 'real basis, on which a legal and political superstructure arises' generates many problems, and in this section I offer a brief overview of my approach to three of them.

The three problems concern the relationship between the economic structure and the legal superstructure only, although analogues of the second and third problems could also be posed with respect to the political superstructure. The solution to the first problem gives rise to the second, and the solution to the second problem gives rise to the third.

To say that the legal superstructure *rises on* the economic base is, I have always presumed, a vivid way of saying that the character of the former is explained by the character of the latter. But a number of critics of Marxism, and notably John Plamenatz,[1] have argued that the Marxist pretension that relations of production (which constitute the economic base) explain superstructural relations of law is necessarily false, since a searching explication of what must be meant, and of what Marx himself meant, by relations of production reveals that, being essentially relations of ownership, they are themselves legal in character. They may therefore not be regarded as non-legal phenomena distinct from and explanatory of legal relations.

We can call that *the problem of legality*. As I have indicated elsewhere,[2] the problem is that the following four statements generate a logical contradiction, yet each of the first three seems to be asserted by the theory, and the fourth is manifestly true:

1. The economic structure is the sum total of production relations.

2. Production relations are relations of ownership.

3. The economic structure is (explanatory of and therefore)[3] distinct from the legal superstructure.

[1] See his *German Marxism*, ch. 2, sect. 1, and *Man and Society*, 279–282.
[2] 'On Some Criticisms', 127–8, *KMTH* 218.
[3] I parenthesize this phrase because its occurrence is not required to generate inconsistency in the quartet of statements.

4. Ownership is a legal relationship.

My solution to the problem of legality is to reject (2), by interpreting 'ownership', 'property' (etc.) in their relevant Marxian uses as denoting not relationships of legal ownership proper, but relationships of *de facto* power. Consider Marx's description of instruments of production which were 'transformed . . . into the property of the direct producers, first of all simply in practice but later also in law'[4]. His formulation implies that, at the first stage, the producer had property in a non-legal sense: Marx must have meant that he first enjoyed over his instruments an effective control structurally analogous to, but unaccompanied by, legal ownership. In the usage I adopted,[5] the said producer first had the powers which *match* (that is, have the same content as) the relevant legal rights of ownership, but not yet those rights themselves. My solution to the problem of legality was to represent production relations, which are commonly described in the language of ownership and rights, as, in fact, relations of effective control, or powers. That a capitalist owns a particular factory is, strictly speaking, a superstructural fact. That he has effective control over it is the matching economic structural fact. His possession of effective control over it is his ability to dispose of it thus and so, *whatever it may be that confers that ability on him.*

But now the theory of base and superstructure faces a second problem. For in the standard case (when, that is, society, being non-transitional, is law-abiding), it is people's (e.g., the capitalist's) superstructural rights that confer on them their economic powers. And if that is so, then how can the economic structure be said to explain the legal superstructure? The explanation seems to go in the wrong direction, from rights to powers. This second problem, which I shall call *the problem of explanatory direction*, is the apparent inconsistency between these statements:

3. The economic structure is explanatory of (and therefore distinct from)[6] the legal superstructure.

5. In the standard case, people have the economic-structural powers they do because they have the legal rights they do.

[4] *Capital*, 933.
[5] See *KMTH* 219 ff., and also sect. 3 below.
[6] This phrase appears in parentheses because it is not required to generate the apparent inconsistency between (3) and (5).

My solution to the problem of explanatory direction was given in Chapter 1 above.[7] The solution denies that there is inconsistency between (3) and (5). It says that, despite (5), (3) may be true, since (5) does not contradict the contention (which, indeed, entails (5)) that, in the standard case, people have the rights they do *because* when they have such rights they consequently have powers matching them. In short, (3) is reconciled with (5) when the explanation ventured in (3) is interpreted as a functional explanation.

But if (3) is interpreted as a functional explanation, then a new problem arises. The new problem is that not all law has pertinent economic effects, from which it seems to follow that the contemplated functional explanation cannot be applied to the whole of the legal superstructure. This third problem, which can be called *the problem of the inapplicability of the explanation*, is the apparent inconsistency between (3) and (6) when (3) is interpreted, as it must be to solve the second problem, as a functional explanation:

> 6. Not all law serves a function for something economic, so, *a fortiori*[8], not all law is functionally explained in terms of the economy.

Now the only way that I know how to reconcile (3) and (6) is to deny that all law counts as part of the legal superstructure. It is not plausible to reconcile them by changing the interpretation of (3) and attempting non-functional economic explanations for *all* of the law for which no functional explanation could be ventured. My own preferred solution is to restrict the legal superstructure to those legal ensembles which have an extensive effect on the economy: see Chapter 9 below. The Marxian contention will then be the not at all truistic (and, no doubt, at most only on the whole true) one that, wherever law indeed has such an extensive effect, it is functionally explained with reference to that effect.

The rest of this chapter answers a critic of my treatment of the problem of legality. But my reply to him also affords me an opportunity to clarify my approach to the problem of explanatory direction, since the two problems are closely related.

---

[7] See pp. 9–10 above, and see *KMTH*, ch. 8, sects. 3, 4 for further elaboration.

[8] This is true *a fortiori* because not all function-serving things are explained by the functions they serve: see p. 13 above.

2. In an article entitled 'Can the Base be Distinguished from the Superstructure?' Steven Lukes purports to refute my solution to the problem of legality, and he returns a negative answer to the question he poses. Some people think that his refutation succeeds, [9] but I think that it fails, and I here offer my reasons for saying so.

In my response to the problem of legality, I undertook a two fold task: first, to present a plausible characterization of relations of production from which legal terms are expunged, and then to argue that relations of production, in the recommended *rechtsfrei* characterization, might reasonably be thought to explain super-structural ownership relations. Lukes is concerned to challenge only the first and relatively 'narrow'[10] part of that exercise, my attempt simply to distinguish between base and superstructure. Accordingly, my obligation here is to defend that distinction and not, except *en passant*, the functional explanation of property law by economics which presupposes it. If that explanation is defensible, then so is the distinction it presupposes, but the converse is not true.

3. The chief instrument of my defence of the distinction between base and superstructure was a distinction between *rights*, in the usual legal sense,[11] and *powers*, which were defined as follows:

a man has the power to ø if and only if he is able to ø, where 'able' is non-normative. 'Able' is used normatively when 'He is not able to ø may be true even though he is ø-ing, a logical feature of legal and moral uses of 'able'. Where 'able' is non-normative, 'He is ø-ing' entails 'He is able to ø'.[12]

Notice that to say that a person has a power, in the defined sense, is to say nothing about what confers the power on him, or sustains his exercise of it. The answer to that question could involve brute force, or ideology, or, of course, the law. And in law-abiding society the law will figure prominently in the answer, since 'in law-abiding society men have the powers they do because they have the rights they do'.[13] But rights and powers even then remain distinct, and one way of seeing the distinction between them is to note that

---

[9] See, e.g., John Dunn's review of Miller and Siedentop (eds.), 535.
[10] 'Can the Base be Distinguished?', 104.
[11] See *KMTH* 62.
[12] Ibid. 220.
[13] Ibid. 232.

the power to ø is what you have *in addition to* the right to ø when your right to ø is effective, and . . . the right to ø is what you have *in addition to* the power to ø when your power to ø is legitimate.[14]

Now relations of production involve what people are effectively able to do, legitimately or otherwise. Hence, while to have a right over some productive force is to stand in a superstructural relation of law, to have a power over some productive force is to stand in a basic relation of production. And the claim that base and superstructure are conceptually distinct now resolves itself into the claims that it is logically possible to have a right without the power you have when the right is effective, and to have a power without the right that would make the power legitimate. Thus ineffective rights and illegitimate powers are proofs of the conceptual distinctness of base and superstructure. And though, as I acknowledged, rights are usually effective and powers are usually legitimated, that truth does not erode the conceptual distinction historical materialism requires. The distinction would be intact even if, what is false, there never existed an ineffective right or an illegitimate power.

Powers are usually legitimate because, as I unequivocally said—this was the title of section 4 of chapter 8 of *KMTH*—'bases need superstructures': legal protection, a covering of legal norm, is generally indispensable to the enjoyment of economic power. I therefore asserted both the conceptual distinctness of norms and powers and the indispensability, in general, of norms to powers. It follows that I did not regard the proposition that powers generally need norms as a suitable premiss for denying that the two are conceptually distinct. Perhaps I was wrong, and the distinction I defend can indeed by impugned on the basis of the premiss I grant, but to show that one must do more than state and reiterate the said premiss. *My main objection to Lukes's critique is that it is largely an emphatic statement of what I already amply acknowledged.* He insists on what I grant, and insist on myself, that powers generally need the support of norms, and he does not spell out why I am not entitled to assert that.

Lukes focusses largely on moral norms,[15] rather than on the legal

---

[14] Ibid. 219.

[15] He thereby fails to 'focus exclusively', as he says ('Can the Base be Distinguished?' 104) he will, on the base–superstructure relationship, since moral norms are not, so I think, superstructural (see *KMTH* 216), but among the 'forms of

ones with which chapter 8 of *KMTH* was concerned, but this does not alter the essence of our dispute. Suppose that he is right that moral norms are generally indispensable to basic relations of power. And suppose, too, that the moral norms observed in economic life are less plausibly explained as functional for the economy than ownership law is. The conjunction of these claims— and Lukes's case rests on them—does not show that moral norms are conceptually implicated in relations of power. The indispensability of A to B, and the fact that A is not explained by B, do not in combination show that B cannot be described in A-free terms.

I need not differ with Lukes when he says that a

stable system of enablements and constraints, to be effective, requires that I and relevant others are generally motivated by certain kinds of shared (teleological) reasons for acting and not acting,[16]

for that is just a version of the indispensability claim. But does it follow that, as Lukes adds, 'these [the reasons] give such enablements and constraints [a] distinctively normative character'? Only, at most, in a trivial and uncontroversial sense. For one might, with a pinch of infelicity, say of an A which requires a B to be stable that it therefore has a B-ish character: a dictatorship to which the support of the Church is indispensable *might* be said to have a religious character (though I would prefer not to say such a thing on merely that basis). But that which the religion stabilizes can certainly be described in religion-free terms. And, similarly, even if powers sustained by norms have in *that* good or bad sense a normative character, we can still separately conceive, in norm-free terms, what the norms are stabilizing, and I need not and do not assert anything stronger.

To achieve clarity in this matter, one must distinguish between a non-normative concept of power, and a concept of non-normative, or non-normatively based, power. I recommend the first concept, not the second, and much of Lukes's critique depends on his having confused the two.

social consciousness' which Marx mentions in distinction from the superstructure at p. 20 of the Preface to *The Critique of Political Economy*. (Note, moreover, that Marx does not, as Lukes reports (*op. cit.* 103–4), say that forms of social consciousness correspond to the superstructure. That is a (polemically irrelevant) misinterpretation which rests on a misreading of the syntax of the Preface sentences Lukes there quotes.)

[16] 'Can the Base be Distinguished?', 113.

To see that he is subject to this charge, consider pages 115–16 of his article. He there distinguishes between a 'pure, non-normative relationship of power—say, of simple coercion', and one which is in some way normatively freighted, because it depends, for example, on the belief that it is morally right to honour agreements: and he then proceeds as though I am committed to the falsehood that all relationships of power are non-normative in his sense. But constructing a non-normative concept of power carries no such commitment. The concept is constructed to cover what Lukesian non-normative and Lukesian normative relationships of power have in common—their being relationships of power. What I call 'powers' are not essentially non-normative (in Lukes's sense of not being supported by norms) but simply not essentially normative, and I have no difficulty in admitting that, in the standard case, 'norms . . . *are* what enables' people to exercise powers.[17] My claim is just that what norms enable are not themselves norms.

In illustration of the point that powers, as I define them, are what mere coercers and benefitters from norms have in common, I said that it is true both of an illegal squatter (whose tenure is secured by, for example, savage dogs whom the legitimate authorities cannot overcome) and a legal landowner that they have the power to use their land and exclude others from it.[18] Lukes objects that, unlike the squatter, the legal landowner can, by virtue of an environment of legal and other norms, do such things as bequeath his property to others. Now it is true that the squatter cannot precisely *bequeath* his land, since bequeathing is an essentially legal activity. But it does not follow, and it is false, that he cannot achieve the effect of bequeathal, by the brute means he favours: he can bring it about that another has over his land the same power he now has over it. And his power to do that complex thing is also enjoyed by the legal landowner, so that Lukes is wrong to conclude that 'one cannot identify powers . . . embodied in norm-governed economic relationships independently of the norms which . . . govern them'.[19]

[17] Ibid. 116.
[18] See *KMTH* 223–4.
[19] 'Can the Base be Distinguished?', 116. For further response to Lukes's criticism see sects. 11, 12 of my 'Reply to Four Critics': the foregoing sect. reproduces sect. 10 of that article. And, for a response to a partly Lukes-like criticism of my views on base and superstructure offered by Hugh Collins in his *Marxism and Law*, see my 'Collins on Base and Superstructure', *Oxford Journal of Legal Studies* (forthcoming).

3

BEING, CONSCIOUSNESS, AND ROLES

> It is not the consciousness of people that determines their being, but, on the contrary, their social being that determines their consciousness. Karl Marx, Preface to *A Contribution to the Critique of Political Economy*, 1859.

1. The statement displayed above does not wear its meaning on its face: it is not immediately clear what thesis we should take it to be conveying. The object of the present chapter is to recover and clarify that thesis, and thereby to defeat the contention that, for deep conceptual reasons, the exhibited statement *cannot* carry a true and interesting message. I shall refute that extremely strong contention, but I shall not seek to establish the unqualified truth of the quoted claim. I believe that, like many milestone doctrines in the history of social science, it is only partly true. But it could not be even partly true if the arguments I shall challenge were sound.

2. Perhaps the most formidable and certainly the most indefatigable purveyor of such arguments was Professor John Plamenatz, who developed them in a number of his works.[1] What Marx and Engels thought must be true, more or less *a priori*,[2] Plamenatz thought could not be true, and could be known not to be true without consulting the evidence of history. He thought that the basic distinctions of historical materialism, between being and consciousness, and between foundation and superstructure, could not properly be drawn, because the elements the historical materialist would distinguish are, as a study of their concepts would prove, too intimately bound up with one another to admit of the needed distinctions. I showed in Chapter 2 above why this may appear to be true but is in fact false with respect to the distinction between the economic structure and its legal superstructure. Here I deal with the problem more generally, although I shall sometimes have occasion to draw on the results of Chapter 2, in so far as they are generalizable.

---

[1] *German Marxism and Russian Communism*; *Man and Society*; *Ideology*.

[2] One may infer that they thought it more or less *a priori* true from the way in which they argued for the explanatory priority of material and economic facts. For a negative assessment of that argumentation, see ch. 9, sect. 7 below.

In *Man and Society* Plamenatz discusses what he calls 'sides of social life' (e.g., the economy, religion, science, politics, art, etc.), and he lodges two claims. The first is that (A) *it is not plausible to regard any 'large' side of social life as derivative from any other.* Unlike many of his anti-Marxist contentions, this one is not argued for on conceptual grounds. It relies, instead, on an appeal to our intuitive appreciation of historical and social facts. The second claim, which is conceptually grounded, is that (B) *moral and other ideas cannot be determined by any side, or combination of sides, of social life, since they enter into every one of them, in virtue of what a side of social life, by definition, is.*

I shall later (in section 5) distinguish the thesis that being determines consciousness from the theory to which it is connected —that the economic foundation determines the character of a non-economic superstructure. We may take claims (A) and (B) as directed, respectively, against the theory and the thesis. Claim (A) challenges the theory, since, if it is correct, then the economy cannot be designated as a 'foundation':

If we take something like fashion in dress, we can show that it greatly depends on certain other things which it hardly influences. But if we take larger sides of social life, like religion or science or government, it is no longer plausible to treat any of them as fundamental or derivative in relation to the others.[3]

Plamenatz is willing to assert that fashion is 'much more affected by the rest of social life, or even by some other part of it, than it affects it'. This is what he means when he allows that it is derivative.[4] Indeed, Plamenatz is prepared to say that this can be *shown*. Most people would find his judgement about fashion intuitively acceptable. But Plamenatz thinks it can be demonstrated, and, if this is so— in fact, even if it is not so—then the intuition must be grounded in a principle of interpretation which, if it were made explicit, might well enable some rational judgement about the relative strength of the larger factors Plamenatz mentions. I am not saying that it is easy to unearth the principle. I am saying that the claim about fashion implies that there is one, and that if we had it, we might be able to say that government is more fundamental than science, or vice versa, in Plamenatz's sense of 'fundamental', even

---

[3] *Man and Society*, 283.
[4] Ibid.

though we can say little using intuitive resources alone. The principle, in conjunction with the available empirical evidence, might license the judgement that one large side of social life influences another more than it is influenced by it.

The force of this objection to Plamenatz is that is is not easy to be sure in advance of conceptual and empirical work what judgements are plausible in this area. We require a clarification of the idea of a side of social life, so that we can establish the identity of each; a clarification of the idea of x affecting y more than y affects x; and a careful study of the historical record, in the light of such clarifications. I realize that this is an enormous programme. But it is inappropriate to make confident judgements without embarking upon it.

I turn to the second contention (claim (B)):

Since claims and duties and mental attitudes are involved in all social relations, in every side of social life, no matter how primitive, since they are part of what we mean when we call a human activity social, we cannot take any side of social life and say that it determines . . . men's moral and customary relations and their attitudes towards one another.[5]

For Plamenatz, x determines y if, given a particular form of x, there arises a particular form of y, or, as we might also put it, if variations in x explain variations in y.[6] On this use of 'determine' it is conceptually in order to assert that the character of men's ideas and customs is determined by the stock of instruments of production available to them, and/or by their level of economic development. Each of the latter can be described without referring to customs and ideas. Plamenatz might respond by saying that in that case what is described is not a 'side of social life'. Be that as it may, Marxists—and it is Marxism Plamenatz is discussing—are not obliged to assert that what they isolate as fundamental may be styled a 'side of social life' in Plamenatz's sense. As I understand historical materialism, economic activity is central only because the economic structure, which is not an activity or set of activities, is central; and while moral and other ideas may enter the activity, the structure may be so conceived that it is free of all such superstructural encumbrances.[7]

---

[5] Ibid. 284–5, Note that, according to Plamenatz's argument, no number of sides of social life, including all of them, could have the contested determining role.

[6] Ibid. 278.

[7] See *KMTH*, ch. 8, and ch. 2 above.

But Plamenatz is wrong even on his own ground. For it is not clear that a side of social life, as he conceives it, is incapable of determining the ideas associated with it, as he understands determination. The ideas associated with a side of social life may vary as and *because* the side as a whole varies, and this will meet his sense of 'determine'. But to make good these objections, I should like to focus on a more extended formulation of claim (B), which derives from Plamenatz's book on *Ideology*.

3. The second of the claims (claim (B)) introduced in the last section disputes the thesis which is our epigraph: Plamenatz maintains that social existence *cannot* determine consciousness because consciousness is integral to, gives shape to, social existence. This is argued at length in chapters 2 and 3 of *Ideology*. The following presentation achieves as close an approximation as any to the structure of his argument, which is never offered in step-wise form. The key terms and phrases are Plamenatz's own:

    1. Social being consists of institutions.
    2. Institutions are conventional modes of behaviour.[8]
∴ 3. Social being consists of conventional modes of behaviour.
    but
    4. Conventional modes of behaviour involve the use of ideas
    and
    5. If x involves y, x cannot determine y.
∴ 6. Conventional modes of behaviour do not determine the ideas they involve.
∴ 7. Social being does not determine the ideas it involves.

The trouble begins with the first premiss, which cannot pass unless it conforms to what Marx meant by 'social being'. I shall

---

[8] Or, as Plamenatz also says, 'forms of social activity': nothing depends on which formulation we select. (By 'conventional modes of behaviour' Plamenatz means all modes of behaviour governed by rules or norms, not just behaviour (like shaking hands to signify welcome) which is, as we say, merely a convention.)

question premiss (1) in the next section. Here I examine the derivation of subconclusions (3) and (6).

In my opinion, the derivation of (3) exploits an ambiguity in the term 'institution'. Setting aside the exegetical issue raised in the last paragraph, premiss (1) can appear (≠ is) acceptable only when we contemplate institutions composed of relations among people[9] (and things), such as a *latifundium*, or a feudal manor, or a corporation, or the Church of England, or a stock exchange. But none of these is—as premiss (2) requires—a conventional mode of behaviour. Premiss (2) can appear acceptable only when we think of institutions which are practices, such as the institutions or practices of slavery, serfdom, marriage, punishment, and so forth. Such practices might indeed be considered conventional modes of behaviour, or concatenations of such modes, but a set of relations is not an institution in this 'practice' sense. It is a locus of practices, but it is not itself a practice. It follows that subconclusion (3) rests upon an equivocation.

I turn to the passage from (4) and (5) to (6). Until we are told what concept of involvement figures in premiss (5), it cannot be assessed, and therefore cannot be accepted. Plamenatz tells us little. Hence it is entirely open that, in any sense of 'involve' in which (4) is true, (5) is false, so that the transition to (6) embodies futher equivocation.

Plamenatz thinks the thesis that all ideas are determined by forms of social activity 'suggests that there are forms of social activity which do not involve the use of ideas.'[10] In the absence of a clarification of 'involvement', one must wonder why he imputes the suggestion, since it does not appear present in causal claims

---

[9] That Plamenatz sometimes has in mind institutions in this sense is shown by the fact that he also says (*Ideology*, 48) that social conditions consist of social relations. Indeed, an alternative version of the argument displayed above would replace its first three propositions by these: 1. Social being consists of social relations. 2. Social relations are defined by conventional modes of behaviour. Hence, 3. Social being is defined by conventional modes of behaviour. The rest would be as before, and the equivocation besetting the original derivation of (3) would give way to difficulties concerning the meaning of 'defined'.

[10] '[T]he contrast [Marx] makes between social existence and consciousness is odd and misleading. Taken literally, it suggests that there are forms of social activity that do not involve the use of ideas' (*Ideology*, 42). From this it appears that Plamenatz takes Marx's 'social being' to be a set of forms of social activity. That unwarranted supposition is refuted in the next section.

generally. I do not suggest that the production of sound is not involved in blowing a trumpet when I say that blowing a trumpet causes sound. In one plain sense of 'involve' causal assertions always suggest the contrary of what Plamenatz says they do, for whenever an effect occurs, one may say that what caused it involved its occurrence.

Plamenatz also espouses this variant of (5), which I shall call (5)(i): if x involves y, y cannot determine x. For he says[11] that 'the thought that forms part of an action' can no more 'affect' the action than 'the shape of something' can 'affect' that thing. The analogy is unhappy, since the shape of a bridge can make it weak, and the shape of a chemical compound, the arrangement of its atoms, can decide what its further properties are. But whatever the merits of the analogy are, one may be satisfied of the dubious character of the principle ((5)(i)) it is intended to illustrate by reflecting that the respiratory organs both cause and are involved in respiration.

If we drop the notion of involvement and express (5) and its variant in the alternative language of wholes and parts, which Plamenatz also employs, we still get negative results. (5) becomes: if y is part of x, x cannot affect y; and (5)(i) becomes: if y is part of x, y cannot affect x. But the surface of a sphere may melt as a consequence of the sphere's rapid rotation, even though, one may add, every sphere necessarily has a surface. That defeats the alternative version of (5). As for its revised variant, it founders on the fact that the engine which is part of a locomotive causes the locomotive (engine included) to move.

Of what relevance, it may be asked, are trumpets, bridges, chemical compounds, respiratory organs, rotating spheres, and locomotives to a discussion of the way *social* phenomena are connected? The answer is as follows. Natural objects and processes may be intimately connected, thoroughly involved with one another, and yet in unquestionably causal relation. Professor Plamenatz writes as though social phenomena are either quite unrelated or related too closely to admit of causal connection. A review of simple facts of nature indicates that he has not catered for the possibility that social facts too may be very closely linked and yet bound together by causation.[12]

---

[11] Ibid. 66

[12] Plamenatz's charge, to put it crudely, is that Marxism tries to separate the inseparable. Some writers more sympathetic than he was to Marxism think that it

4. We must now inquire whether premiss (1) ('Social being consists of institutions') harmonizes with the sense Marx attached to 'social being' when he said that it determines consciousness. Harmony is required, since the conclusion of Plamenatz's argument is intended as a denial of Marx's thesis.

Marx wrote: 'It is not the consciousness of people that determines their being, but . . . their social being that determines their consciousness.' I believe that his statement is open to the following construal, which is supported by cognate texts: *the consciousness of a person is determined by the social being of that person.* That the statement may be expressed in this individualized form may not be so evident from its familiar abbreviations ('Being determines consciousness', 'Social being determines consciousness'), but the fuller formulation commands priority from an interpretive point of view, and it is friendly to my construal.[13] In my reading of the statement, it is a generalization one instance of which is Marx's claim that the 'illusions of the jurists [and] politicians . . . is explained perfectly easily from their practical position in life, their job, and the division of labour'.[14]

One may reasonably add that it is not the whole consciousness of a person, not, that is, all of his ideas and thought-processes, which Marx here claims is explained by his social position. It is, rather, what is called, two sentences before the one bearing our thesis appears in the Preface, his 'social consciousness', by which we may understand his beliefs about society and the values which explain his social activity.

I do not contend that the only possible way of taking the being/consciousness thesis is the one I have just defended. I claim that it is an eminently eligible way of taking it, and that what the thesis says when we so take it is something that Marx definitely thought. One might, nevertheless, also take the thesis in a less individualized

does not, and that presentations of it like my own are strained attempts to split apart what Marx brought together. I criticize that point of view in a discussion of Milton Fisk at pp. 209–10 of my 'Reply to Four Critics' and at pp. 220–1 of my review of Melvin Rader's *Marx's Interpretation of History.*

[13] The individualized reading is also supported by a *German Ideology* passage (p. 37) in which Marx, having admonished us that 'it is not consciousness that determines life, but life that determines consciousness', proceeds to explain that, in his 'approach', what matters are 'the real living individuals themselves, and consciousness is considered solely as *their* consciousness'.

[14] *The German Ideology*, 62.

form. One might take it as meaning (what Marx also thought—it is, indeed, a closely related thought—)that the ideas about society prevailing in a society are explained by the economic structure of that society. Such a less individualized thesis is illustrated by the claim that 'the concepts honour, loyalty, etc., were dominant' 'during the time that the aristocracy was dominant', and because it was dominant, and that 'the concepts freedom, equality, etc.' were dominant 'during the dominance of the bourgeoisie', and because of that dominance.[15] But whichever construal is closer to what Marx meant, it is a useful exercise to show how my own perfectly eligible and 'tighter' construal of the thesis can be defended; and something like the tighter thesis is in any case needed, alongside the looser one, if Marxists are to explain the different distributions of conviction in the dominant ideas, and their different variations, among members of the different social classes.

(Marx refers in the Preface to 'morality, religion, metaphysics, all the rest of ideology *and* their corresponding forms of consciousness':[16] one might take the less individualized thesis as relating to ideology and my own preferred individualized form of it as relating to the conscious manifestation of ideology in the minds of individuals. One might also distinguish, more subtly, between *forms* of consciousness, which are abstract entities, and *consciousness* itself, which is a process in people's heads, and one might align them respectively with the less and more individualized theses. But while this last proposal has a satisfying ontological neatness, it would tend to make forms of consciousness much the same thing as ideology, instead of being, as the wording of the foregoing quotation suggests, something co-ordinate with the latter.)

Let us now examine premiss (1) of the Plamenatz argument, in the light of our individualized interpretation of the being/consciousness dictum. Premiss (1) says that social being consists of institutions. But can an institution, in any relevant sense, *be* the social being of a person? Certainly not, if by an 'institution'[17] we understand a practice. And if by an 'institution'[18] we understand a set of social relations, then a person's social being is surely not an institution itself, but his emplacement, his particular situation,

---

[15] Ibid. 60.
[16] *Critique of Political Economy*, 20 (my emphasis).
[17] See sect. 3 above.
[18] See, again, sect. 3 above.

within that set. A person's social being, I am proposing, is his *place* in society, the role(s) he occupies in the institution(s) to which he belongs. But of course we must add that what Marx mainly[19] meant by 'social being' was a particular one or set of a person's social roles, namely, his economic role(s).[20] Taken by itself, and in its individualized construal, the structure of Marx's sentence leads us to identify social being with social role. Its occurrence inside Marx's thought ensures that the role is usually an economic one, and I shall, for simplicity, ignore superstructural roles in the sequel.

One may now say that, for Marx, a person's social being is the economic role he occupies. And although role-defined behaviour, the *performance* of a role, may ($\neq$ does) involve the use of ideas in a causation-excluding sense of 'involve', nothing like that can be said about a person's *occupancy* of a role.[21] 'If a person occupies the role of a shopkeeper, he will have the ideas of a shopkeeper as a result' suffers from no conceptual difficulties, not even apparent ones.[22] The desired causal claim is perfectly assertable. The extent to which such assertions are true is, of course, another matter. I think that they are to an important extent, and that, when they are false, this is due to empirical facts about how people function in society, and not to conceptual difficulties.

5. One merit of the construal which I have put on the being/consciousness thesis is that it enables us to locate the thesis within the total doctrine of the Preface of 1859. The individualized construal facilitates clarification of the relationship[23] between being and consciousness on the one hand and foundation and superstructure on the other. They are connected but distinct pairs. The foundation is an economic structure, a set of production

[19] 'Mainly', because there are also superstructural roles, such as those occupied by the jurists and politicians referred to on p. 43 above. What Marx calls their 'practical position' is, by the way, precisely what I mean by their 'place' or 'role'.

[20] To avoid further typographical barbarity, I shall henceforth use 'economic role' to mean 'economic role or roles'. The set of economic roles occupied by one person may be thought of as a single composite economic role.

[21] The italicized distinction is elaborated and defended in sect. 6 below.

[22] *Apparent* ones attach to this different claim: 'If a person does what a shopkeeper does, if he performs that role, he will have shopkeeper-like ideas as a result.'

[23] See Plamenatz, *Ideology*, 47 for an expression of uncertainty about that relationship, which is generally neglected in discussions of historical materialism.

relations, whereas the social being of a person is his position in it; and the superstructure is a set of non-economic institutions (of law, politics, religion, education, etc.) in which persons participate with a consciousness grounded in their being.[24]

The heart of the theory of the Preface is that as society increases the volume of productive power at its disposal, changes in its division of labour (work roles) and in its division of property (ownership roles) are functionally required. An array of roles well suited to the achieved level of the productive forces tends to be established because it is so suited and tends to perdure as long as it remains so. The arrays of roles in the period of history to which the theory is addressed divide role-occupants into classes bearing antagonistic interests. Accordingly, there is a permanent disposition towards class struggle, victory tending to go to the class capable of and interested in maintaining or introducing the array of roles indicated by the current technology. The function of superstructural institutions is to stabilize, by many means, the existing role-array, but they also become (what they always are in some measure) the theatre of social conflict when convulsive changes are in the offing. None of this occurs except through the agency of human beings, whose actions are inspired by their ideas, but whose ideas are more or less determined by their economic roles.

Plamenatz experiences difficulty when he confronts Marxian theoretical constructions because he is disposed to see in society only a collection of activities, not positions; or, what comes to the same thing, he concentrates on what he calls 'social life' and fails to distinguish it from the social structure in which it occurs. Hence he takes it for granted[25] that anyone who speaks of 'social existence' must or should have something like 'forms of social activity' or 'conventional modes of behaviour' in mind, when the phrase invites or at the very least permits a quite different interpretation. In his emphasis on people engaged in sundry social behaviours, Plamenatz misses what Marx aptly called the *anatomy* of society.[26]

Plamenatz writes:

---

[24] Recall that 'forms of social consciousness' are mentioned in the 1859 Preface alongside reference to the superstructure, and not as a part of it: see *Critique of Political Economy*, 20.

[25] See n. 10 above.

[26] *Critique of Political Economy*, 20. In the unpublished (by Marx) Introduction to that work, Marx used a similar image, referring to society's 'skeleton structure': see *Grundrisse*, 110.

Social conditions consist, presumably, in social relations, and these relations are defined in terms of conventional modes of behaviour. John is the husband of Mary (1) if he behaves towards her in the ways required or expected of a husband, or (2) if it is recognised that he has the right and duty to do so.[27]

What is first said about John is strictly speaking false. His behaving in that or in any other way is not sufficient for his being Mary's husband. Nor is it necessary, since if it were, husbands could not be criticized for failing their wives. The second characterization of husbandhood is closer to the truth, though it would be closer still if it were put the other way around ('If John is the husband of Mary, then it is recognized . . .), since John could acquire the relevant rights and duties other than by marrying Mary.

Speaking less strictly, one may allow that each definition captures a sense of 'husband', regardless of the rules laid down by Church and state. But my principal criticism is that Plamenatz conceals the large difference between the alternatives when he casually juxtaposes them. The difference between definitions featuring behaviour and definitions featuring rights and duties is that the first specify the kinds of actions performed in society and the second specify its roles. Only the second may be used to reveal the network of ties connecting society's members. The social network and social activity are of course intimately related, just as the anatomy and physiology of an organism are. But the network and the activity are nevertheless different, not least with respect to their relevance and propriety in explanations of social phenomena.

In the last two sections I have leaned heavily on the concept of a role, which must now be explained.

6. We need a specially tailored concept of role for our purposes. I shall distinguish three familiar concepts ordinarily expressed by the term 'role': the concepts of a social role, a dramatic role, and a function. The technical concept we need is a development of the first of these commonplace concepts.

'Judge', 'industrialist', 'farmer', 'soldier', 'teacher', 'physician', 'electrician'—such descriptions may be used to denote persons in virtue of the social roles they occupy. Each such role imposes duties

---

[27] *Ideology*, 48 (numbers added by me).

upon and affords rights to its occupant. Right and duty are frequently identical in content. Thus a physician has the right and the duty to dispense medicine, a soldier the right and the duty to bear arms. I have elsewhere[28] defined 'social role' as follows: 'A description under which a person falls allocates him to a social role or position in the measure that the attribution to him of some rights and/or duties follows from the application of the description.'

The phrase 'or position' is added to highlight the fact that one can occupy a role without playing it, for[29] one naturally speaks of occupying rather than playing a position. People occupy roles without playing them when they lack the will or ability to play, or when obstacles prevent their doing so. They retain their rights and duties, but they do not exercise and fulfil them. The distinction between occupancy and performance helps us to see how the first may causally explain the second. What is more, a role which is not even occupied may be part of the social structure. Examples will be found in the 'Situations Vacant' columns of newspapers. Not every post advertised there is well enough established to qualify as an unoccupied role in the social structure, but some are. Certainly, the role of president has not disappeared from those American universities which have lost their presidents and have not yet hired new ones.[30]

Now if one specifies and relates all the social roles in a society, one has characterized it as a social structure. The relevant relations between roles show up in the rights and duties occupants of roles have by virtue of their occupancy *vis-à-vis* occupants of other roles by virtue of their occupancy.

But society is not only a structure. It is also to some extent, or in certain ways, a drama; and to some extent, or in certain ways, a system. And there is a concept of role corresponding to each of these two further ways of conceiving society. (The sociologist Erving Goffman is the acknowledged master of the dramaturgical conception of society. Talcott Parsons is the most famous exponent of the systemic view. Each makes crucial but quite different use of the term 'role'.)

The role of Hamlet is not a social role. Typically, the social role

---

[28] See 'Beliefs and Roles', 56–7, which also contains further discussion of the definition.

[29] Outside the special contexts of sports and games, which are not discussed here. I am not attempting an exhaustive account of 'role' and its cognates.

[30] That was true of a number of American universities in the early 1970s, when the first version of this chapter was written.

of the person who plays the role of Hamlet is that of an actor. And even if an actor plays Hamlet and no other role every night for decades, his social role is that of an actor, more specifically, of an actor of the role of Hamlet, not the role of Hamlet. It is his right and duty to play Hamlet, which is not a social but a dramatic role. It may seem odd to attribute this right and duty to him, but not when one reflects that he might legitimately complain if he is prevented from appearing on stage as Hamlet, and that others may legitimately complain if he decides not to appear.

The term 'role', then, may denote a position in society, a part in a play, and—this is our third concept—a function in a system or scheme. When we say of a piston that it plays a role within a mechanical system, we mean that it fulfills a function within that system. Functions may also attach to persons, as in 'Corporal Smith's function in the strategic scheme is to detect the enemy's movements.' Bagehot thought that the function or role of the monarch in the British political system is to dignify the constitution, or, as we might unkindly put it, to deflect attention from the sordid doings of government. But that is not the monarch's social role in the sense I have defined.

Having distinguished three types of role, we may now note that there usually are dramatic and functional aspects to social roles proper. Consider a judge. His social role is defined by his duty to render sound verdicts and sentences, his right to question counsel and so on. But judges often perform that role with a great show of solemnity and sobriety. One may then say that they play a role, and thereby draw attention not to their performance of a social role in the defined sense, but to the dramatic quality of that performance. (The histrionic aspect can become mandatory, and then one may say that it is part of the judge's (social) role to play a (dramatic) role). Finally, one may say that it is the role of a judge to help maintain social stability, thereby specifying the judge's function. The social role is so articulated that its effective performance should contribute to the fulfilment of the associated function. But the means does not always secure the end, and the space between them is the difference between social roles and roles in the sense of functions.

Other examples. One may say of grandmothers that it is part of their role (in the sense of function) to preserve and transmit tradition, but that they may peradventure fail to do so while impeccably carrying out the duties of their social role. One may suggest, with Schumpeter, that the function of the entrepreneur is to introduce innovations, but his social role, the position which, if Schumpeter is right, enables him to do that, will be defined, differently, in terms of his rights and duties *vis-à-vis* shareholders, managers, workers, other entrepreneurs, etc.

Persons standing in the production relations which compose an economic structure occupy economic roles, which are a species of social role. Typical economic roles are those of landowner, serf, wage-labourer, shopkeeper, and merchant. A person's 'being', in the sense of Marx's thesis, is the economic role he occupies. Enough has been said to show that his occupancy of it does not involve his having a particular consciousness in a sense which excludes its being a result of that occupancy. 'Derivative' elements are not integral to social being in that way. But, if we left the analysis here, they would be integral in another way, for a different reason.

For social roles have here been defined with reference to rights and duties which, being normative attributes, are inadmissible by historical materialism as constitutive features of economic positions: they belong in the superstructure. The remedy is to construct a concept of social role parallel to the one defined, but which is not normative. That is achieved by replacing reference to rights and duties with reference to powers and constraints. Economic roles in the required technical sense are determined not by what persons are *de jure* entitled and obliged to do, but by what they are *de facto* able and constrained (= not able not) to do. The procedure for constructing power-analogues of rights has been set out in detail elsewhere,[31] and the construction of constraints corresponding to duties may be accomplished in a similar fashion. I have also shown how an historical materialist may acknowledge, without damage to his theory, that it is usually rights and duties which guarantees powers and constraints. The 'concession' is unembarrassing, since it is compatible with the thesis that rights and duties have the content they do because their having it helps to maintain powers and constraints appropriate to the given state of the productive forces. The relationship between the positive and the normative is an aspect of the fact, which every clear-minded Marxist should insist on, that *the base needs a superstructure*. An elaboration of that claim is provided elsewhere.[32]

---

[31] See *KMTH* 219–22, 236–40 and, for a résumé, ch. 3, sect. 3 above.
[32] See *KMTH*, ch. 8, sect. 4.

4

HISTORICAL INEVITABILITY AND
REVOLUTIONARY AGENCY

1. Marx and Engels considered it inevitable that a socialist revolution would overturn capitalism. They express that belief in the *Communist Manifesto*, when they say that the 'fall [of the bourgeoisie] and the victory of the proletariat are equally inevitable'.[1] Now, the *Communist Manifesto* is famous as a call to arms. It encourages political activity to bring socialism about, and its very publication was part of just such political activity. But, if the advent of socialism is inevitable, then why should Marx and Engels, and those whom they hoped to activate, strive to achieve socialism? How can their activity be rational, if they think that socialism is *bound* to come? These questions pose what I shall call *the consistency problem*, since they suggest that it is not consistent to believe both that socialism is inevitable and that it is rational to struggle to bring it about. The present chapter is an attempt to solve this problem.[2]

What needs to be shown is that rational people who believe in the inevitability of socialist revolution can also think that they have reasons *of a certain primary kind* for joining the revolutionary movement. It is, of course, possible to believe that the advent of socialism is inevitable while joining the socialist movement for some or other ancillary reason: because you want to march on the winning side, because you find battle against the class enemy exhilarating, because you want to be where the action is, or tell your grandchildren that you were, and so on. When people join the revolutionary movement for reasons of that secondary order, they

---

[1] *The Communist Manifesto*, 496. Cf. *Capital*, i. 619, where Marx predicts 'the inevitable conquest of political power by the working class'.

[2] To solve the consistency problem, I need to describe beliefs which render it consistent to hold both that socialism is inevitable and that it is rational to strive to bring it about. One may distinguish three degrees of strength in proposed solutions to the problem. Solutions of weakest strength attribute to revolutionaries further beliefs which are merely *logically possible*: even lunatic beliefs can therefore supply a solution of this weakest type. The strongest solutions attribute *true* beliefs, and solutions of medium strength attribute beliefs which are neither merely logically possible, nor definitely true, but *plausible*. It is a solution of that medium degree of strength which I try to provide in this chapter.

need not believe that they are contributing to its success. Marxist revolutionaries plainly do have that belief, and the problem is to reconcile it with their further belief that revolutionary success is inevitable.

Notice that it is not only Marxists who assign inevitability to a goal which inspires them to a great deal of advocacy and energy. Politicians of milder complexion often say of policies which they spend a lot of effort promoting that they are bound to be adopted. The Marxist goal is, of course, grander than that of most politicians, but that has no bearing on the relative conceptual coherence of the Marxist stance. The consistency problem arises both in the dramatic Marxist case and in the more ordinary one.

Some Marxist beliefs about historical inevitability may generate difficulties which do not also afflict drabber political doctrines. Marxists think that a number of large historical transformations which, to others, seem manifestly at the mercy of circumstance, are inevitable, and that distinctively Marxist belief might well raise special philosophical problems: it certainly raises historical ones. But, whatever those problems may be, they are not immediately at issue in the present exercise. My present purpose is to show that the Marxist political practice of trying to bring socialism about is compatible with the Marxist belief that its advent is inevitable. I do not seek to defend that belief itself, although a defence of it against certain charges will emerge as a by-product of my attempt to sustain the stated compatibility claim.

2. One way of handling the consistency problem is *the birth pangs solution*.[3] It runs as follows: 'Although it is inevitable that a socialist revolution will come, it is not inevitable how long it will take for it to come. It is therefore rational for us to dedicate ourselves to the revolutionary movement, in order to make socialism come sooner rather than later. The sooner socialism comes, the smaller will be the amount of suffering imposed on people by continuing capitalist oppression.' The birth pangs solution says that those who believe that socialism is inevitable can hope to cause the transition to it to occur comparatively quickly, even if they cannot, *ex hypothesi*, hope to make the very

[3] The phrase 'birth-pangs' comes from the Preface to the 1st edn. of *Capital* (i. 92).

achievement of socialism more likely. They strive to bring about socialism not because it will not otherwise occur, but because it will otherwise occur later than necessary. (Note that the birth pangs solution does not invoke the consideration that participants in the revolutionary movement can try to reduce the amount of agony that occurs in the course of the revolution itself. This distinct consideration, which the phrase 'birth pangs' readily brings to mind, will be examined in section 5 below).

Since the birth pangs solution attributes to revolutionaries a concern for the welfare of other people, it presupposes that they are not selfishly inspired. But that is not an objection to the solution, since revolutionaries are not, on the whole, selfishly inspired, and, what is here more relevant, Marx and Engels did not believe that they were. Had Marx supposed that proletarian revolutionaries would be actuated by self-interest alone, he could not have thought it 'self-evident that in the impending bloody conflicts, as in all earlier ones, it is the workers who, in the main, will have to win the victory by their courage, determination and self-sacrifice'[4]

Now it might be thought that the birth pangs solution is defeated by the consideration that, even if all prospective revolutionaries would, together, make socialism come sooner, it is still not rational for any of them to devote his energy to the revolution, since the difference one person can make to how soon it is likely to come is too small relative to the costs and risks of revolutionary participation. It might be objected, in short, that the birth pangs solution succumbs to a free rider problem. (Note that the objection does not suppose that revolutionaries are unwilling to sacrifice anything for the cause, but only that, if they are rational, then they proportion the size of the sacrifice they will contemplate to the difference they can expect to make to what happens, and that the relationship between those two magnitudes tells against participation in the present case.)

But even if a free rider problem indeed undoes the rationality of individuals' trying to hasten the transition to socialism, it would not follow that the *inevitability* of socialism renders the birth pangs motivation for revolutionary participation irrational. If a free rider problem looms here, then it does so whether or not socialist revolution is inevitable, and the birth pangs solution was not introduced to solve that further and different problem.

[4] 'Address of the Central Authority to the Communist League', 282.

A simple thought experiment will show that the problem of reconciling the inevitability of revolution with the rationality of engaging in it is independent of any free rider problem that may here supervene. Suppose that, for whatever good or bad reason, all those who want socialism are unalterably committed to acting in such a way that, if all so act, then the goals of each are achieved. That supposition rules out free rider problems by fiat. But, even when they have been thus ruled out, we can still ask the assembled revolutionaries, 'Why are you (*pl.*) engaging in revolution, when you think that the advent of socialism is inevitable?' The birth pangs solution recommends that they answer, 'Because we can thereby hasten its advent', and the cogency of that answer to the consistency question is not impugned if it is incapable of providing each individual with an answer to the different question as to why *he* participates in the pangs-reducing effort.

That different question may be hard to answer, because of the free rider problem, but a proponent of the birth pangs solution is not obliged to answer it. The birth pangs idea does repel the challenge to revolutionaries that their belief in the inevitability of revolution deprives them of reason to struggle. It is not intended to vindicate the rationality of struggling against *every* challenge, and, in particular, it does not have to show how the free rider objection to struggling can be overcome.

Marxist revolutionaries who solve the consistency problem through recourse to the birth pangs solution think it inevitable that a socialist revolution will occur sooner or later, but they do not think it inevitable that one will occur as early as they are trying to make one occur. They are like a team of scientists who think it inevitable that a cure for AIDS will one day be discovered, but who bend themselves to the task of discovering it because they want the cure to come as soon as possible. The birth pangs solution depends on this distinction, between the inevitability, which it affirms, of an event of type E at some or other future time, and the inevitability, which it denies, of an event of type E within the period in which the agents are trying to make E occur. (I mean, by that period, the time within which, if the agents are successful, E occurs, and not the time when they spend their E-promoting effort, which could wholly or partly precede the period in which E occurs.)

I now want to increase the severity of the consistency problem, by eliminating the distinction on which the birth pangs solution turns, and thereby disqualifying that solution. I shall now suppose that those who dedicate themselves to the movement believe not only that revolution is inevitable sooner or later but also that a revolution is inevitable within the very period in which they are striving to bring one about. (It does not matter, for our purposes, whether or not they think the first inevitability depends on the second—whether, that is, they think revolution would be bound to come even if it were not bound to come soon.) Under that supposition, the birth pangs solution fails, since it depends on denying the inevitability of the *impending* revolution.

This strengthening of the consistency problem is justified by a fact about the posture of revolutionaries: when they believe that an imminent revolution is inevitable, they are not deterred from fighting hard to bring the revolution about. The birth pangs solution is incapable of dispelling the appearance of irrationality in that relatively familiar combination of belief and action. It must therefore give way to the different solution to the consistency problem which I offer in the next section.

3. We are now contemplating revolutionaries who believe that it is inevitable that there will be a socialist revolution within, say, five years, and that it is rational to struggle to bring about revolution within that very period (and not in order to make it occur earlier in that period than it otherwise would). How can such struggling be rational? Does not the inevitability of the revolution entail that it is going to occur no matter what they, or others, do?

But the inevitability of an event does not, in fact, entail that it will occur no matter what anyone does. For something is inevitable if it is bound to happen[5] (if, that is, it is certain to occur), and it can be bound to happen not no matter what people do, but because of what people are bound, predictably, to do. One reason, moreover, why they might be bound to do something is that it is their most rational course. And that is the reason which operates in the case at hand: I am sure that the ground of the Marxian claim that the advent of socialism is inevitable is that a sufficient number of workers are so placed that it is rational for them, in the light of all

---

[5] Note that I am not here making the converse claim, that, if something is inevitable, then it is bound to happen. Some people (not including me) would regard the radioactivity case (see sect. 6 below) as a counter-example to that claim.

their interests and values,[6] to join the struggle to bring socialism about. When capitalism is in decline, and socialism is achievable, there are bound to be so many workers who have good reasons for waging the fight against capitalism that a successful socialist revolution will inevitably ensue. If you put the consistency problem to the revolutionary workers, they will say: 'The socialist revolution is bound to happen because we are irreversibly resolved to bring it about, and we are thus resolved because of the excellent reasons we have for bringing it about'.[7]

Now, when this is the ground of an inevitability claim, one cannot say that the inevitable thing will happen no matter what people do, for that would contradict the very basis on which the thing is said to be inevitable. The basis for saying that the advent of socialism is inevitable makes it absurd to ask why people should bother to struggle for it if its coming is inevitable. One does not ask why an overwhelmingly strong army bothers to fight, when its victory is inevitable. For its victory, when inevitable, is not inevitable whether or not an army fights. Its victory is inevitable only if, and because, it will fight. If something is bound to happen, then it is inevitable, but it scarcely follows that it will happen even if nothing (for example, no human being) brings it about. No one concludes that he need not bother to do *A* when he realizes that, because he has such good reasons for doing *A*, he *is* going to do *A*. I shall call this *the good reasons solution* to the consistency problem.[8] Unlike the birth pangs solution, the good reasons solution meets the condition that the revolutionaries think that the very revolution, identified by the time of its occurrence, for which they will be responsible is itself inevitable.

---

[6] Not, that is, in the light of their self-interest alone: no such absurd restriction on the ends of rational action is contemplated here. For present purposes, we may, following Elster, define rational action as action which is the best means to realizing (whatever may be) one's goals, given beliefs which are themselves justified by the evidence at one's disposal. See Jon Elster, 'Weakness of Will and the Free Rider Problem', 240.

[7] Note that I do not represent them as saying: 'and we are therefore bound to bring it about'. That self-characterization could be criticized from the Hampshirean point of view which insists that one cannot say of oneself, in a standardly predicting way, that one is bound to do something, for one could only, in saying such a thing, be announcing one's decision to do it. No such Hampshirean objection applies to what I have represented the revolutionaries as saying.

[8] Philosophers versed in the free will controversy might suppose that the good reasons solution embodies a compatibilist attitude to the free will problem. In fact, however, my own sympathy is with incompatibilism, and I show that the good reasons solution does not require compatibilism in sect. 10 below.

In my view, the good reasons solution is an entirely adequate answer to the questions with which this chapter began. I must, however, deal with three plausible objections to it, which are treated in sections 4–7.

4. I begin with the redundancy objection, which is the most potent of the three, and which will, I fear, exact a long and complex reply.

According to the redundancy objection, (almost[9]) no revolutionary who believes that the advent of socialism is inevitable can also think that his participation in the revolution will raise the chances of its success: hence no revolutionary has any reason to join the revolutionary movement (apart from irrelevant reasons of the secondary kind which were set aside at the beginning of this chapter).

To one who gives the good reasons answer to the charge that it is irrational for him to join the revolution when he thinks its success is inevitable, the redundancy objector replies as follows: 'Your answer would stand if you had reason to think that there will be *just* enough similarly motivated revolutionary agents, one of whom is you, for the movement to succeed. For then your participation would be required for the revolution's success, and it would also ensure that success, so that you could both be rationally resolved to participate and (therefore) confident of the inevitability of success. On the unlikely hypothesis that there are *just* enough revolutionaries bent on struggle, the good reasons solution works, because the contribution of each revolutionary is *pivotal*.

'But you have no reason to think that you are, in fact, pivotal. Now, it does not follow from that alone that it is irrational for you to join the movement. You might reason that since you do not know how many others will join, you should participate *in case* you are pivotal, since so much is at stake.[10] But that rationale for participation is unavailable to you once you believe as, *ex hypothesi*, you do, that the revolution is inevitable. *You* cannot think that you might be pivotal. For you might be pivotal only if there might be, without you, just one revolutionary fewer than are needed. But if you believe, as you must to believe that you might be pivotal, that there might be a deficit of one, you must also believe

---

[9] Possible exceptions are people like Lenin, but, since such exceptional people have no bearing on the argument, I shall ignore them throughout.

[10] See Derek Parfit, *Reasons and Persons*, 73–5.

that there might be a deficit of two. (It is, to be sure, possible to believe that there might be a deficit of one and yet disbelieve that there might be a deficit of two, but reckoning what might happen is in this domain so difficult that no one could reasonably hold that conjunction of views.) But, if there might be a deficit of two, then successful revolution is not inevitable.

'Let me pose the problem in a different way. Revolution is, on your solution, inevitable if and only if either just enough or more than enough workers are resolved to make it happen. But you cannot believe that there might be just enough, since your belief that revolution is inevitable must reflect a belief that there are certain to be more than enough. But then you must believe that your own contribution is redundant, and you therefore lose your reason for participation.'

The redundancy objection presses a particular sort of free rider problem, with two distinctive features. First, the problem is not posed 'neat', but under the assumption that the revolution is inevitable; and second, the problem here is that the individual can make *no* difference to the prospect of success, and not merely, as is generally true in free rider problems, that he can make at most only a tiny difference.[11]

Now, when I defended the birth pangs solution against a free rider problem, I said that the claim that the birth pangs solution rationalizes revolutionary engagement in the face of the inevitability of revolution is not defeated if, for reasons other than the inevitability of revolution, the birth pangs idea fails as an inspiration to rational action (see section 2 above). But it would be a mistake to think that the good reasons solution can be similarly insulated against the free rider problem raised by the redundancy objection. For that free rider problem has an immediate and ineliminable bearing against the good reasons solution.

That different bearing reflects the fact that, unlike the birth pangs solution, the good reasons solution offers—indeed, rests upon—an account of why socialism's advent is thought to be inevitable. The good reasons solution has two parts. Its first part says that socialism is inevitable because enough workers have good reason to fight for it. Its second part says that it therefore cannot be

---

[11] Note that free rider problems in which the individual makes *no* difference are not amenable to the solution expounded in the Parfit pages cited in the preceeding note.

irrational for them to fight for it simply because it is inevitable, since it is not irrational to act for good reasons. In the good reasons solution, the very thing that makes the revolution inevitable makes it not irrational to struggle to bring it about.

The free rider problem facing the good reasons solution pertains to its first part. The redundancy objector can grant that, if socialism is indeed inevitable because workers have good reasons to fight for it, then the consistency problem disappears. But he doubts that workers do have good reasons to fight for socialism, because of the free rider problem. He says that the good reasons solution fails because, if socialism is supposed to be inevitable in virtue of the reasons workers have for fighting for it, then the claim that it is inevitable cannot be sustained.

To show that the birth pangs solution solved a problem which was independent of the free rider problem, I supposed that the assembled revolutionaries, when asked, 'Why are you engaging in revolution when the advent of socialism is inevitable?' could answer 'Because we thereby hasten its advent'. The good reasons solution invites them to answer that question as follows: 'Socialism is bound to come because enough of us have good reasons for striving to bring it about, and we therefore shall bring it about. It follows, trivially, that we do have good reasons for engaging in revolution.' Now collectives of people may, by appropriate action, hasten the advent of outcomes, but, if their members are rational, they do not act to achieve what each of them seeks where it is not rational for any member to engage in such action. It follows that the word 'we', in the answer the collective gives under the good reasons solution, unlike the word 'we' in its birth pangs solution answer, must (at least *inter alia*) be taken distributively.[12] And, since that is so, the free rider problem now possesses an immediate relevance which it lacked in the case of the birth pangs solution.

The redundancy objection proceeds from an unchallengeable premiss and reaches its destructive conclusion through two inferences:

A revolutionary who thinks that the success of the revolution is inevitable cannot believe that his participation raises the probability of that success.

---

[12] It must, that is, mean 'each one of us', whereas, in the birth pangs solution, it need only mean 'all of us together'.

He therefore cannot believe that his participation makes a (relevant)[13] significant difference to what happens.

He therefore cannot believe that he has a reason (of a primary kind) to participate in the revolution.

The second inference presents the free rider component in the redundancy objection.

Because its opening premiss is unchallengeable, only the inferences of the redundancy objection can be questioned. I first consider, and then set aside, a reply to the objection which rejects its second inference. I then proceed to my own reply, which rejects its first inference.

The second inference depends on a doctrine about rational action which some have challenged. The doctrine says that the only difference that should make a difference to what I do is the difference I can make by doing it. According to its challengers, this doctrine overlooks an alternative rationale for doing something: although my action may by itself make no difference, it may be one of a set of actions which *together* make a difference.[14] If those who challenge the doctrine are right, the second inference of the redundancy objection is fallacious, and an articulate revolutionary could reject it as follows: 'Suppose that I indeed make no difference by joining the movement, since more are going to take part in the struggle than are necessary for the revolution to succeed. Yet, although I am surplus to requirements, it is rational for me to enter the revolutionary ranks, because I want to be among those, which is to say all the revolutionary agents, who *together* ensure that the revolution succeeds.'[15]

[13] A relevant difference here is one which is such that socialist revolution is inevitable when enough people are moved by the attempt to produce that difference.

[14] See statements 4 and 4*a* on p. 238 of John Mackie's 'Norms and Dilemmas'. Note that Mackie's endorsement of the idea he expounds is incomplete, in that he contends only that things go better if people think in this collective fashion, from which it does not follow that it is a rational way to think. (In *Reasons and Persons* Derek Parfit propounds a similar, but emphatically not identical, doctrine about collective action: see pp. 70–3, 75–86, on the 'third mistake in moral mathematics'. The Parfit position differs from Mackie's in that Parfit is careful to restrict the scope of the 'what we do' rationale to cases where the individual is *not* redundant. What Parfit maintains is, nevertheless, subject to variants of the difficulties (see n. 16 below) which afflict Mackie's position.)

[15] Suppose that I chop off his head while you stick a dagger in his heart. Then each of us ensures that he dies, although neither of us makes a difference to whether or not he dies. Suppose now that *n* revolutionaries are needed for success, and that *m* (*m*>*n*) in fact participate. Then no one of the *m* makes a difference to whether or not

I do not think that the stated rationale for redundant participation in collective action is tenable. There are a number of
apparently strong objections to it, and I do not think that they can
all be met.[16] I consequently do not endorse this first reply to the
redundancy objection, and I proceed to my own reply, which
questions its first inference. I believe that *something* like this
different reply is satisfactory (*something* like it, since, as will
become evident, the structure of my reply is not as clear as I should
like it to be).

My reply says that the individual revolutionary may make a
significant difference to what happens even though he does not
raise the probability of revolutionary success. To indicate what that
difference is, I shall employ a simplifying analogy.

Suppose that there is a car whose battery is low, and, since it is a
big car, three people must push it to get it to go. As it happens, there
are three people near the car, each of whom very much wants it to
move, and the car's situation and their own motivations are
common knowledge among them. Then each can consistently
believe both that it is inevitable that the car will move and that it is
rational for him to join in pushing it: each appropriately motivated
person is pivotal here.

But now let us make the example harder, and more closely
analogous to the situation of the revolutionaries. Once again, three
people are needed to push the car, but now each of four is resolved
to push it, provided that at least two others will, and each of them,
because their inclinations are common knowledge, believes that it is
inevitable that it will be pushed. The redundancy objector asks

the revolution occurs, but each one belongs to a set of coalitions each of which has *n*
members and each of which ensures that it occurs. Because he belongs to such sets,
the individual is among those who ensure that the revolution occurs.

[16] The idea that what I achieve together with others can motivate me even where
it would make no difference to what is achieved if I dropped out has psychological
reality: I am sure that people have this motivation as a matter of fact, when, for
example, they vote in mass electorate constituencies. But I doubt that the motivation
constitutes a rational justification for action. Capsule statements of objections to its
rationality: i. How should I compare, with a view to deciding what to do, the good
effects of my redundant collaboration with others with the good effects I can bring
about on my own? ii. Don't I needlessly sacrifice production of those latter good
effects by joining redundantly with others? iii. How, without reasoning according to
the differences I can make, should I decide which good-effects-producing group to
join? iv. Why should redundantly collaborating with other people make sense when
no one would suppose that redundantly collaborating with natural agencies does so?

what good reason any of them can have to push when he knows that he is surplus to requirements. If the doctrine about 'what *we* do' were right, then each would have as a reason for pushing that he would then belong to a group which gets the car to go. But I do not think that the doctrine is right, and I therefore offer the following different reply to the objection.

If an individual pushes, then although, *ex hypothesi*, he does not raise the probability that the car will move, he reduces the burden on each of the other pushers. This suggests a good reason for pushing it, namely, that *each pusher wants to reduce the burden on the others in achieving what they all seek, by assuming some of it himself*. It is that burden, *so described*, that he wants to reduce. He does not want to reduce the burden of the others because he has a general policy of reducing people's burdens, which happens to be activated in this context. A well-disposed passer-by who had no independent concern that the car should move might join in the pushing to help the others, but our pusher joins in because he thereby takes some of the load off the others and thereby contributes to achieving what he and they seek. (If the pushers' motivational structures were like the passer-by's, the car would not, of course, be moving. His is the merely conditional desire to help whoever might be pushing. Theirs is the categorical desire that there be other pushers whom they are helping, a desire which they are all able to fulfil.) Nor is it constitutively his concern simply to alleviate the cost to other pushers of their pushing. Let us assume that, if he mopped their brows, that would reduce their discomfort, but not the amount of effort they must put in. On that assumption, brow mopping would not fulfil his aim, which is, to express it differently, to bring it about that the car moves as a result of others' putting in less effort as a result of his putting in some effort. And the way that he reduces the effort of the others is through his own pushing of the car, through his own input into the achievement of the sought result. That result would, *ex hypothesi*, supervene without his input, but not as he wants to supervene, with less effort from others because of the effort he himself supplies.

The picture offered here, of interlocking mutual assistance, might help to explain the appeal of the 'what we do' doctrine, which I rejected above. In my solution solidarity is, I hope, unmysteriously rational: it is easy to see to what *effect* it is exercised, whereas, in pure 'what we do', it is exercised (literally) to no effect. Still, I have no objection to the suggestion that my own solution is a refinement of 'what we do' theory, that it represents an elaboration of what its exponents have in mind.[17]

The application of the car-pushing model to the circumstance of the revolutionaries is fairly straightforward. Each one of them, in joining the struggle, does not, *ex hypothesi*, render its success more likely, but he puts himself in a position palpably to diminish the burden on other revolutionaries. To see that this is so, observe that a revolution is a concatenation of particular engagements at particular sites. At each such site, a single individual can frequently make the task of the other revolutionaries there easier. To be sure, at some sites swelling the number of agents could be counter-productive, because of crowding effects, so that the revolutionary has to choose his site with care, but there is always an opportunity for him to make a relieving contribution somewhere.

The reason, then, which each revolutionary has to participate is that he can thereby reduce the burden on other revolutionaries in the task of achieving what they all seek. And it is, as in the car-pushing case, that burden, so described, which figures in his motivation: he does not join the revolution because he generally wants to reduce people's burdens and the revolutionary process happens to offer an excellent opportunity for doing so. Since each revolutionary is, moreover, sufficiently confident that enough others will be similarly motivated, each can believe that successful revolution is inevitable while rationally deciding to participate in the movement.

The redundancy objector might now say that, even if this reply fashions a solution to the consistency problem, it does not vindicate the good reasons solution as that was originally described. In its initial presentation (see section 3 above), the solution, when stated by the revolutionaries themselves, ran as follows: 'The socialist revolution is bound to happen because we are irreversibly resolved to bring it about, and we are thus resolved because of the excellent reasons we have for bringing it about.' But now the individual seems not to join the movement in order to bring about socialism

---

[17] See Mackie, 'Norms and Dilemmas', 240 for a comment on his statement 4 which suggests an interpretation of it along my lines, although it is hard to see how the interpretation could be extended to his statement 4*a*.

but for the seemingly secondary reason that he wants to reduce the burden on other revolutionaries. The goal of achieving socialism seems no longer to play its required central role.

I have tried to forestall that objection by drawing attention to the nature of the burden which the revolutionaries are seeking to reduce: it is the burden of bringing about socialism, considered as such—the burden, that is, of helping to realize what all the revolutionaries seek. The goal of achieving socialism is, consequently, integral to the burden which they want to reduce: what each aims to do, and can do, is to bring it about that socialism arrives with less effort from others because of the effort he devotes himself.

Not all workers will join the revolution for the reason I have stated (or, indeed, for any other reason). So let me say more about the form of the good reasons solution, and about the assumptions it makes about the extent to which people in general and workers in particular are rational. Those assumptions are less extravagant than may thus far have appeared.

Each worker finds himself in a particular objective situation, with a particular set of interests and values, and, consequently, a particular optimally rational course of action.[18] Call his interests and values his *motivation*, and call a motivation which makes participation in revolution rational a *revolutionary motivation*. Then note that the good reasons solution does not say that, given merely their objective situation, workers are bound to have revolutionary motivations. Their motivations connect vagariously with their situations, and, for many workers, participation in revolution will not be their most rational course. What the good reasons solution does say is that, in virtue of the mix of situations in which they are placed, and a predictable distribution of psychological variations, there are bound to be so many proletarians with revolutionary motivations so many of whom are rational that there are bound to be enough who join the revolutionary movement to ensure its success.

No one's situation means that he is bound to have a revolutionary motivation: at the level of the individual, the tie between

---

[18] Recall the definition of 'rational action' given at n. 6 above, which governs the present discussion.

situation and motivation is neither rationally dictated nor inevitable. But, at the collective level, it is inevitable (though not a dictate of rationality) that there will be enough motivations which rationally dictate revolutionary engagement for a socialist revolution to be inevitable.

The good reasons solution says that participation in the revolution is not, despite its inevitability, irrational, since the inevitability of the revolution is founded on the good reasons those who participate in it have for doing so, and it is not irrational to act for good reasons. The solution does not require that all workers are rational, nor that all rational workers will have a revolutionary motivation, but only that there are bound to be enough who are both rational and possessed of the right motivation for revolution to occur. We need not suppose that the entire proletariat undergoes the socialization which Marx had in mind when he said that workers would be 'trained, united and organized by the very mechanism of the capitalist process of production'.[19] We need not even suppose, less implausibly, that a large majority of the class undergoes that socialization. All that we need suppose is that a minority of it that is big enough to overturn capitalism will be on the march.

According to the good reasons solution to the consistency problem, socialism is inevitable because of what enough people, being rational, are bound to do. Notice, though, that socialism could be bound to come because people are bound to bring it about other than in exercise of their rationality. A person who acts in intemperate anger against something he hates might thereby be making a quite irrational choice. Suppose now that oppression by capitalists motivates so many workers to act in a violent and irrational fashion that the demise of the system is, in consequence, inevitable. Each agent wants (as it were) to throw a brick at the system. He wants to do that so much that he will do it whether or not he expects anyone else to do something similar, and even though, on his incomplete information, all that he can expect to achieve is a severe punishment. But, when he reaches the street with his brick, he finds many others there who are similarly inclined and equipped, and together their violence brings down the system. In this scenario, socialist revolution is inevitable not despite but because of what people will do, but it is not a scenario which substantiates the good reasons solution to the consistency problem.

The 'anger scenario' is an element in a different solution to the consistency problem, and not one on which I can rely here, since I do not think that it is an appropriately Marxist solution. In this different solution, socialism comes not because people act with good reasons but because, as it were, they explode; yet it can be rational for an individual to join the revolutionary movement because, for example, he wants to reduce his angry fellows' burden, or because (see section 5) he wants to help to moderate socialism's birth agony. The anger scenario shows how it can be rational for an individual to participate in a revolution whose success he thinks is inevitable, but it does not, *ex hypothesi*, and unlike the good reasons solution, show how *all* the participants in a revolution which *all* think inevitable can be rationally moved to participate in it.

5. Before proceeding to the second objection to the good reasons solution, I want to discuss a strategy, which I did not consider in section 4, for handling the free rider problem which the redundancy objection raises. This alternative strategy emphasizes the fact that an individual can lessen the amount of agony that occurs in the course of the revolution, and, in that sense, reduce the birth pangs of socialism.[20] Recall (see page 63 above) that the revolution concatenates particular engagements at particular sites. If, at a particular site, six revolutionaries are engaged, instead of five, the four counter-revolutionaries there may come more quietly as a result, with a further result being less injury and death, on both sides. This blocks the free rider problem, by showing how one individual's action can make a palpable difference. It would be absurd to ask someone why he bothers to take part, when all he can do is make the tiny difference that 5,000 people die instead of 5,001. His powerful reply will be that saving one human life is an enormous thing for a single individual to achieve.[21]

---

[20] This sort of 'birth pangs' consideration was mentioned and set aside in the first paragraph of sect. 2. It differs from the consideration that the individual can try to make socialism come sooner, though there is *sometimes* an extensional equivalence between the two aims.

[21] It is not similarly devastating to point out, in defence of what I called the 'birth pangs solution' in sect. 2, that a single individual can make socialism come five minutes sooner.

Now this is indeed a reason for joining the struggle, but it is not a reason which revolutionaries distinctively have, since there is no more reason to reduce the agony of the revolution if you are in favour of socialism than there is if you are against it. Minimizing the agony of the process is an essentially secondary motive for socialist revolutionaries, considered as such: wanting to minimize it neither makes them revolutionaries nor reflects the fact that that is what they are. The individual cannot both participate in order to reduce the agony of the process and believe that revolution is inevitable because enough will be motivated to participate for the same reason that he has. For that would imply that the revolution is inevitable even if no one is in favour of it, and that implication is plainly absurd.

One cannot similarly dismiss the consideration on which I did rely when I sought to nullify the redundancy objection, namely, that the individual wants to help those who are working to bring socialism about *because* that is their goal. Only someone who favours socialism can have his sort of motivation.[22] A thus-motivated socialist does not enter the revolutionary process without being governed by its goal: his commitment to the socialist goal is part of the explanation of his desire to assist those who are striving to achieve it (by assisting those who are striving to achieve it by assisting those who are striving to achieve it . . . and so on).

The iteration of the phrase in that last parenthesis exposes the peculiar structure of my reply to the redundancy objection. As I said (see page 61 above), I am not at present able to make that structure as clear as I should like it to be. But something *like* this must, I think, be right. For remember the car-pushing analogy, which raises all the relevant problems.[23] No pusher makes a difference to whether the car will move, or even, we could add, to how fast it will move. Yet each has the good reason to push that it will reduce the burden others shoulder in the achievement of what they all want, and each can be certain that the car will move just because enough others are motivated in exactly the way he is.

There are a number of conditions which an adequate reply to the

[22] It is, in that way, like the motivation of wanting to make socialism come sooner, as opposed to with less bloodshed.
[23] A good way of seeing that the car-pushing case raises all the relevant problems is by supposing that one can make the revolution by killing the President, who is at the bottom of a narrow alley down which the car can be pushed.

free rider objection to the good reasons solution must meet. The reply must identify a reason motivating revolutionaries (*a*) which is consistent with the fact that no individual makes a difference to whether or not socialism comes, (*b*) to which the goal of achieving socialism is nevertheless integral, and (*c*) which each revolutionary can believe is motivating enough others so that socialism is bound to come, as a result of their being so motivated. The agony-reducing reason meets condition (*a*), but not conditions (*b*) and (*c*). It is like the desire to succour the car-pushers by wiping the sweat off their brows, where, as I assumed at page 62 above, that service makes them push with less discomfort, but not more effectively. Both the pure 'what we do' solution and my own satisfy all three of the above conditions. But, unlike 'what we do', my own solution also satisfies a further condition, which I think mandatory: it identifies a pertinent difference which the individual makes through his participation.[24]

6. The second objection to the good reasons solution is the *preventability objection*. I shall develop it as it applies to the case of the overwhelmingly strong army's impending inevitable victory (see section 3 above), which is a model for the good reasons solution.

The preventability objection says that, for something to be inevitable, it must be unpreventable, and that, for these purposes, refraining from bringing something about (when no one else proceeds to bring it about) counts as preventing it. It follows that the army's victory is not inevitable, since its commander could frustrate it, if, as we may suppose, his troops would obey a surprising change of orders. And a sufficient number of other ranks could also prevent their own army's victory, if, as we also may suppose, they are able to act with sufficient co-ordination.

The preventability objector thinks that it follows from the fact that something could be prevented that it is not bound to happen. He is wrong. A thing is bound to happen even if it could be prevented, as long as whoever has the power to prevent it is bound not to prevent it,[25] and that, we may suppose, is true in the case of

---

[24] It is because it fails to meet that further condition that the unreconstructed 'what we do' doctrine falls subject to the objections listed in n. 16 above.

[25] Someone might think that, if a person really has the power to prevent something, then he is not bound not to prevent it. But that thought is best developed as the freedom objection, which is different from the preventability objection, and which I deal with in the next section.

the army's victory. If something might be prevented, then it is not bound to occur. But the fact that it *could* be prevented does not mean that it *might* be, because of the case in which all those who could prevent it are bound not to. The preventability objection therefore depends upon an invalid inference. If something is bound to happen, and bound not to be prevented, the claim that it is inevitable is not defeated by the consideration that it could be prevented. The military victory is inevitable when the only people who could prevent it are, being rational, bound not to.

The preventability objection misidentifies a relational property of events, which the word 'unavoidability' always signifies, with a non-relational property, which the word 'inevitability' at least sometimes signifies. The words 'inevitable' and 'unavoidable' do not always mean the same thing—which is not to say that they never do—and it is indicative of the semantic difference between them that there are no living words 'evit' and 'evitable' which mean 'avoid' and 'avoidable'. The preventability objector takes inevitability to be unavoidability but that is neither the only sense of 'inevitability' nor its best sense, and it is not the sense which the relevant German term has in its pertinent occurrences in the writings of Marx and Engels.

'Unavoidability' denotes a relational property in that, if something is said to be unavoidable, then we can ask: for whom is it unavoidable? Sometimes the answer will be: for these people, though not for those; and sometimes the answer will be: for everybody. But when something is said to be inevitable, in the sense of the term in which I prefer to use it, it is not inevitable *for* some people and not for others, or even for everyone, since its inevitability is not *in relation* to anyone at all. In the present sense of 'inevitable', if something is inevitable, it is inevitable *tout court*. This is a better sense of 'inevitable' than the sense (if there is one) in which it means 'unavoidable', for it is a defect in any such sense of the term that the words 'evit' and 'evitable' hardly exist. The sense I prefer matches, moreover, the term which Marx and Engels used in the present connection, for the German language nicely marks the distinction between the indicated relational and non-relational properties with the two words '*unvermeidbar*' and '*unvermeidlich*', and it is the latter word which Marx and Engels used in the passages cited in note 1 above.

But, whatever the contested *words* may mean, the substantial point is that one must not confuse the non-relational property I have in mind with the relational one. Since that is the crucial point, I shall disagree with, but not try further to refute, someone who insists that he finds it more comfortable to deny that, if something is bound to happen, it is inevitable, than to accept that, if something is inevitable, it need not be unavoidable. He can read this chapter as an attempt to show how fighting for socialism can be rational on the part of those who believe that it is bound to come. On that reading of my purpose, the important point made in this section is that what is bound to happen need not be unavoidable. I shall continue to mean, by 'inevitable', 'bound to happen', and anyone who finds that unacceptable can mentally translate the term that way whenever it appears in this chapter.

Now, if there exists a power on someone's part to avoid something, then for him that thing is avoidable. But this need not detract from its inevitability, since to say that something is inevitable is not to say that no one is able to avoid it. That something is bound to happen establishes that it is inevitable, whoever may have or lack the power to avoid it: it might be bound to happen because everyone with the power to avoid it is irreversibly resolved not to use it. The fact that something is inevitable does not settle whether anyone has that power, and we can ask, of something that is inevitable, whether or not it is, for anyone, avoidable. And, while an inevitable event is avoidable for whoever can prevent it, preventability does not defeat inevitability itself.

Some inevitable things—such as all, or, anyway, most, volcanic eruptions— are unavoidable for everyone. Most inevitable military victories, and also the advent of socialism, if it is inevitable, are, by contrast, not unavoidable for everyone. The victory of its opponent is unavoidable for the other army, and for all coalitions in the resolute and overwhelmingly strong army which are unable to frustrate its victory, including almost all members of that army taken singly. On a Marxian view, the advent of socialism is, analogously, unavoidable for the capitalist class, and for each member of the working class, but it is not unavoidable for the working class as a whole. Action-dependent occurrences in history are, unlike volcanic eruptions, never unavoidable for everyone, but, where they are bound to occur, they are nevertheless inevitable.

People who think that a civil war in Northern Ireland is now inevitable need not think that it is unavoidable. For they might think that Northern Irish Protestants have the power not to resist an evolution towards rule by Dublin, and that Northern Irish Catholics have the power to accept Protestant rule, even though each group is bound not to do those things. Note that one could say, *in anger*, that a civil war is now inevitable: one's belief that it is (though inevitable) avoidable would explain one's anger.

My claim that the inevitable (i.e., that which is bound to happen) may be avoidable should not be confused with an uncontroversial statement, which the same words could be used to express. It is not controversial to say that a resident of Northern Ireland could avoid its inevitable civil war by emigrating, or that drivers can sometimes avoid an inevitable landslide by detouring around it. The unavoidability claims which, in my controversial submission, are not entailed by corresponding inevitability claims are best expressed in sentences of the forms 'it is unavoidable for x that e will occur', or 'the occurrence of e is unavoidable for x', as opposed to in sentences of the form 'e is unavoidable by x'. I controversially say that there can be people for whom the occurrence of something inevitable is avoidable, and not merely that people can sometimes avoid an inevitable occurrence.

If I am right, that something which will happen is unavoidable for everyone is not a necessary condition of its inevitability. And it might be argued that it is not a sufficient condition of it either, if what is inevitable is bound to happen. For an actual occurrence which was not bound to happen might nevertheless have been universally unavoidable, in the here relevant sense that no one could have prevented it. In illustration of this claim, consider the case of a mass of radioactive substance which is so placed that, if it undergoes a certain amount of decay before 9 o'clock, then a certain number of lambs on a nearby farm will undergo genetic damage. Suppose that it is now ten minutes to nine, and that it is impossible for anyone to get to the substance within ten minutes, because everyone is too far away. Now the probability of the required amount of decay occurring before 9 o'clock is, according to quantum physics, less than 100 per cent, and we may suppose, for vividness, that it is even less than 10 per cent. Nevertheless, if the decay will occur, it will occur no matter what anyone does, and so, therefore, will the unwanted genetic damage. Suppose that the decay and the damage will indeed occur. Then although the genetic damage is now universally unavoidable, it is (though going to happen) not bound to happen, and, so one might think, it is therefore not inevitable. It would follow that universal unavoidability is not a sufficient condition of inevitability.

But whether or not universal unavoidability is, as I just suggested, insufficient for inevitability, I am confident that it is not necessary for inevitability, and that is enough to silence the preventability objection to the good reasons solution.

The preventability objector denied that the army's victory was inevitable. His ground for saying so was that a number of people could have prevented it. He might also have suggested that it was not inevitable on the partly similar ground that a freak snowstorm could have prevented it. Whoever finds the first suggestion more powerful than the second will probably sympathize with the freedom objection, to which I now turn.

7. I have argued that, if the advent of socialism is inevitable, then that is because enough workers have good reasons for fighting for it, and that it is therefore not irrational for them to fight for the society whose advent they think is inevitable: its advent is inevitable precisely because, being rational, they are bound to fight for it. Now someone might agree that inevitability does not require unpreventability, but he might still object to the good reasons solution on the following grounds, which compose what I shall call the freedom objection.

The good reasons solution founds the inevitability of socialist revolution on the development of revolutionary motivations[26] which elicit revolutionary action from rational individuals. The freedom objector begins by insisting that rational action is, by its nature, free action, and that, when an action is free, then, although the probability that it will occur may be very high, it is never as high as 100 per cent.[27] But if the probability of an occurrence is less than 100 per cent, it is not bound to happen, and it is therefore not inevitable. It follows that inevitability cannot be founded on

---

[26] The concept of a revolutionary motivation is explained at p. 64 above.

[27] Or he might say, instead, that rational action is preceded by a free choice, which, being free, cannot occur with 100 per cent probability. It here makes no difference at what point in the run-up to rational action a certainty-defeating exercise of freedom is claimed to occur.

rationality in the way I suggested. The very thing which is supposed to show that socialism is inevitable ensures that it is not.

The freedom objection conjoins four claims:

1. If an action is rational, then it is free.
2. If an action is free, then the probability of its occurrence is less than 100 per cent.
3. If the probability of an occurrence is less than 100 per cent, then it is not bound to happen.
4. If something is not bound to happen, then it is not inevitable.

I shall address the first three claims of the freedom objection in a moment. But I want first to note that its fourth claim might be challenged. It will be challenged by those who disagree, in a particular way, with my handling of the radioactivity case in the foregoing section. I said that the genetic damage was universally unavoidable but, because not bound to occur, not inevitable. But some will think that it suffices for the inevitability of an occurrence that it will happen and that it cannot be stopped. They can infer that, since that is sufficient for inevitability, it is not necessary, in addition, that what is inevitable be bound to happen. Their position entails that although the genetic damage was not bound to occur, it remains true that because, as a matter of fact, it was going to occur, and could not be prevented, it was inevitable that it would occur. If they are right, the occurrence of the damage was an event which, though inevitable, was not bound to happen, and claim (4) fails.

In my opinion, this challenge to claim (4) is ineffective: I think it brings inevitability and unavoidability too close together. But even if the radioactivity case does show that being bound to happen is not required for inevitability, so that claim (4) fails, the freedom objection against the good reasons solution can be saved. For the inevitability claim regarding the advent of socialism *is* based on a belief that it is bound to happen. Hence the challenge to (4), while it might be thought to raise an interesting question about the concept of inevitability, does not substantially do away with the freedom objection. The objection sustains itself under this modest restatement of (4):

4a. If something is not bound to happen, then it is not inevitable for the reason Marx and Engels supposed they had for thinking that the advent of socialism was inevitable (i.e., that it was bound to happen).

Since Marx and Engels confidently predicted the revolution they said was inevitable, precisely by saying that it was inevitable, they thought that it was bound to happen. If you say, in advance of its occurrence, that something is inevitable, then you must believe that, unlike the perhaps inevitable genetic damage, it is bound to happen. But how can a revolution be bound to happen in virtue of human rationality when, to rehearse the freedom objection's first three claims, rationality entails freedom, freedom entails less than 100 per cent probability, and the probability of something which is bound to happen is 100 per cent?

Does rationality entail freedom? Some would deny that it does, but I am not going to resist the freedom objection by joining them, since, whether or not rationality entails freedom, I am sure that Marx and Engels thought rational revolutionary action was in a central sense free, and, I think, in that sense of 'free' in which, according to some, if an action is free, then the probability of its occurrence falls short of 100 per cent.

But are they right? Must an action which is rational and (in the putatively consequent sense) free be less than 100 per cent probable? Some philosophers think that, being free, it cannot be 100 per cent probable; some that, though free, it can be;[28] and still others that, being rational, it must be 100 per cent probable, as long as no other course is also rational. For these last philosophers rational action is, though free, necessitated by the demands of reason, and, for an Hegelianizing subset of them, it is free *because* it is necessitated by the demands of reason.[29] And even if we do not sympathize with the stated Hegelian claim, we can understand the idea that, if a being is rational, and the factors affecting its decision make just one decision rational, then anyone who knew what all those factors were could predict its decision with certainty.

Now I shall not venture an opinion on these matters. For suppose

---

[28] For a plausible argument to that effect, see Peter Van Inwagen, *An Essay on Free Will*, 64. Philosophers who think that a free choice can be 100% probable might press a different freedom objection from the one developed here. They might claim that a free choice is, even when 100% probable, nevertheless avoidable, and, therefore, not inevitable. My reply to that objection was given in the previous section.

[29] For this view, see Brand Blanshard, 'The Case for Determinism', 27 ff. Thomas Nagel would, I think, reject Blanshard's view: see his *View from Nowhere*, 116 n. 3.

that the most adverse answer (to, that is, the good reasons solution) is right, namely, that if an action is free, then it is not 100 per cent probable. Then either its lesser probability is consistent with its being bound to happen,[30] in which case the objection fails, or, so it seems to me, it must be consistent with the supposed freedom of rational action that it is *virtually* predictable and, therefore, *virtually* bound to happen. If it detracts from your freedom to say that you will certainly choose the item you love and not the item you hate from a two-item menu, it detracts from your rationality to say that the probability of your doing so falls *appreciably* below 100 per cent.

I conclude that, if workers fight for socialism because it is rational for them to do so, then, even if it follows that socialism is not 100 per cent predictable, it may nevertheless be overwhelmingly likely and, therefore, at least virtually inevitable. But there is no reason to think that Marx and Engels either meant or needed to mean something stronger than virtual inevitability when they said that a socialist revolution was inevitable. So even if true inevitability cannot be founded on human rationality, the inevitability Marx and Engels had in mind can be.

Note that the modest concession in deference to those who affirm (2), which the defender of the good reasons solution here makes, to wit, that socialism is only virtually inevitable, does not do away with the consistency problem. You do not credibly answer the question why you fight for socialism when its coming is inevitable by pointing out that it is only virtually inevitable.

8. I have tried to show that action can be rational even when the agent undertakes it on behalf of a goal whose achievement he thinks (virtually) inevitable. But I do not defend the idea that the inevitability of a goal's achievement can *make* it appropriate to work for such a goal. It can be both rational and honourable to work for a goal whose achievement is inevitable, but it is either irrational or dishonourable to work for it precisely *because* its achievement is inevitable. To support socialism just because its advent is inevitable is to display either irrationality or a disreputable wish to be on the winning side because it is the winning side.

[30] I insert this disjunct for argumentative completeness only: I do not believe that it describes a consistent possibility.

Nothing in the works of Marx and Engels warrants attribution to them of the view that its inevitability is a good reason for pursuing a goal. The idea that they thought so is an invention of enemies of Marxism. But various thoughts with which the misattribution I have just rejected might be confused may help to explain its persistence.

The first thought is that it is, of course, irrational to try to prevent the coming of something which is (known by the agent to be) inevitable (though it is not irrational to try to postpone its coming: if a deluge must come, and I can affect whether or not it will be *après moi*, I have a good reason to build a dam). But the irrationality of trying to prevent the inevitable does not entail that it is irrational *not* to work for it, nor that it is rational to work for it *just because* it is inevitable.

A second relevant consideration is that embattled revolutionaries might reflect that the advent of socialism is inevitable in order to reassure themselves that their effort is not futile. They might note, exultantly, that history is on their side. But it is not dishonourable to take comfort from that thought, as long as history is not on their side *simply* because they wish to be on its side, and they have carried out that wish.

I emphasize 'simply' because of a third consideration, which is that Marx and Engels believed that the tendency of history is progressive. As history proceeds, increasingly higher levels of productive power are attained, with widely liberating consequences. Hence, if a social transformation is inevitable, it will follow, on the historical materialist theory, that it is not only inevitable but welcome. One might then say that one is working for the transformation because it is desirable, and that *it is desirable because it is inevitable*, meaning, however, by the italicized clause, that its inevitability is evidence or proof that it is desirable, as opposed to what constitutes it as desirable. One would not then in any disreputable sense be working for it because it is inevitable. Yet one might *say* that one is working for it because it is inevitable, where that carries a non-disreputable meaning. It is a general truth that, in a sentence of the form 'I choose O because it is F', the feature denoted by 'F' need not be what makes O worth choosing, but just a feature which indicates that O has a further feature which makes it worth choosing. I might say that I shall travel in that aeroplane because its tail is red, even though it is not its red tail, but the associated fact that the aeroplane belongs to British Airways (who take good care of you) which makes it worth choosing.

9. I have up to now supposed that, when Marxists say that a socialist revolution is inevitable, or historically necessary, what they say entails that a socialist revolution will happen. But terms like 'necessary' and 'unavoidable' and (perhaps somewhat less naturally) 'inevitable' can also be used in a sense in which that entailment is lacking, and not because, in the case of 'unavoidable', the unavoidable thing is not unavoidable for everyone.

To begin with a banal example, notice that the sentence 'The repair of the roof is now unavoidable' does not, in its most familiar occurrences, entail that the roof will now be repaired. It has that entailment only in the unfamiliar case where what is meant is that no one could prevent the resolute workmen from repairing the roof. Usually, when a roof's repair is said to be unavoidable, or necessary, or, this being less common, inevitable, what is meant is that no alternative to repairing it is acceptable. One could also say, in that case, that its repair is imperative, so I shall use the (somewhat inelegant) phrase *imperative inevitability* here. Something is imperatively inevitable when whether or not it occurs is within human control and no alternative to its occurrence is acceptable.

Sometimes, when Marx and Engels said that socialism was necessary, they meant that without it there would be barbarism, or, at any rate, a terrible waste of human potential.[31] They meant that it was imperatively inevitable. Under that meaning of inevitability, the inevitability of the revolution is an excellent reason for bringing it about, and the consistency problem with which this essay began does not arise. If the roof's repair is now (in this sense) unavoidable, then that is an excellent reason for repairing it.

Here is an important example of Marx's use of 'historical necessity' (*historische Notwendigkeit*) in an imperative sense. Having said that capitalism is an historical necessity, he adds that it is 'merely an historical necessity, a necessity for the development of productive power from a definite historical starting-point or basis, but in no way an *absolute* necessity of production'.[32] Whatever else

---

[31] See *KMTH* 159–60.
[32] *The Grundrisse*, 831–2.

Marx meant here, he meant that, unless capitalism had supervened on pre-capitalist class society, human productive power would never have reached the desirably high level at which class society and, therefore, capitalism, are no longer necessary for productive progress.

If we call this *imperative* inevitability, we can call the inevitability discussed in sections 1–8 *predictive* inevitability. We can then say that it is a Marxian thesis that, because socialism is imperatively inevitable, it is, in virtue of human rationality, predictively inevitable. If socialism is necessary because no alternative to it is acceptable, necessary (or unavoidable), that is, in a sense in which one who says so does not commit himself to saying that it is (virtually) bound to come; then it is, as a result, necessary in just that further and predictive sense: people are too rational to permit barbarism to occur when they can choose socialism.[33]

Within predictive inevitability, we can distinguish between *categorical* inevitability, which has been the main topic of this chapter, and *conditional* inevitability, which should not be confused with imperative inevitability, and which has not yet been discussed. An event is conditionally inevitable if it is bound to occur should certain conditions, which might not obtain, in fact be realized. Many of Marx's predictions about the future of capitalism, in its later stages, are conditional inevitability statements, since their truth is intended to be conditional on the persistence of capitalism (and, perhaps, on other things too). Examples are his statements that capital will become increasingly concentrated, that the economy-wide rate of profit will decline, and (the exegetically problematic thesis) that workers will undergo increasing misery. In making these forecasts, Marx was not rejecting the possibility that a socialist revolution would occur so soon that their categorical counterparts would be falsified: (some of) the projected eventualities would be robbed of the time they need to unfold by an early socialist revolution.

10. I have sought to reconcile the Marxist belief in the inevitability of the advent of socialism with the Marxist commitment to bringing socialism about. I have not tried to establish that the

[33] The texts cited at *KMTH* 159–60 can be understood as asserting predictive inevitability on the basis of imperative inevitability.

inevitability belief itself is true, but I have, implicitly and incidentally, defended it against certain charges. That is because of the leading role which rationality plays in my solution to the consistency problem.

The belief that socialism is inevitable may be resisted for a number of reasons. When it is defended by reference to rationality, it will be resisted by those who do not believe that socialism is in the interests of the workers, and by those who think that, even if it is in their interests, it is not rational for them to struggle for it, because the relevant free rider problem is insoluble, or because the costs of transition to socialism make the struggle for it a bad bet.[34] I do not, in this section, address those reasons for thinking that the advent of socialism cannot be inevitable, two of which go beyond the scope of this chapter, and one of which (the free rider problem) was treated in section 4.

What I seek to do here is to allay suspicions about Marxist inevitabilitarian claims which reflect over-assimilation of inevitability to concepts distinct from it. Three such concepts are unavoidability (as explicated above), nomological determinism, and automaticity. People sometimes oppose the belief that the advent of socialism is inevitable because they mistakenly think that it presupposes or implies claims about unavoidability, nomological determination, and automaticity which they regard as false and/or dangerous.

Having dealt with the difference between inevitability and unavoidability, I turn here to nomological determination. (I call it *nomological* determination in deference to those who think that a future event might be determined because it figures in the uniquely rational course of a rational agent, and not in virtue of laws of nature.) An event is nomologically determined if and only if the statement that it will occur is entailed by laws of nature and statements describing antecedent conditions. The thesis of *determinism* says that all events are nomologically determined.

---

[34] This last reason for saying that the workers' interest in socialism need not generate an interest in struggling for it is independent of the free rider problem. The idea is that the power of the capitalist class to resist the revolutionary movement and to commit sabotage against a fledgling socialism means that socialism's birth agony will be so severe that it is not, on balance, worth fighting for. On the suggested gloomy hypothesis, no revolutionary would stand to gain from the struggle for socialism, even if all workers were to join that struggle. This can be called the 'Przeworski problem', because of Adam Przeworski's brilliant exploration of it in his *Capitalism and Social Democracy*.

Now whether or not determinism is true, and whatever the consequences of believing it may be for our practice of holding people responsible for their actions and for our sense of ourselves as deliberatively choosing agents, it is emphatically false that Marx and Engels based their belief in the inevitability of socialism on determinism. Had they done so, they could not have distinguished between the advent of socialism, which they thought inevitable, and the time and manner of its advent, which they did not think inevitable. To prevent misunderstanding, I emphasize that I am not saying that, if they had affirmed determinism, they could not have believed that the way socialism would come was partly a matter of free human choice. That inference requires a denial of compatibilism, or an attribution to Marx and Engels of a denial of it, where compatibilism is the doctrine that genuinely free choice is compatible with determinism. And while I happen myself to be an incompatibilist, the main claims of this essay do not oblige me to take a position on the truth of compatibilism, or on the question whether or not Marx and Engels accepted it.[35] My present point is the simple one that, since Marx and Engels did not think everything was inevitable, they could not have derived the inevitability of what they did think inevitable from determinism (whether or not they believed in determinism), for if that makes anything that happens inevitable, it makes everything that happens inevitable.

What is the relationship between the claim that an event is nomologically determined and the claim that it is inevitable? If an event is nomologically determined, then, so I believe, it is bound to happen, and, being an incompatibilist, I also believe that no one can prevent it. Hence nomologically determined events are, I believe, inevitable, on any view of what inevitability is.[36] But it does not follow that they are *historically* inevitable. For we can reasonably restrict that predicate to inevitabilities which are such in virtue of broad historical conditions, as opposed to just any conditions at all. Suppose that it was nomologically, because neurologically, deter-

---

[35] I affirm that belief in inevitability is consistent with the rationality of striving to bring the inevitable about. That consistency claim requires compatibilism only if inevitability entails nomological determinism and rational action entails genuine choice, and I affirm neither of those entailments in this chapter.

[36] That is, both on the view of inevitability according to which the genetic damage of p. 71 above was inevitable (because it could not have been prevented) and on the view of inevitability according to which (although it could not have been prevented) it was not inevitable.

mined that Napoleon would suffer a lapse of concentration at a crucial moment at Waterloo, and therefore lose the battle he would otherwise have won, and that, only because of all that, it was nomologically determined that the Metternich reaction would come to prevail. Then if, as I believe, what is nomologically determined is inevitable, all that would be inevitable, but it would not be historically inevitable, since not the broad historical situation but facts which, relative to it, were accidents, would have ensured the fateful chain of events. If the kingdom was lost for the want of a horseshoe nail, its loss might have been inevitable, but the point of the poem is that it was not *historically* inevitable.[37]

Turning to the converse implication, let us ask whether the inevitability of an event (and, therefore, its historical inevitability) implies that it is nomologically determined. The implication will be denied by those who think that unpreventability suffices for inevitability (see page 73 above), and by those who think that, when something is inevitable in virtue of human rationality, it need not be nomologically determined.

Even if everything which is inevitable is nomologically determined, the doctrine of historical inevitability, as it was held by Hegel and Marx, does not entail the thesis of determinism. For, although they thought that the main course of history was inevitable, they did not think that everything in history was inevitable. The issues of determinism and historical inevitability in the Hegelio-Marxian sense should not be identified, as they *sometimes* are by Isaiah Berlin, to the detriment of his famous lecture on this subject.[38]

Finally, a word about a less common confusion. Inevitability and automaticity are distinct, so a certain picture of history is not imposed upon us even if everything that happens in history is

---

[37] 'For want of a nail, the shoe was lost; / For want of a shoe, the horse was lost; / For want of a horse, the rider was lost; / For want of a rider, the message was lost; / For want of a message, the kingdom was lost; / And all for the want of a horseshoe nail'. It was, perhaps, inevitable, once the nail was gone, that the kingdom would be lost, but, if I am right, it was never *historically* inevitable.

[38] The identification is implicit at *Historical Inevitability*, 33; but note, too, p. 25, where Berlin acknowledges that Hegelio-Marxian historical inevitability is consistent with the existence of human free choice. Since Berlin is an incompatibilist, what he there acknowledges entails, for him, that historical inevitability is consistent with the falsehood of determinism.

For illuminating remarks on determinism and historical inevitability see Allen Wood, *Karl Marx*, 113–16.

(historically) inevitable. The proposition that something will happen inevitably neither entails nor is entailed by the proposition that it will happen automatically. It could be true that the machine will shut itself off automatically, even though it is not bound to shut itself off, since someone might (but in fact no one will) disturb its operation. And economic processes under capitalism might have automatic but non-inevitable results, since the mechanism producing them is amenable to interference, and people are not bound not to interfere with it. And if socialism were inevitable for the sorts of reasons canvassed in this chapter, it would not follow that it would come automatically. Much struggle would nevertheless be needed.

5

HUMAN NATURE AND SOCIAL CHANGE IN THE MARXIST CONCEPTION OF HISTORY[1]

1. According to *KMTH*, the fundamental explanation of the course of social change lies in facts which are in an important sense asocial, and, in one sense of the word, material.[2] The relevant fundamental facts are asocial in that no information about social *structure* enters into their formulation, under the following understanding of *social structure*: a statement formulates a fact about social structure if and only if it entails an ascription to (specified and unspecified) persons of rights or effective powers *vis-à-vis* other persons.[3] Examples of material facts in the present partly technical sense are the general one that human beings are able to sacrifice present gratification for the sake of greater future gratification, and the particular one that the productive resources available to European humanity in 1250 ensured that most labour in Europe would be agricultural labour.

KMTH offers an argument[4] in which exclusively asocial premisses are used to support a grand conclusion of an asocial kind about the whole course of human history, to wit, that there has been, across that course, a tendency for the productive power of humanity to grow. This claim was called, in *KMTH*, the Development Thesis, and it was formulated as follows:

1. The productive forces tend to develop throughout history.[5]

As just indicated, the tendency posited by (1) is supposed not to be due to the character of social structures. If it obtained only because of favourable social relations of production which were not themselves materially explained, it would then lack the autonomy with respect to social structures which *KMTH* assigns to it. One

---

[1] Written with Will Kymlicka.
[2] See *KMTH* Ch. 4 for an attempt to specify that sense.
[3] This characterization of social structure is adapted from *KMTH* 94.
[4] Ibid. 152–3. The argument is summarized in sect. 2 below.
[5] *KMTH* 134.

may, accordingly, enter the following alternative statement of the Development Thesis:

>   2. There is an autonomous tendency for the productive forces to develop.

(2) will be called the *Full* Development Thesis.

Since productive forces are not unmoved movers, the autonomy here assigned to their tendency to develop is not an absolute one. The tendency's autonomy is just its independence of social structure, its rootedness in fundamental material facts of human nature and the human situation. Throughout this chapter, *nothing more, or less, will be meant by the autonomy of the tendency of the forces to develop.*

Now the tendency to development here asserted on an asocial basis is supposed, in *KMTH*, to explain some very important social facts, and, in particular, the supposed fact that

>   3. Social structures have, by and large, been propitious for the development of the productive forces.[6]

(2) would explain (3) in that, if there is an autonomous tendency for the productive forces to develop, then social relations must be such as to allow it.[7] It is convenient to give the claim that (2) explains (3) an independent billing:

>   4. Because there is an autonomous tendency for the productive forces to develop in history, social structures are so shaped or selected as to allow for that development.

Now which relations of production are propitious at a given stage of development, and, hence, which relations will be selected at that stage, depends on the level of productive power already achieved at that stage. Thus (4) sustains (5), which was called, in *KMTH*, the Primacy Thesis,[8] since it assigns explanatory primacy to the productive forces over the production relations:

>   5. The nature of the production relations of a society is explained by the level of development of its productive forces.

---

[6] We shall sometimes express (3) by saying, more tersely, that social structures have been (or are) propitious.

[7] For a fuller exposition of the derivation of (3) from (2), see *KMTH* 158–9. For a fuller one still, see Andrew Levine and Erik Wright, 'Rationality and Class Struggle', 51–6.   [8] *KMTH* 134.

In an impressive critical notice of *KMTH*, Joshua Cohen maintained, among other things, that the argument described above is fatally flawed, since asocial premisses could not, he contended, suffice to justify the claim (claim (1)) that the productive forces tend to develop throughout history. If claim (1) is true, then the fact that social structures have been propitious (claim (3)) is an irreducible part of its explanation. It would follow that any tendency for the productive forces to develop is not autonomous, and, consequently, that the primacy thesis is false: a tendency to productive development could not explain why social relations are propitious if their being so is part of the explanation of that very tendency. Joshua Cohen concluded that there is an unavoidable circle in the argument for (5), or a circle to be avoided only by abandoning the attempt to explain (1), and, *a fortiori*, the attempt to explain it by reference to asocial facts only. But to avoid the circle by adopting the latter course is, so Joshua Cohen claimed, to 'enfeeble'[9] the argument for the Development Thesis.

2. In this chapter, we refute Joshua Cohen's claim that *KMTH*'s argument for the Development Thesis is circular or feeble, after first addressing an earlier critique of the argument made by Andrew Levine and Erik Wright,[10] which to some degree anticipates Joshua Cohen's objections to it. But before we take up those tasks, more must be said about the nature of the argument for the Development Thesis.

The argument employs three premisses.[11] The first is that the historical[12] situation of humanity is one of material scarcity: given the character of external nature and the forces available for dealing with it, human beings can satisfy their wants only if most of them spend the better part of their existence engaged in more or less repugnant labour. The second premiss is that people have the intellectual and other capacities needed to discover new resources

---

[9] Joshua Cohen, review of *KMTH*, 265.

[10] 'Rationality and Class Struggle', esp. 61–3.

[11] *KMTH*. 152. Joshua Cohen calls them the 'Smithian premisses' (review of *KMTH*, 263).

[12] On the present meaning of 'historical', see *KMTH* 23, 152, and p. 126 of ch. 7 below. The historical situation of humanity excludes conditions in which nature is bountiful without human assistance, and those in which, by virtue of centuries of human effort, it has been made bountiful.

and to devise productivity-enhancing skills and tools. And the third premiss is that they are rational enough to be able to seize the occasions their capacities create to make inroads against the scarcity under which they labour. In brief: given their rationality, and their naturally inclement situation, people will not endlessly forgo the opportunity to expand productive power recurrently presented to them, and productive power will, consequently, tend, if not always continuously, then at least sporadically, to expand.

Now *KMTH* did not say what was meant by 'tendency' in the present context, and we shall not give a full answer to that question here. It will suffice to say that the tendency must not be a *mere* tendency, where that means at least that it must not be regularly unfulfilled because relations of production are unpropitious.[13] That leaves a lot of reasons why it might, in particular cases, be unfulfilled. Non-fulfilment might be due to material misfortune, such as an earthquake, or a gradual depletion of a needed resource. It might also be due to the scarcity of a particular resource not previously needed, but now needed for further advancement (for example, a certain sort of metal). It might, again, be due to the impossibility, under any production relations, of generating a surplus of dimensions now necessary for progress, because, for example, progress now requires a vast irrigation system; or, more improbably, to a defective physical theory whose errors have not, up to now, created impediments to progress. The relevant common feature of these possible blockers of productive progress is that in each case progress is blocked for reasons unconnected with the character of the governing social structure. If such material blockers were very common, then it might be inappropriate to posit a standing tendency of the productive forces to develop, but we conjecture that they are not very common, and no one has criticized *KMTH* by urging that they might be.

In short, the asocial premisses are intended to establish the existence of a normally fulfilled tendency, one which might be unfulfilled, but which is not regularly unfulfilled for social reasons. And the point of placing this burden on those premisses is that they would otherwise not support a Development Thesis from which the Primacy Thesis could be derived. In a different context from the present one, one might speak of a tendency to development which was rooted in subsocial conditions but regularly blocked by social

[13] Cf. Cohen, review of *KMTH* 262–3.

structures, but that is not our usage here, since such a tendency could not explain the character of social structures.[14]

Note that the claim that there is an autonomous and, by and large, fulfilled, tendency for the productive forces to develop, differs in two important ways from the statement that the forces *do*, by and large, develop. The first is that they might develop for a miscellany of reasons, and not in fulfilment of any tendency. And the second is that they might tend to develop simply because relations tend to be propitious, and that explanation of their tendency to develop would deprive the tendency of its autonomy.

It bears mentioning that G. A. Cohen was aware that the premisses of the argument for the Development Thesis were remarkably exiguous, given the fullness of its conclusion.[15] He said that attempting any such argument was 'venturesome and perhaps foolhardy'.[16] He proceeded nevertheless, because he thought it would be worth finding out what was wrong with an argument of this degree of simplicity and ambition. We shall claim that, whatever else may be wrong with it, it does not suffer from any circularity of the sort its critics discern in it.

3. According to the argument for the Development Thesis, human beings are rational and innovative creatures who have a scarcity problem, which they contrive to alleviate by improving their forces of production. A natural, but, as we have seen,[17] incorrect understanding of the argument sees it as requiring that the agents who actually introduce better forces do so in order that their own burden of labour will be lightened. The picture unintentionally suggested by *KMTH* is of individual producers, or co-operating groups of them, striving to upgrade their skills and means of production, so that labour will lie less heavily upon them, a picture in which global productive progress is the aggregate result of those

---

[14] The critics addressed below lacked the benefit of the foregoing partial clarification of 'tendency', but, to the extent that the clarification modifies *KMTH*, it makes it *more* vulnerable to their arguments.

[15] Later, the argument is somewhat enriched, through the addition of a sub-argument which is meant to handle certain objections to it. See *KMTH* 153 ff. and the summary in sect. 10 below.

[16] *KMTH* 150.

[17] See ch. 1, sect. 3 above, and, for further elaboration of the point, see sect. 5 below.

several strivings. Following Levine and Wright,[18] we have called this the Rational Adaptive Practices (or RAP) view of the development of the forces, and it is to their criticism of the Development Thesis, so understood—for that is how they understand it—that we first turn.

4. Levine and Wright claim that the RAP account of productive development is falsified by the known record of history: in the feudal period, for example, the motivation for such productive development as actually occurred came from the relations of production, and not from the material situation of producers, considered in abstraction from those relations. The 'impulse' to progress, to the extent that there was one, reflected the 'class-specific rationality' associated with the position of feudal lords within the prevailing relations of production. From the peasant producer's point of view, 'there was nothing "rational" about the way in which feudalism allowed for the development of the productive forces'.[19] Development did not occur because of 'a rational desire to augment productive capacities in the face of material scarcity, but as an indirect effect of feudal relations'.[20]

Having satisfied themselves that the RAP view of productive development is false, Levine and Wright go on to suggest a remodelled argument for the Development Thesis which accords with the facts upsetting the RAP account. There might be a tendency to productive progress in virtue of the successive 'class-specific rationalities' that arise out of successive sets of social relations. But this fresh case for the Development Thesis—for, that is, (1)—would be purchased at the expense of rejecting (2). Productive development would no longer be autonomous, and the attempt to explain material progress in material terms would be abandoned. Moreover, and relatedly, one could now no longer use (1), the Development Thesis, as a basis for asserting the Primacy Thesis (i.e., (5)). For such a use of the Development Thesis requires that it explain why relations of production are propitious (why, that is, (3) is true), and the revised argument for (1) bases the defence of (1) on an independent assertion of (3). That revised argument is, consequently, a failure, since, as Levine and Wright

[18] 'Rationality and Class Struggle', 54: see p. 23 of ch. 1 above.
[19] Levine and Wright, 'Rationality and Class Struggle', 63.
[20] Ibid. 62.

correctly say, 'the explanatory asymmetry Cohen accords the productive forces depends upon an independent argument for the development of the productive forces, one that does not itself hinge on the form of the relations of production'.[21]

One cannot, without vitiating circularity, defend (1) by means of (3) and *also* derive (5) from (1). Circularity is avoided if one reverts to the RAP account of the Development Thesis, in which the impulse to productive progress lies outside the relations of production. But the RAP account is empirically false. The upshot is a dilemma. Either (i) maintain a RAP account of the Development Thesis, thereby preserving the autonomy of the tendency to development, and enabling a non-circular derivation of the primacy thesis, the entire procedure, however, resting upon an empirically false premiss; or (ii) adopt an empirically defensible 'class-specific rationality' interpretation of the Development Thesis, but then the autonomy of productive development is lost and the attempt to infer the Primacy Thesis involves a vitiating circle. Asocial premisses cannot explain a tendency to development which obtains only because class-specific rationalities have the character they do.

5. We now show that the Levine/Wright critique mislocates the autonomy which the tendency to productive development is meant to possess. Once that autonomy is properly sited, it will be possible to offer a non-RAP account of the Development Thesis which accommodates the facts upsetting the RAP account, preserves the autonomy of the tendency to productive progress, and enables a non-circular derivation of the Primacy Thesis.

The key point is that the Full Development Thesis, to wit, that

2. There is an autonomous tendency for the productive forces to develop,

is different from the claim with which Levine and Wright[22] evidently identify it, namely that

[21] Ibid. 63. Levine and Wright add that 'the development thesis cannot both follow from the primacy thesis and, at the same time, be a presupposition of it.' But that statement misdescribes the putative circularity. It is not the primacy thesis, (5), which is used in the remodelled argument for (1). That remodelled argument bases (1) on (3), and the problem is that, when (1) is based on (3), (1) cannot be used as a basis for asserting (5).

[22] Others, too, lean towards this identification, such as Richard Miller, when he writes that 'in a Marxist technological determinism, economic structures . . . have

6. There is a tendency for the productive forces to develop autonomously,

(6) says that the forces tend to develop without assistance, and, therefore, without the assistance of the relations. But (2) does not entail (6). (2) assigns autonomy to the tendency of the forces to develop, not to the development it is a tendency to.

A child has an autonomous tendency to grow up. He is born with a disposition to do so which is not externally instilled in him by, for example, his parents. But it does not follow that he has a tendency to grow up autonomously, where that means independently of parental and other assistance. The asserted autonomy of the tendency of productive power to grow is relevantly similar. The tendency's explanation lies not within social relations, but in the sub-social facts about humanity rehearsed in section 2 above. Yet it does not follow that productive power grows without social relational assistance, nor even that social relations cannot be, what they are in Levine and Wright's presentation of the feudal case, and what they certainly are in the case of capitalism, the *immediate* source of the development of the forces.[23] That the tendency of the forces to develop is realized through the specific social relations of particular societies does not contradict the claim that it is rooted in material and, therefore, socially unspecific circumstances of human nature and the human condition.

This clarification of autonomy enables us to present a non-RAP account of the development of the forces, one which, moreover, is congruent with certain utterances of Marx. Recall the statement[24] in his letter to P. V. Annenkov of 1846:

. . . in order that they may not be deprived of the result attained, and forfeit the fruits of civilization, [people] are obliged from the moment when

some impact on productive forces (otherwise they could not facilitate their growth) but the most basic changes in the productive forces result from their own expansion in people's pursuit of greater productive efficiency' (*Analysing Marx*, 180). Counterposing the result of that pursuit to the impact of economic structures strongly suggests that the pursuit achieves its result independently of the impact of those structures, and that is the RAP view.

[23] On the compatibility between the Full Development Thesis and the fact that capitalist relations induce productive development, see ch. 1, sect. 3 above, a few sentences of which are reproduced in the present section.

[24] It was quoted at p. 23 of ch. 1 above.

their mode of intercourse no longer corresponds to the productive forces acquired, to change all their traditional social forms.[25]

Texts like the Annenkov letter confer a Marxian pedigree on the use of human rationality as a basis for asserting the Development Thesis. But now rationality functions at a different point from that at which it figures on the RAP view, which such texts do not support. The non-RAP claim is not that rational producers introduce superior forces in order to lighten their own labour: that this occurs is not denied, but it is not put forward as the general case. Instead, the claim is that, being rational, people retain and reject relations of production according as the latter do and do not allow productive improvement to continue. In the singularly apt formulation of Philippe Van Parijs,[26] the non-RAP claim does not posit a 'search-and-selection process which operates directly on the . . . productive forces' but 'one which operates on the relations of production, which in turn control the search-and-selection of productive forces'. This non–RAP reading of the argument for the Development Thesis preserves the autonomy of the tendency of the forces to develop. The tendency is not now seen as an effect of the 'class-specific rationalities' attached to given sets of social relations. On the contrary. Particular class-specific rationalities prevail only as long as they are associated with class structures which serve a more basically grounded impulsion to productive progress.

In this new use of them, our three asocial premisses (see section 2 above) generate a (Full) Development Thesis from which the Primacy Thesis can now, without circularity, be derived. For we can now say that the dilemma formulated at the end of section 4 rests upon a false dichotomy. According to Levine and Wright, productive progress under feudalism is *either* the effect of feudal relations *or* the result of rationality, intelligence, and scarcity. Yet propitious relations, and their associated class-specific rationalities, might prevail precisely *because* there is a 'universal impulse for human beings to improve their condition by virtue of the kind of animal they are'.[27] The 'rational desire to augment productive

---

[25] *Selected Correspondence*, 31; see *KMTH* 159–60 for comparable statements from other works. (In 1846 'mode of intercourse' occupied the conceptual niche in which Marx later placed '(social) relations of production'.)

[26] 'Marxism's Central Puzzle', 96.

[27] 'Rationality and Class Struggle', 62. Or, more accurately, by virtue of the kind of animal they are *and* the fundamental material features of their situation.

capacity in the face of material scarcity'[28] might explain why productivity-enhancing relations obtain. If they indeed obtain, then, by definition, productivity is enhanced because of them, but the sense in which that is true by definition does not deprive the tendency to productive development of its autonomy.[29]

The *KMTH* argument may be faulty, and it is certainly not conclusive, but it neither moves in a circle nor denies the truth that relations of production are (at least often) the proximate spring of productive progress. What the argument does deny is that relations of production constitute any part of the ultimate reason why development tends to occur. For it locates that ultimate reason in the facts that people are rational, innovative, and afflicted by scarcity. The conclusion from those facts, that productive forces will tend to develop, would not be true unless social relations were characteristically propitious. But the fact that they are propitious is not why the tendency to development obtains, nor even why, in the final analysis, it is fulfilled, since, in the final analysis, it is because of that autonomous tendency that relations are as they are.

The following analogy might illuminate our reply to the circularity objection. One might argue that there will be a tendency for people's illnesses to be cured by other people, who get better over time at curing illnesses, simply because people dislike being ill, something which is not, in the present sense, a social fact. Yet suppose, quite plausibly, that, without appropriate medical organization, which is a social structure, little curing, or progress in curing, would occur. The basic explanation of the tendency of illness to be cured, and of its fulfilment, might nevertheless remain, as was claimed, people's hatred of illness, which could also be adduced to explain, through the tendency to improvement in cures which it generates, the existence of propitious medical organization. The route to the latter claim does not seem to involve a circle, and it looks as though, if there is no circularity here, then there is no circularity in the apparently parallel argument for the primacy of the productive forces over the production relations. The relevant general point is that the fact that proposition q is a necessary condition of the truth of proposition p does not disqualify the claim that p explains why q is true. That structure involves no circularity in general, so why should one think that a circularity appears when *p* says that the productive forces tend to develop and *q* says that social structures are propitious for their development?

6. Joshua Cohen purports to supply an answer to that question. His answer is that it is impossible to explain the tendency to development, if there is one, without drawing on the proposition that relations of production are propitious. But if that social fact is an irreducible part of the explanation of material progress, then one cannot, on pain of circularity, invoke a tendency to material progress in explanation of that very same social fact.

Joshua Cohen might accept that, as we argued against Levine and Wright, the fact that the Development Thesis is true only if social relations are propitious does not itself preclude an asocial explanation of the Development Thesis. But he believes that no asocial explanation of it will work: unless one invokes the propitiousness of social relations, one will be unable to explain any tendency to development. (Joshua Cohen's argument for that conclusion is presented in sections 7 and 11 below.)

Now Joshua Cohen notes that one might adduce the social fact that relations have allowed development to proceed not in order to explain, but in order to provide further evidence for, the Development Thesis, beyond the evidence for it which the asocial premisses provide. That he correctly observes, is how, G. A Cohen used the fact that relations have been propitious in a bolstering sub-argument for the Development Thesis, which is summarized in section 10 below. But, so Joshua Cohen claims, unless one puts that fact to explanatory use, one will not have explained 'why there is a tendency to productive progress, and, *a fortiori*', one will not have explained 'this tendency in terms of a few elementary facts about human nature', or, more generally, in purely material terms. He concludes, similarly to Levine and Wright, but on partly different grounds,[30] that the Primacy Thesis cannot be derived from the Development Thesis. Such a derivation requires that the Development Thesis be established 'on non-social grounds, i.e. without

[30] For Levine and Wright, history shows that productive progress comes from class-specific rationality: it is therefore not, as a matter of fact, asocially explained. By contrast, Joshua Cohen thinks a tendency to productive progress could not, as a matter of principle, be asocially explained. His circularity objection does not depend upon the historical record: see sect. 7, 11 below.

making reference to social forms (especially property relations)'. But then the case for the primacy of the productive forces collapses, since there cannot be an 'asocially based (autonomous) tendency to productive growth'.[31]

Joshua Cohen's challenge can be presented as a trilemma. One alternative is to cite no social facts at all in arguing for the Development Thesis: but then the argument for it is too feeble, as G. A. Cohen recognized—hence his introduction of a sub-argument, in which social facts are cited. The second alternative, embraced by G. A. Cohen, is to cite social facts as further and indirect evidence for the Development Thesis, without relying on them to explain it. This may improve the case for believing the Development Thesis, but now it remains unexplained, since, so Joshua Cohen contends, the asocial premises are unable, by themselves, to explain it. The third alternative is to accept that social facts must appear in the explanation of the Development Thesis, but then the Primacy Thesis cannot be based on the Development Thesis without patent circularity.[32]

7. We shall defend the second alternative, by arguing that Joshua Cohen has not shown that social facts are needed to explain a tendency to development.

The crucial social fact is that 'social structures have been such that individual pursuit of material advantage has issued in productive growth.'[33] Joshua Cohen holds that we cannot forswear

---

[31] Cohen, review of *KMTH*, 261–2.

[32] We construct this trilemma on the basis of an important but difficult paragraph in Cohen's review, which overlaps p. 264 and 265. We have interpreted it under Joshua Cohen's guidance. The paragraph is difficult because of an apparent shift in its author's intention which occurs at p. 265 l. 9. Up until that line, the problem seems to be this: *either* one says that structures have (merely) as a matter of *fact* been propitious for productive development, in which case the argument for the Development Thesis is too feeble, since no *tendency* to productive growth could be inferred; *or* one says that it is in the *nature* of structures that they tend to be propitious, in which case one can indeed infer that the Development Thesis is true, but one may not then, on pain of circularity, use it to argue for the Primacy Thesis. After the ninth line, the problem seems, instead, to be this: *either* one uses the social fact that structures are (or tend to be) propitious to explain the Development Thesis, in which case circularity results; *or* one uses it merely as evidence for the Development Thesis, in which case the latter will lack a convincing explanation. (We have opted for the second interpretation, since it is the one Joshua Cohen chose in conversation with G. A. Cohen.)

[33] Cohen, review of *KMTH* 265.

explanatory use of that fact. For if, in particular, we rely for explanation of the tendency to development on the asocial premises alone, we shall be defeated by the 'co-ordination problem', which is that 'the promptings of reason are directed to individuals, whereas the deeds of society depend upon the actions of groups of individuals, *diversely prompted by reason*.'[34] There is, as G. A. Cohen put it, a 'shadow between what reason suggests and what society does',[35] which the asocial premises cannot remove.

Now Joshua Cohen seems to be raising two rather different problems here, each of which is undoubtedly pertinent, but only the first of which should be called a co-ordination problem.

i. The first problem is the well-known problem of collective action. Although a given materially possible enhancement of productivity might be in everyone's interest, it might never occur, because it is not in everyone's (and perhaps in no one's) individual interest to initiate, and/or to contribute to, the effort required to bring it about. Though each person would benefit from productive progress, his pay-off structure would be that of a free rider, and so no progress would result. Joshua Cohen grants that this would not always be so, but he argues that 'in the abstract', that is, on the basis of asocial premises alone, there is no reason not to expect 'structural arrangements' which 'generate undesirable outcomes from individually rational outcomes' to predominate.[36] For all that the asocial premises show, it is just as likely that individuals will be caught in situations without collectively optimal solutions as it is that such solutions will be accessible to them, and there is therefore no general asocially based tendency for development to occur.

This first problem is a genuine co-ordination problem. Notice, however, that it has nothing to do with the '*diverse* promptings of reason', on one natural interpretation of that phrase. For in many contexts of collective irrationality,[37] such as, for example, the

---

[34] Ibid. 264.
[35] *KMTH* 153.
[36] Review of *KMTH* 257. The full sentence reads: 'For in the abstract there seems no reason to expect "invisible hands" to predominate over "prisoner's dilemmas" or other structural arrangements that generate undesirable outcomes from individually rational actions'. It would be unfair to place too much weight on this invocation of 'invisible hands', but it is important to note that they are by no means the only way that collective action problems are solved or averted. There exist deliberate ways of coping with collective action problems which the metaphor of '*invisible* hands' could not be thought to cover.
[37] We use 'collective irrationality' merely as a label for the Pareto suboptimal

original Prisoners' Dilemma, everyone is prompted to act in the same direction (because, for example, everyone has the same pay-off orderings), but, unfortunately, they are all prompted away from co-operation. The first problem, then, is that the promptings of reason are directed at individuals rather than at groups, not that individuals (or groups) are *diversely* prompted by reason.

ii. The second problem, which is not aptly called a co-ordination problem, is the problem of (what Levine and Wright called) class-specific rationality. When people are considered in terms of their asocial condition, they indeed appear to have an interest in productive progress, but they may lack that interest, all things (including social conditions) considered, because of the roles they occupy in the social structure. A feudal lord's desire to protect and improve his own material situation would give him an interest *against* productive progress when productive progress would induce changes in social relations which threaten his superior position. The lord's optimal course would then be to oppose improvements in technology, while extracting as much as he could from his peasant dependents. More generally:

> the fact that individuals have an *interest* in improving their material situation, and are intelligent enough to devise ways of doing so, does *not* so far provide them with an interest in *improving the forces of production.* Only under *specific structural* conditions is the interest in material advantage tied to an interest in a strategy of productivity-enhancing investment.[38]

The second problem, then, is that the asocial premises do not ensure that people's class positions will endow them with an interest in productive progress. It is not the problem that reason prompts individuals rather than groups, for it would obtain even if, for example, reason prompted feudal lords as a class, rather than as individuals. The problem arises because, in virtue of their specific social positions, reason prompts individuals *and/or* groups *diversely*, and regardless of the presence or absence of collective action problems within groups.

upshot of unsolved collective action problems. We take no stand on the controversial question whether such upshots display genuine irrationality, as opposed to just adversity.

[38] Cohen, review of *KMTH* 268.

The first problem is the discrepancy between individual and collective rationality, while the second problem is the discrepancy between what is rational, asocially considered, and what is rational, all things, including class position, considered. But both 'discrepant rationality' problems could be thought to generate the same conclusion, which is that, for all that the asocial premisses show, 'interests and powers' might be 'so organized that progress is blocked, with nothing "outside" the structure to guarantee its transformation in a way that allows continued progress.'[39]

Hence, if there is a tendency to productive development, then not only, and non-fatally, must social structures have a certain shape, but also, and this is the fatal point, the tendency has to be explained (in part) by reference to the fact that they have that shape. The tendency is therefore not autonomous, and it therefore cannot be used to explain the nature of relations of production.

8. Since Joshua Cohen appears to take the Development Thesis in a RAP sense,[40] one might respond to the discrepant rationality problems by exploiting its non-RAP interpretation, as follows: social structures tend to be propitious because, in the last analysis, people do not tolerate them when they are severely unpropitious. And that intolerance has an asocial explanation. It reflects the interest people have, under conditions of scarcity, in progress-inducing relations of production. They are biased in favour of propitious relations, and that political circumstance is, in the relevant sense, something '"outside" the structure' which tends to ensure that relations continue to be propitious.

9. But that reply to the discrepant rationality problems is open to an obvious objection. For whether or not the 'search-and-selection process which operates on the relations of production' (see page 91 above) counts as '"outside" the structure' (by virtue of being 'outside' the economy), that process occurs on a level (within, one might say, a political superstructure) at which both kinds of discrepant rationality problems will once again arise. Thus Joshua Cohen could now ask: What ensures that political superstructures

---

[39] Ibid. 257.
[40] See ibid. 263.

will enable individuals to organize progressive political change, instead of trapping them in Prisoners' Dilemmas? And: Why should classes with an interest in enhancing productivity also have the power to replace politically incumbent classes which lack it? If political selection overcomes the discrepant rationality problems at the level of the economic structure, what overcomes those problems at the level of the political superstructure itself? If the asocial premisses do not explain the triumph over rationality problems directly, so that political selection must be invoked, then why suppose that those premisses directly explain the absence of defeating rationality problems in the political superstructure?

Joshua Cohen would conclude that the argument remains 'stuck between circularity and enfeeblement'.[41] Our new hypothesis is that, if and when economic structures present insurmountable rationality problems, political superstructures facilitate their replacement. If that hypothesis is intended as an explanatory premiss for the conclusion that the forces tend to develop, then their tendency to do so is not autonomous, and the project of explaining the social by the material collapses into circularity. Recourse to the political superstructure merely expands the circle, for it is part of the social *explanandum* that superstructures are congenial to propitious economic structures, and that *explanandum* is here being used to help to explain its material supposed *explanans*. If, on the other hand, the congeniality of superstructures is, instead, adduced as mere further (non-explaining) evidence for the Development Thesis, then the explanation of the Development Thesis is enfeebled. For asocial premisses cannot explain why rationality problems do not arise at the political level, and they therefore do not explain how they are overcome at the economic level.

10. Although neither of the discrepant rationality problems described in section 7 above was expressly formulated in *KMTH*, the existence of problems of that general kind was noted, and the circularity objection which they threaten to sustain was more or less envisaged.[42] Then, to show that, despite such problems, the asocial premisses might strongly support the Development Thesis, a sub-argument was offered. Its premiss—called by Joshua Cohen

---

[41] Ibid. 265.
[42] *KMTH* 153.

'the Alleged Facts'[43]—was that societies frequently replace productive forces by better ones, and only very infrequently by inferior ones. Its conclusion was that, although there exist obstacles to the expression of rationality, the asocial premisses formulate circumstances which do have a big impact on the world, since, unless one supposes that they do, one cannot explain the contrast between the frequency of productive progress and the rarity of productive regression. Part of the explanation of lack of regression might, of course, be sheer social inertia, but 'inertia is too unselective to explain, by itself', a general 'lack of regression in face of the fact that there is often conspicuous progress'.[44]

The sub-argument's conclusion is that the asocial premisses have considerable general explanatory power. That conclusion is intended to suggest that they might have enough explanatory power to justify the claim that there is a tendency to productive progress, which is the conclusion of the main argument. Thus the frequency of *actual* progress, in face of the rarity of actual regress, is used to defend the operation of inferring a *tendency* to productive progress from the asocial premisses. 'The facts which best explain why the productive forces frequently advance, but rarely regress, also make it reasonable to believe that the productive forces have a natural propensity to expand.'[45]

11. Now Joshua Cohen denies the Alleged Facts, on which the subargument is based, and we confront that denial in section 14. But he also maintains that the Alleged Facts do little to overcome the discrepant rationality objection *even if they are exactly as alleged.* We italicize that clause because we find the thought it expresses extraordinary, and we emphasize that, from now until the end of section 13, we shall suppose, with full polemical propriety, that the Facts are exactly as Alleged.

According to *KMTH*, the asocial premisses provide a good explanation of the Alleged Facts, and we may therefore conclude that the conditions those premisses formulate powerfully constrain the structure of society. Joshua Cohen disputes the starting-point of that argument. He thinks that, whatever would be the real

[43] Review of *KMTH* 264.
[44] *KMTH* 154.
[45] William Shaw, 'Historical Materialism and the Development Thesis', 209.

explanation of the Alleged Facts, the asocial premises simply could not explain them adequately. 'What the facts, if they were as alleged, would show is that structures have been such that individual pursuit of material advantage has issued in productive growth.'[46] They would show that self-interested rationality regularly finds a way through the reefs of suboptimality and counter-finality. But rationality can do that only if there is a way to be found, and the asocial premises cannot explain why such a way is available. The conditions they formulate are powerless to prevent either of the discrepant rationality problems from being insoluble.

Take, first, the collective action problem. We could imagine a society in which a universal interest in progress was not satisfied, because people were locked into an unmodifiable multi-person Prisoners' Dilemma. Or, to take the class-specific rationality problem, imagine a society which meets the following specifications: Eighty per cent of its members live off the labour of the rest. Productive progress would so upset social relations as to render that exploiting majority much worse off. And the producers, who have an interest in productive progress, and the technical capacity to bring it about, are politically unable to challenge the majority class.[47]

No matter how rational, intelligent and motivated to pursue material advantage individuals are, no tendency to productive progress would ensue in these logically possible societies. But, for all that any asocial premises show, all historical societies could have been relevantly like one or other of them. Hence no asocial premises can yield the Development Thesis. To derive the Development Thesis, one needs the asocially inexplicable premiss that social structures have as a matter of fact contained channels along which rationality could flow. To explain a tendency to development, that would be required as an independent premiss. And that restores the circularity-or-enfeeblement dilemma.

G. A. Cohen's sub-argument was offered in mitigation of 'two large gaps' in the original argument for the development thesis. The first was that individuals might not care enough about their material problem, since they have other problems to contend with too. The second was the one already mentioned, that 'it is not evident that societies are disposed to bring about what rationality

---

[46] Review of *KMTH* 265.
[47] Cf. ibid. 268–9.

would lead men to choose.[48] Joshua Cohen allows that the sub-argument is a 'plausible response to the *first* difficulty'. But he denies that it helps with the second. For 'it is not facts about *individuals* that are now in question, but facts about the *structures* that determine the outcomes of individual acts.'[49] The circularity-or-enfeeblement dilemma is unavoidable, since asocial constraints could never ensure that structures will offer opportunities for overcoming discrepant rationality problems. If the Facts are indeed as Alleged, then that must be because social structures have, on the whole, been favourable to development, and not in virtue of any extra-social development tendency.

12. The objection of section 11 does not challenge the Alleged Facts. It therefore does not say that societies of the logically possible sort it describes occur universally, for it follows from the Alleged Facts that propitious social relations are very common. What the objection says is that their being common could not be materially explained.

We reply that no good argument has been provided for that conclusion. For one way in which the asocial conditions (whose weight the sub-argument seeks to enhance) might assert themselves is precisely by militating against widespread occurrence of logically possible societies of an unpropitious kind. Though logically possible, they might, for material reasons, be contingently unlikely, and then the objection of section 11 would fail.

How might the facts recorded in the asocial premisses make obstructive structures materially improbable? Those premisses concern not only the motivations and capacities of individuals, but also the fundamental material features of their situation. One such feature is the limited amount of productive power available to them, and that feature is relevant to both of the examples described in section 11.

Thus, to address the first example, Prisoners' Dilemmas are inescapable only when people are unable to modify each other's pay-off structures in certain ways. But even when they cannot do so, the result might not be so dire, because of the uncertainties and

---

[48] *KMTH* 153.
[49] Review of *KMTH* 264–5.

interdependencies imposed by material scarcity. Interdependency tends to make Prisoners' Dilemmas occur in indefinitely long series, and it is by now well known that such seriality facilitates their solution. Material conditions might also, moreover, enable 'political entrepreneurs' to modify pay-off structures, to beat the decision environment into such a shape that the free rider quandary is transcended.

Consider, now, the second example of section 11. A society in which a bare twenty per cent of the population does all the work is, by definition, at a very high level of productive power. But that would have liberating consequences for the political capacity of the exploited class, so that the features characterizing the society, while logically compatible, might never co-occur, for material reasons.

Structures do organize 'interests and powers',[50] but they do not generate them *ex nihilo*, and the material constraints under which historical structures arise might regularly open ways for individuals to ensure that productive progress occurs. That seems to be a possible conclusion from the Alleged Facts. It is not, perhaps, a mandatory one, but it is not in principle excluded in the fashion argued in section 11.

Despite the fact that economic and political structures are not unproblematically congenial to progress, the Alleged Facts entail that progress wins through. The sub-argument then presents this challenge: either accept that the asocial premises have great explanatory power, or offer an alternative explanation of the contrast between frequency of progress and infrequency of regress. Note that the *greater* the propensity of social structures to throw up rationality problems is, the *better* grounded is the conclusion of the sub-argument, if, as we are here allowed to suppose, the Alleged Facts obtain. Despite the potential for suboptimality and counter-finality in social structures, the Facts say that progress often occurs and regress hardly ever does, and that suggests that the asocial conditions of human nature and circumstances are strongly efficacious, for they seem to have the strong effect of subverting persistingly unprogressive structures in favour of progressive ones.

We conclude that the sub-argument's challenge is intact. Nothing Joshua Cohen says succeeds in dissipating its force.

---

[50] Ibid. 257: see p. 97 above.

13. Here is a further illustration of the importance of material constraints on structures.

Joshua Cohen remarks that the Alleged Facts are supposed to answer G. A. Cohen's first objection (see page 100 above) to his argument for the Development Thesis by 'providing indirect evidence that material interests are in fact of paramount significance for individuals'.[51] But the Alleged Facts might sustain an answer to that objection which takes an interestingly different form,[52] because it does not imply anything 'definite about the priorities among' people's 'different goals'.[53] Material constraints might ensure that people's non-material interests, though not at all secondary, tend not to conflict with their material interests in progress-defeating ways. It might even be that their other goals are 'preferred to productive development whenever they conflict with it, but' that they 'conflict with this goal so infrequently', or at such non-critical junctures, 'that they never endanger a materialist account of history'.[54] That conjecture might, of course, be empirically implausible, but the way to show that is to assess the fidelity of the materialist account to the facts of history. The claim that there is an inevitable circularity in any attempt to argue for the account cannot be sustained.

14. Now Joshua Cohen does, also, construct a factual case against historical materialism, when he addresses himself to the sub-argument's claims about the historical record. He does not, of course, question the Alleged Fact that 'productive forces are frequently replaced by better ones', but he denies the sub-argument's other allegation, which is that 'societies rarely replace a given set of productive forces by an inferior one', that there is, in other words, 'little productive regression' in history.[55]

Joshua Cohen counter-claims 'that there is *substantial* regression and stagnation, alongside productive progress'.[56] Now (prolonged)

[51] Review of *KMTH*.
[52] To be fair, we note that *KMTH* provided no hint of this different form of answer.
[53] Allen Wood, *Karl Marx*, 30.
[54] Ibid.
[55] Review of *KMTH* 264.
[56] Ibid. 266.

stagnation is, in a general way, *prima facie* evidence against historical materialism, but it is not evidence against either of the Alleged Facts, and here, in an admittedly somewhat narrow way, we shall stick to our brief and examine the adequacy of Joshua Cohen's case for the claim that the record shows '*substantial regression*'.

Joshua Cohen's first example is the 'long period' of Chinese history 'roughly corresponding to the Ming and Ch'ing dynasties', in which, he says, there was 'little evidence of . . . development of productive forces, though . . . no apparent regression either'.[57] The latter concession makes the example irrelevant here: what we have is, at most, an example of stagnation. And it is not clear that we have even that much. For Joshua Cohen also says that, in the given period, 'agricultural output continues to expand on the basis of the extension of cultivation and increased output per acre on increasingly fragmented holdings'[58] and the exploitation of new resources implied by the extension of cultivation could count as an expansion of productive power. Any increase in output per person, or, more accurately, in potential output per person, qualifies, for non-arbitrary reasons,[59] as a development of the productive forces, whether or not the increase is based on an improvement in productive technique. Joshua Cohen thinks the China example is a case of stagnation only because he misidentifies the development of the productive forces with the development of technology alone.

In the second paragraph of his historical review[60] Joshua Cohen mentions more cases of putative stagnation, and only one case of a putatively 'genuine regression in agricultural productivity, resulting from the "second serfdom", i.e., from the imposition of substantial labour services on the Polish peasantry'.[61]

Now the 'second serfdom' was certainly a regression in *relations* of production, since it replaced relatively free by relatively bound labour. One can, moreover, agree with Joshua Cohen that the 'imposition of services guaranteed to the Polish lords what was certainly more important to them than an increase in the forces of production, viz., control over the surplus produced in agriculture'.[62] But three considerations undermine Joshua Cohen's hope that the example will serve his polemical purposes. i. The fact that

---

[57] Ibid. 267.
[58] Ibid.
[59] See *KMTH* 60–1.

[60] Review of *KMTH* 267–8.
[61] Ibid. 267.
[62] Ibid.

control over the surplus was *more* important to the lords does not mean that they would not also have cared how big that surplus was, and, therefore, how effective the agricultural productive forces were. ii. What needs to be shown, to establish regression in the level of development of the forces, is that potential output per person dropped, because, e.g., of a loss of agricutural skill, or a destruction of good means of production. The Polish nobles might have accepted a trade-off in which existing forces were underused, or badly used, but that would not mean that the power of the stock of forces available to them was diminished. iii. If the revived serf relations later crumbled because the forces they employed were actually and/or potentially underproductive, then that would support the Development Thesis in an indirect way: it would be evidence that forms of society which do not share in the tendency of the forces to develop are likely to go under.

These brief rejoinders do not, of course, settle the historical issue in our favour. What they do show is that it is more difficult to refute our case than one might think when crucial distinctions are overlooked: between stagnation and regression, between actual and potential output per person, and between technical progress and productive progress in a comprehensive sense. Not being historians, all we can offer are these potent conceptual reminders—and one important non-conceptual point:

In light of the fact that it is only relatively recently that historians have come to appreciate the full extent of technical progress both under feudalism and within the ancient world—both of which had long been thought innocent of technical innovation—one needs to avoid facilely writing off earlier societies as devoid of productive progress.[63]

15. Underlying Joshua Cohen's criticisms is, he says, a 'scepticism' about *KMTH*'s 'ambition',[64] which is 'to defend a non-theological theory of history in which progress is the central tendency'.[65] Such a defence, he rightly says, requires 'some extra-social factor . . . controlling historical change'.[66]

---

[63] Shaw, 'Historical Materialism and the Development Thesis', 205. For an excellent account of pre-capitalist productive progress, and of the mechanisms driving it, see Gunnar Perssons's *Pre-Industrial Economic Growth in Europe*.

[64] Review of *KMTH* 254–5.

[65] Ibid. 257.

[66] Ibid. 273.

In a domain as uncertain as the present one, everybody is entitled to be sceptical: no one could claim to *know* that extra-social features of human nature and the human situation operate powerfully enough to generate an historical tendency capable of overcoming recalcitrant social structures. But material conditions patently constrain social structures to *some* degree, and our chief complaint is against an *a priori* denial that the constraints are strong enough to induce the mooted extra-social tendency. Joshua Cohen's circularity objection (though not his objection to the Alleged Facts) amounts to such an *a priori* denial.

We have acknowledged that social structures must be of a certain shape if there is to be a tendency for the forces of production to develop. But we have denied that that is a reason for rejecting the extra-social explanations of historical materialism. If it were such a reason, then there would be (equally *a priori*) reasons for ruling out such contributions to social understanding as Marvin Harris's *Cultural Materialism*,[67] and the whole field of human sociobiology. (Whatever may be the defects of sociobiology, it is surely not to be dismissed on the mere ground that complaisant social structures are required to realize the tendencies it posits.)

[67] See, in particular, ch. 4 of that book.

2
Historical Materialism—Criticism and Revision

6

FETTERING

1. I found a lot of ambiguity in traditional statements of historical materialism, and much of *KMTH* was, consequently, an exercise in disambiguation. But I have become aware, partly as a result of the large amount of excellent criticism to which the book has been subjected, that it contains at least as much ambiguity as it dispels.

One important ambiguity was spotted by Richard Miller.[1] It is the vacillation, in *KMTH*, between contrasting conceptions of what it is for relations of production to *fetter* productive forces, conceptions which, following Miller, we can call those of *Absolute Stagnation* and *Relative Inferiority*. On the Absolute conception, fettering relations prevent all further improvement in productivity. On the Relative conception, they may or may not do so, and there is no reason to think that in general they do so, for on the Relative conception there is fettering when different feasible relations of production would develop the productive forces faster, and not just temporarily, but over a considerable period of time. On the Relative conception fettering obtains when existing relations are not optimal for further development of the productive forces.

It is natural, at this point, to try to choose between the two conceptions, but, as we shall see, it is difficult to favour either. An adequate conception of fettering must meet two constraints, imposed by the 1859 Preface sentences which introduce the notion of fettering:

At a certain stage of their development, the material productive forces of society come in conflict with the existing relations of production . . . From forms of development of the productive forces these relations turn into their fetters. Then begins an epoch of social revolution.

The first two sentences lay down what may be called the *predictability constraint*: it must be plausible to suppose that, under continued development of the productive forces, relations do,

---

[1] See his 'Productive Forces and the Forces of Change', 96–7. Miller's reference to *KMTH* 175 is particularly telling.

sooner or later, become fetters. The *revolution constraint*, which comes from the third sentence, is that it must be plausible to suppose that when relations become fetters they are revolutionized. (Further sentences entail that productively superior relations of production are installed in the course of the epoch of social revolution. But that will not here figure as a constraint. For *present* purposes, it is possible that the revolution should prove abortive and induce no progress at all. An epoch of social revolution could be a struggle between socialism and barbarism which barbarism wins.)

Let me say what is meant by calling the foregoing *constraints* on an adequate conception of fettering. The constraints derive from what Marx wrote, but how well a given conception of fettering meets them depends on how true the conception is to independently plausible statements about how people and societies operate. To illustrate for the case of the revolution constraint: since Marx said that fettering is followed by revolution, an adequate conception of fettering must make it likely, *given how the world works*, that fettering would indeed be followed by revolution.

Now the reason why it is, as I said, hard to favour either the Absolute Stagnation or the Relative Inferiority conceptions of fettering is that neither seems able to meet both the predictability and the revolution constraints. The Absolute conception perhaps meets the revolution constraint, but I doubt that it meets the predictability constraint: is there reason to think that, were capitalism, for example, to last forever, then the development of the productive forces would at some point entirely cease, even if there is abundant reason to think that, *were* their development to stop, an epoch of revolution would ensue? (Certain devotees of the Law of the Tendency of the Rate of Profit to Fall think that not merely increases in productivity but production itself will stop, for ever, if capitalism lasts. They have no difficulty espousing the Absolute conception of fettering, but non-communicants of their sect are not in the same position.) There may not even be good reason to think that a persisting capitalism would, in time, display a deceleration in the rate of development of the productive forces: Absolute Stagnation is, of course, the extreme case—apart from actual retrogression[2]—of such deceleration.

---

[2] On retrogression as the stimulus to revolution see the discussion of McMurtry in sect. 7 below, and see p. 122 of that discussion for a suggestion that, contrary to the doubt expressed in the paragraph above, even actual retrogression in productive power might be an eventual consequence of capitalist relations of production.

The Relative Inferiority conception meets the predictability constraint better: it seems probable that all class-bound relations of production are only finitely flexible, and that with continued development of productive power they become less good than other relations would be at facilitating further productive progress. But Relative Inferiority satisfies the revolution constraint less readily. For the costs and dangers of revolution, both to those initiating it and to those who follow them, make it unreasonable to expect a society to undergo revolution just because relations which are better at developing the productive forces are possible, especially when those relations have not already been formed elsewhere and been seen to be better.[3] Note that relations might be Relative fetters even when they are stimulating faster productive development than has ever before occurred. Is it plausible to suppose that revolution would be risked at a time of *accelerated* development of the productive forces, just because there would be still faster development under different relations? Would workers overthrow a capitalism which has reduced the length of each computer generation to one year because socialism promises to make it nine months?

My doubt that the Relative conception satisfies the revolution constraint is not based on the false proposition that people revolt only when it is in their selfish interest to do so: arguably, the structure of collective action is such that almost none would revolt, under any conditions, and therefore on any conception of fettering,

---

[3] This point is stressed by Elster at *Making Sense of Marx*, 293. One might try to reply to it as follows: let it be granted that workers will not make a revolution just because the relevant counterfactual is true. Still, a transition to new relations might be made in one or two societies for reasons unconnected with contradiction between forces and relations of production. The new relations would then display their superiority, and consequently, through imitation, be generalized, so that, globally speaking, there would be social transformation because of Relative Inferiority fettering. (See ch. 1, sect. 4 above on the meaning of 'globally speaking' here.)

It might be objected that the circumstance that relations fetter forces is meant to be not only a sufficient but also a necessary condition of revolution, so that, contrary to the envisaged reply, there cannot be a single revolution which is not a response to fettering. But a proponent of the reply could rejoin that the claim that fettering is a necessary condition of revolution itself applies globally, and not to each society, and that would preserve the viability of his model of initial chance variation and deliberate subsequent selection.

The foregoing reply to the Elster objection to Relative-Development fettering would also serve, *mutatis mutandis*, against analogous objections to the notions of Relative Use Fettering and Net Fettering, which are introduced in sects. 2 and 5 below. (Elster anticipates and rejects the reply to his objection given above, but I do not share his confidence in the general application of his reasons for rejecting it: see *Making Sense of Marx*, 293 ff.)

if that false proposition were true.[4] But one can affirm that unselfish inspiration is a necessary condition of revolutionary action and still believe that people are unlikely to embark on revolution when the *status quo* is not intolerable, the costs and dangers of insurgency are severe, and success is uncertain, and that is enough to generate doubt that the Relative conception satisfies the revolution constraint.

Neither Absolute Stagnation nor Relative Inferiority, in their unqualifed forms,[5] will do, and the right conclusion might be that the notion that revolution follows on fettering of the *development* of the productive forces cannot be saved. It might be that a quite different formulation of the Marxist theory of social change is required.

2. Perhaps we shall reach the required formulation by exploring the idea that the fettering which provokes revolution is of the *use*, rather than of the *development*, of the productive forces. The development of the productive forces is growth in their productive power, or increase in how much *can be* (not *is being*) produced.[6] Fettering the development of the productive forces is, accordingly, restricting the growth of a capacity. It is, for example, reducing the rate of growth of productive capacity to zero, as in the Absolute Stagnation conception, or rendering that rate lower than it could be, as in the Relative Inferiority conception. But whether growth in productive capacity is in some way being impeded is a quite different issue from whether, and to what extent, productive capacity is being effectively used. And perhaps the latter issue is the more important one from the point of view of the dynamics of social change.

---

[4] See ch. 4, sect. 2 above.

[5] Each condition could be made stronger and/or more plausible through the addition of qualifications, and complex conditions could be devised which combine absolute and relative elements. In this highly preliminary and experimental discussion I do not explore those further possibilities, and I consequently fail to provide a comprehensive treatment of my topic. I hope to stimulate sufficient interest in the problem to provoke others to attempt a better solution to it than anything I offer here.

[6] The relevant 'concept of productivity differs from the one the economist uses when he compares the physical productivity of labour in different societies. Productivity in our sense is the maximum to which productivity in that sense could be raised, with existing means and knowledge' (*KMTH* 56).

I now attempt two supporting illustrations of this suggestion.

Early modern forms of division of labour in what Marx called 'manufacture' demanded the concentration in one place of large numbers of workers. Such concentration was variously forbidden and hampered by feudal and semi-feudal bonds and regulations, which tied producers to particular lords and masters in dispersed locations. Here, then, the relations of production fettered the use of the productive forces and, moreover, those relations came under pressure for that reason. Change occurred because of the gap between what *could* be achieved and what *was* being achieved, rather than because of the gap between how fast capacity was improving and how fast it could be improved: the second gap existed but it is hard to believe that it was comparably powerful as a precipitant of social change.

Another illustration. I would claim that capitalist relations of production impede optimal use of the high technology those relations are so good at creating. Under capitalism advances in computer and electronic engineering cause economic dislocation, unemployment, and the degradation of work sometimes called 'deskilling', whereas under different arrangements the same forces of production could be used to bring about a benign realignment of labour, leisure, and education. I think, too, that there might be increasing recognition of the irrationality of the existing use of contemporary technological marvels and, as a result, socialist social change. If that happened, the change would occur not at all because capitalism does not replace a given generation of computers quickly enough, but because it does not make good use of any generation of computers. Once again, the operative discrepancy would be not between how fast what can be done improves and how fast it could improve, but between what is done and what could be done.

We can call the recommended new conception Use Fettering,[7] as opposed to Development Fettering. Like Development Fettering, Use Fettering has absolute and relative variants, but only its relative variant deserves examination. Absolute Use Fettering means a complete unemployment of all factors of production, so it fails to

---

[7] Use Fettering is invoked in many *KMTH* formulations, such as ones at pp. 160 and 282, and, some would say, throughout the whole of ch. 11. William Shaw's *Marx's Theory of History* emphasizes Use Fettering at pp. 98–101. John McMurtry (*The Structure of Marx's World-View*, 209 n. 11) *defines* 'fettering' as impeding full use, yet at p. 207 he seems to treat 'hindering technological development' as a form of fettering. (For further discussion of McMurtry, see sect. 7 below.)

meet the predictability constraint quite as massively as it meets the revolution constraint. Relative Use Fettering meets the predictability constraint better than Absolute Development Fettering does, and, indeed, tolerably well, since, as I had occasion to remark above (page 111), all class-bound economic systems are only finitely flexible: it is therefore likely that they are sooner or later unable to make optimal use of the developments in productive capacity which they induce or allow.[8] In addition, Relative Use Fettering meets the revolution constraint better than Relative Development Fettering does, since the discrepancy between capacity and use is more perceptible than, and is, therefore, a more potent stimulant of unrest, protest, and change than, the shortfall in rate of development implied by Relative Development Fettering. (Still, one must not exaggerate the perceptibility of Relative Use Fettering, since it obtains *not* merely when less than 100 per cent of capacity is used, but when *more* capacity would be used by some feasible alternative system.)

3. Someone might claim that I have overplayed the difference between Development Fettering and Use Fettering. He might say that relations which make better use of existing productive capacity will tend also to be better at enhancing it. But I see no reason for believing that that is in general true. Many socialists would now concede that nothing can match capitalism as a stimulant to progress in productive power, but they nevertheless favour socialism since they think somewhat slower productive progress is a reasonable price to pay for better use of productive power at every stage.[9] Perhaps those socialists are being unduly pessimistic, but they are not wrong because of a law which connects the various virtues economic structures can have.

4. A critic sympathetic to Use Fettering might contend that what needs revision is what I created out of Marx, not Marx himself, who already preferred Use to Development Fettering. But I think that we have reached the recommended new path by exploring

---

[8] 'Induce or allow' is, of course, an all-too-pregnant disjunction. For a partial delivery of its meaning, see *KMTH*, ch. 6, sect. 7.

[9] According to Jon Elster (*Making Sense of Marx*, 259), Marx would have shown some sympathy for this view.

ambiguities of which Marx was not, in a lively way, aware, and he certainly did not have Use Fettering distinctly in mind when he wrote the Preface sentence ('From forms of development of the productive forces these relations turn into their fetters') which is my topic in this chapter. In the natural reading of that sentence, relations which have become fetters cannot also still be forms of development of the productive forces. But relations which fetter the use of the productive forces could still be forms of development of the productive forces. Hence Marx did not mean 'fetters on the use of the productive forces' when he wrote 'fetters' in the above sentence.

Now, while Marx did not *mean* 'fetters on use' when he wrote 'fetters' in the Preface, he might, nevertheless, have thought that development-fettering relations are, by their nature, also use-fettering ones, and, even if he did not think that very strong thing, I am sure that he did think that Use Fettering often accompanies Development Fettering. And although the Preface formulation tends to represent Development Fettering alone as significant from a revolutionary point of view, I am sure that Marx also thought that Use Fettering had dynamic implications.

Sometimes (though not in the Preface), Marx meant by 'the *development* of the productive forces' a process which I would subsume under the concept of their *use*. For there is an ambiguity, on which I have not yet had occasion to remark, in the word 'develop' (and in the corresponding German '*entwicklen*') which induces an ambiguity in the phrase 'the development of the productive forces'. 'Develop' can mean, what I have so far always here meant by it, *improve*, but it can also mean actualize, or *bring a potential to fruition*. Hence 'the development of the productive forces' can mean not only an increase in the power of the productive forces, and/or the replacement of inferior productive forces by better ones, but also (not improving on existing technique but) embodying already existing technique in concrete exemplars. A capitalist depression might prevent the application of a now known technique. The technique is then a productive force prevented by capitalism from being developed, not in the sense that it stops it being improved, but in the sense that it prevents it being actualized in functioning means of production. And this form of non-development is a form of non-use of the productive force in question.

The Preface uses 'forms of development' in the 'improvement' sense of 'development', for it is at a certain *stage* of the development of the forces that relations become fetters on them, and stages of development, in the Preface sense, go with development as improvement, not development as implementation or embodiment, the production of tokens of a type. Elsewhere, however, Marx does use 'development' in the embodiment, use-related sense. Here is a case where the fettering of the development of the forces under pre-capitalist social relations is a matter of preventing them from being used:

[In petty industry] the peasant owns the land he cultivates, or the artisan owns the tool with which he is an accomplished performer.

This mode of production presupposes the fragmentation of holdings, and the dispersal of the other means of production. As it excludes the concentration of these means of production, so it also excludes co-operation, division of labour within each separate process of production, the social control and regulation of the forces of nature, the free development of the productive forces of society.[10]

The last phrase on Marx's list names something of a piece with what is named by the phrases preceding it, and we might even interpret it as summing up the list that precedes it. The thrust of the passage is that petty industry fetters the productive forces not in the sense that it prevents them from proceeding to a higher stage (though that is no doubt also, and relatedly, true) but in the sense that it prevents their most efficient, their 'free', use. Hence, despite his employment of the *word* 'development' to denote what is blocked here, I am confident that the passage gives evidence both of Marx's exercise of the concept of Use Fettering and of his belief that it tends to lead to remedial social change. (The second contention is based on the rest of the paragraph, in which, by the way, Marx goes on to use 'development' and 'fetters' in a straightforwardly development-fettering fashion.)

5. If we have to choose between Use Fettering and Development Fettering, then, given the Preface constraints, Use Fettering should be preferred. But there is a third conception of fettering which, for

---

[10] *Capital*, i. 927. (I have eliminated the 'and' before the final phrase, since it does not appear in the orginal German.)

reasons to be given presently, I shall call Net Fettering, and which might well be thought preferable to each of the two conceptions which we have looked at so far.

To motivate the introduction of Net Fettering, I note that there was an unacceptable bias in some of the comparisons I employed to justify the displacement of Development Fettering by Use Fettering. I plausibly suggested that workers would not overthrow a capitalism where the length of each computer generation is one year just because socialism promises to make it nine months. But what if socialism would reduce it to one month, or, more generally, would be so much more efficient dynamically that, even though, let us also suppose, it would be much less good at using the power its dynamic efficiency granted it, the net effect of shifting to socialism would be greater *used* productive power at any point in the future? Social form A is arguably superior to social form B if, although A uses the forces to degree .6 and B to degree .95, A develops them so much faster than B that comparison of their trajectories shows a net effect of greater used productive power in A. A might, indeed, need to underuse the forces in order to develop them as quickly as it does, as Schumpeter dialectically noted:

A system—any system, economic or other—that at *every* given point of time fully utilizes its possibilities to the best advantage may yet in the long run be inferior to a system that does so at *no* given point of time, because the latter's failure to do so may be a condition for the level or speed of long-run performance.[11]

Schumpeter's point supports the following procedure for judging the comparative quality of economic systems: look neither merely at how fast they develop the forces nor merely at how well they use them but at the trajectories they promise of *used productive power*, which is a multiple of level of development and degree of use. And call a system *fettering* if, given both the rate at which it develops the forces and how well it uses them, the amount of productive power it harnesses at given future times is less than what some alternative feasible system would harness. That is the Net Fettering proposal.

Net Fettering has two major advantages over Use Fettering. The first depends on the historical materialist idea that fettering economic systems go because it is irrational for people to go on

[11] *Capitalism, Socialism, and Democracy*, 83.

tolerating them.[12] For it would be irrational to prefer society *A* to society *B*, if *B* is use fettering relative to *A* but *A* is net fettering relative to *B*.

Net Fettering is also superior to Use Fettering from the point of view of the unity of historical materialism. Recall the basic claim of that theory, with which this book began:

1. History is, fundamentally, the growth of human productive power, and forms of society rise and fall according as they enable and promote, or prevent and discourage, that growth.

If we shift to Use Fettering, then we can (as we must) retain the first conjunct of (1), but its second conjunct will be altered, since, under Use Fettering, encouraging and preventing *growth* is no longer the key to preservation and change of relations of production. The smallest amendment to (1) imposed by the shift to Use Fettering would yield something like the following:

2. History is, fundamentally, the growth of human productive power, and forms of society rise and fall according as they enable and promote, or prevent and discourage, use of the productive capacity whose expansion that growth is.

In formulation (1), enduring economic structures promote growth in productive power, and social change is induced when a given economic structure no longer promotes that growth: the theory has an agreeable unity to it. In (2), nothing is said about what promotes growth in productive power. We could, of course, expand (2), by adding that the economic structures which are retained or rejected according as they encourage or frustrate *use* of the productive forces also serve to promote the development of the forces. But it then looks strange that social change is not, as in (1), induced when economic structures fetter growth, as opposed to use, of productive power. With the shift to Use Fettering, historical materialism becomes disjointed.[13]

Under Net Fettering, by contrast, there is a fairly obvious and simple emendation of (1) which restores unity to the theory. Instead of saying that history is the growth of productive power, we say that it is the growth of *used* productive power (where that is a

---

[12] See *KMTH*, ch. 6 sect. 4, and the defence of its doctrine in ch. 5 above.

[13] Or, as Elster rather hyperbolically says, 'blatantly inconsistent' (*Making Sense of Marx*, 264. Cf. also Ibid. 266 and *Explaining Technical Change*, 212.)

function of level of development and degree of use). When 'used' is thus inserted in the first conjunct of (1), theoretical unity is maintained, since we shall now mean by 'growth' at the end of the formulation not growth of productive power but growth of used productive power. The relevant fettering will now be of that net quantity, although we could also say, in particular cases, that there is Use or Development Fettering according as it is a static or a dynamic inefficiency which is largely accounting for the Net Fettering itself.

6. We have now distinguished three forms of relative fettering. Relative Development Fettering occurs when productive power (that is, the capacity to produce output) grows more slowly than it could. Relative Use Fettering occurs when output from the available productive forces is less that it could be. And Relative Net Fettering occurs when the trajectory of output levels is less high than it could be.

Each of the three forms of fettering is defined in terms (*inter alia*) of the concept of output. But what does 'output', as it figures in their definitions, mean?

The simplest thing to mean by 'output' is gross national product, or 'GNP'. If we so use 'output', then a social form A is superior to a social form B from the use point of view if and only if A produces more GNP with the given forces than B does. But when I suggested, in section 2 above, that, under socialist relations, the productive forces could be used to produce a benign realignment of labour, leisure, and education,[14] the implied notion of output was not GNP, since it involved strongly qualitative judgments of what sorts of uses of productive forces would be most worth while. (I say '*strongly* qualitative' since some judgments of the quality of output are necessary to the application of even the GNP concept.) I would not say that the prospects are zero for establishing a defensible metric for the quality or qualities in question, but it is fairly obvious that the metric used to measure GNP is too crude to serve in this connection.

---

[14] When capitalism's prevention of that realignment is regarded as its chief fettering effect, one may say, with Elster, that 'the contradiction between the productive forces and the relations of production' is coextensive with 'spiritual alienation' (*Making Sense of Marx*, 265–6).

Suppose someone holds that, while capitalism is superior to socialism from the point of view of Development Fettering, socialism is superior from a Net Fettering point of view, because it is superior from a Use Fettering point of view. Then, as I shall now show, he almost certainly requires a notion of output which is more qualitative than the bare GNP notion.

Suppose that one has in mind a GNP conception of output when one judges that socialism, though inferior in developmental terms, is superior on the net criterion. Then one's judgment is unlikely to be true of anything but the present and the near future. For even if one allows that capitalism's rate of development is only modestly higher than socialism's, say 3 per cent *per annum* as against 2 per cent, capitalism will eventually overtake socialism on the net criterion unless its use of the forces is, in comparison with socialism's, constantly diminishing: and that is hardly likely. Given, moreover, the rapidity with which compound interest zooms up, unless one posits crazy numerical values for the relevant variables, capitalism will overtake socialism not merely eventually, but rather soon. Suppose, for example, that growth rates are as stipulated above but that capitalism uses only four-fifths of the proportion of productive power that socialism does, which is a strong assumption. It would then take a mere twenty-three years for capitalism to overtake socialism in net terms, and it would thereafter sustain its superiority indefinitely.

We have shifted in the course of this chapter from Development Fettering to Use Fettering to Net Fettering. We now find that, if we construe Net Fettering in GNP terms, then we are moving back towards our starting-point, since the arithmetic of compound interest means that a society which is superior from a developmental point of view will be a net superior before very long. The scope for Net Fettering in the absence of Development Fettering is not very great. One instance would be a pair of societies neither of which was superior to the other from a developmental point of view but one of which outclassed the other from a use point of view.

Suppose, now, that we abandon the GNP conception of output, and assess from a more qualitative point of view the standard of living that a set of productive forces is used to produce. Then we can indeed concede that capitalism develops the productive forces more quickly while insisting that socialism is an enduringly superior form of society. I conclude that socialists who accept the superiority of capitalism as a developer of productive power can defend their preference for socialism on the ground of how it uses productive power only by affirming that socialism offers a better way of life. (That is not, of course, a paltry reason for preferring socialism.)

Note that I have not said that that is now the only reason one might have for favouring socialism. My argument is that, among the sorts of reasons discussed in this chapter,[15] the claim that it offers a qualitatively superior way of life is the only one supporting socialism *if* one concedes that capitalism develops the forces more rapidly.[16]

7. Put in its most general form, the question I have addressed in this chapter is: what circumstance leads to the revolutionary displacement of existing relations of production? I have taken it for granted that the relevant circumstance is a fettering of the forces by the relations, and I have sought to understand what we should take such fettering to be. The Preface sentences quoted near the beginning of this chapter amply support the view that the answer to the stated quesion is: fettering of some or other kind.

Basing himself on different stretches of text, John McMurtry proposes a different answer to the general question. He says that revolution occurs when, unless it occurred, the existing level of development of the productive forces would be *forfeited*. This means that revolution occurs when, in its absence, the forces would not only not grow in power, but actually decline.[17] McMurtry rightly says that forfeiture, so defined, is a much stronger requirement than mere fettering. He does not claim that Marx relied unambiguously on forfeiture rather than fettering in his theory of revolution, for he says that in separating the two he is refining a distinction which is 'inchoate' in Marx.[18] But McMurtry does think that the forfeiture notion is present, indistinctly, in

[15] Which do not include assessments of societies from the point of view, for example, of how just they are.

[16] One interesting reason for *not* offering that concession is described by Elster at *Making Sense of Marx* 261–2: see the quotation in ch. 8, sect. 12 below. Another reason relates to the issue about pollution and resources raised in sect. 7 below.

[17] See McMurtry, *The Structure of Marx's World-View*, 205 ff.

[18] Ibid. 209.

Marx, and that it is the basis of a theory of revolution which has advantages over the theory the notion of fettering supplies.

In assessing McMurtry's proposal, we should separate the exegetical question of how attributable the forfeiture theory of revolution is to Marx from the substantive question of how tenable a theory of revolution it is.

As to the substantive question, the forfeiture theory is certainly sensitive to the revolution constraint, and that, no doubt, was a large part of McMurtry's reason for favouring it: as he remarked, in correspondence on this chapter, 'people individually and collectively are by their nature moved by loss of the bird in the hand far more than by the lack of two in the bush'. But does forfeiture meet the predictability constraint?[19] The best case for an affirmative answer, with respect to capitalism, would turn on the systematic pollution and depletion of resources induced by capitalist production. If the current reckless deforestation, exhaustion of water supplies, desertification, perforation of the ozone layer, dissemination of nuclear waste, and so on cannot be arrested except by supersession (as opposed to modification) of capitalist relations of production, then the forfeiture theory amply satisfies the predictability constraint. Planetary enviromental degradation is, of course, consistent with continued progress in technical knowledge, but productive forces include not just knowledge but also the resource endowment to which it is applied, and the forfeiture theory might meet the predictability constraint because of that latter determinant of productive power.[20]

I now turn to the exegetical question. Here are the principal texts on which McMurtry grounds his attribution of the forfeiture idea to Marx:

As the main thing is not to be deprived of the fruits of civilization, of the acquired productive forces, the traditional forms in which they were produced must be smashed.[21]

Men never relinquish what they have won, but this does not mean that they never relinquish the social form in which they have acquired certain

---

[19] For the two constraints just mentioned, see sect. 1 above. They were there introduced as constraints on an adequate notion of fettering, but they readily generalize to constraints on an adequate notion of the circumstance that generates revolution, and may therefore be applied to the forfeiture proposal as well.

[20] On the importance of natural resources as a determinant of productive power, see *KMTH* 61.

[21] *The Poverty of Philosophy*, 175.

productive forces. On the contrary, in order that they may not be deprived of the result attained, and forfeit the fruits of civilization, they are obliged, from the moment when their mode of intercourse no longer corresponds to the productive forces acquired, to change all their traditional social forms.[22]

I concede that, when those texts are taken literally, and in isolation, they abundantly confirm McMurtry's interpretation. When I myself commented on the same texts, I hastily took for granted that forfeiture meant not, as McMurtry takes it, losing productive power itself, but losing the 'opportunity of further inroads against scarcity' which their present level creates, but which only new relations would permit society to seize.[23] I associated the texts exhibited above with the *Capital* passage which says that it is the fact that capitalism eventually 'excludes all rational improvement' that destines it to go under.[24] The *Capital* passage employs the absolute-stagnation view of fettering. The McMurtry proposal goes beyond absolute stagnation to actual retrogression (see page 110 above). In my unprovable opinion, Marx would have settled for absolute stagnation rather than the more demanding McMurtrian forfeiture had he been asked to choose between them (whatever choice he would have made between absolute stagnation itself and the other fettering notions reviewed in this chapter). He would, I think, have agreed that the texts which, taken literally, support the forfeiture proposal present a hyperbolical formulation of the idea of absolute stagnation.

[22] Letter to Annenkov, 23 Dec. 1846 (*Selected Correspondence*, 31).
[23] *KMTH* 159–60.
[24] *Capital*, i. 612.

7

ON AN ARGUMENT FOR HISTORICAL
MATERIALISM

1. In this chapter, and in the two that follow, the focus of inquiry widens. The chapters do not concern the inner articulation of historical materialism. They address two large questions: Is the general approach of the theory, its assignment of priority to the material and economic features of society, more or less sound? And what sort of evidence, in broad terms, would confirm or upset their priority: what does their priority mean?

Now many people who, like me, were brought up in the Marxist tradition think that questions about what historical materialism means and whether it is true are easy to answer. For there is a short piece of reasoning which is widely regarded, in Marxist circles, as at once a sufficient explication and a compelling defence of the basic outlook of historical materialism. The purpose of the present brief chapter is to clear the ground for the two that follow by disposing of the reasoning in question. I shall look at the form it takes in a stretch of argument presented by Engels in the course of his speech at Marx's funeral. Arguments akin to the one Engels offered there have been propounded by many Marxists, including, as we shall see, Karl Marx himself.

2. According to Engels,

Marx discovered the law of development of human history: the simple fact, hitherto concealed by an overgrowth of ideology, that mankind must first of all eat, have shelter and clothing, before it can pursue politics, science, art, religion, etc.; that *therefore* the production of the immediate material means of subsistence and *consequently* the degree of economic development attained by a given people or during a given epoch form the foundation upon which the state institutions, the legal conceptions, art, and even the ideas on religion of the people concerned have been evolved, and in the light of which they must, *therefore*, be explained, instead of *vice versa*, as had hitherto been the case.[1]

I shall not ask whether what Engels argues for should be called a 'law of development', whether or not his reasoning is successful.

---

[1] 'Speech at the Graveside of Karl Marx', 167, emphases added.

Let us assess that reasoning without requiring that its conclusion state a law of development, or, indeed, of anything else.

The passage contains four inferences. The first inference is implicit: it is presupposed by the second one. The last three inferences are signalled by the words 'therefore', 'consequently' and 'therefore', in that order. The structure of the argument is as follows:

1. People must eat (etc.) if they are to engage in politics (etc.).
∴ 2. People must produce food (etc.) if they are to engage in those activities.
∴ 3. Material production is the foundation on which those activities rest. (*See first 'therefore'.*)

and

4. The degree of economic development is also part of that foundation. (*See 'consequently'.*)
∴ 5. Material production (together with the degree of economic development) explains those activities. (*See second 'therefore'.*)

Let us call (2) the 'indispensability claim'. It says that material production is indispensable to all other human activity. I shall first comment on the inferences exposed above, and then offer some additional remarks on the indispensability claim.

Consider, first, the inference from (1) to (2). I think we can assume that Engels would not have regarded (2) as pertinently true had he not believed that material production[2] absorbed a great deal of human energy. He would have abandoned his argument had he thought that the typical historical working day was, say, thirty minutes long. Engels meant to affirm not merely that people must produce, but that the task demands a lot of time and effort (and also, perhaps, that it is not intrinsically attractive[3]). I gloss (2) in this way because no one who thought that material production occupied a negligible amount of human energy could hope to reach the conclusion of Engel's argument ((5)) on the basis of (2).

[2] Throughout this examination of Engels's argument I shall mean by 'material production' what he called 'the production of the immediate material means of subsistence'. It is important to bear this in mind, since the phrase 'material production' is also open to other construals, which would be out of place here.

[3] This further feature of material production makes it more plausible to suppose that activities beyond material production serve its needs: in particular, the need to get people to stick to rebarbative labour. You have to weigh the head down with a superstructure to keep the nose to the grindstone. Cf. *KMTH*, ch. 7, sect. 7.

Does (2), thus glossed, follow from (1)? I think it does in all relevant circumstances. A look at the irrelevant ones will disclose my meaning.

They are those in which the writ of the Curse of Adam does not run, and the earth supplies the requisites of survival with little human help. Marx said that nature is then 'too lavish', for she

'keeps man in hand, like a child in leading-strings'. She does not make humanity's own development a nature-imposed necessity. It is the necessity of bringing a natural force under the control of society, of economising on its energy, of appropriating it or subduing it on a large scale by the work of the human hand, that plays the most decisive role in the history of industry,[4]

and, hence, we may safely add by way of interpretation, in history *sans phrase*. In Arcadia the fruit falls from the tree into people's laps and they make no history because they do not have to. For Marxism, 'people have history because they must *produce* their life'[5]: history is a substitute for nature.[6] But Engels calls what he is trying to demonstrate 'the law of development of human history', and, whatever he thinks that is, he cannot expect it to hold where he would say that history is in abeyance. If, then, we set aside Arcadian cases, and consider nature as it usually is, and as Engels was thinking of it, to wit, as niggardly, and as resistant to human desire and design, then we can confidently endorse the derivation of the indispensability claim, as I glossed it above, from proposition (1). (Note that I have not endorsed the Marxist view that there is no history where nature is lavish. I have simply used the fact that it is a Marxist view to put an exegetically required restriction on the scope of Engel's claims.)

It will simplify our inquiry, without unfairly biassing it, if we decline to inspect one of the three remaining inferences, that carried by the word 'consequently', and which leads us from (3) to (4). Let us delete proposition (4) and therefore also the parenthesis in proposition (5). This leaves us with two inferences to consider, from (2) to (3) and from (3) to (a simplified) (5). If we now call the pursuits of politics, science, art, religion, and so on *spiritual*

[4] *Capital*, i. 649.
[5] *The German Ideology*, 43.
[6] This is why history (sometimes called 'pre-history') stops once nature has been made fit for human habitation. Marxian optimism about the future complements Marxian pessimism about the past.

activity, we can rewrite the inferences we have yet to examine as follows:

2. People must engage in material production if they are to pursue any spiritual activity.

∴ 3. Material production is the foundation of all spiritual activity.

∴ 5. Spiritual activity is to be explained in terms of material production.

Now the argument which those two inferences compose is, as it stands,[7] a bad one. It is an instance of the fallacy of equivocation: the word 'foundation' has to be used with two different meanings for the argument to go through. In saying that material production is the foundation of spiritual activity, one may mean, what is true, that spiritual activity is impossible in the absence of material production: one may mean, that is, what the premiss of the argument ((2)) says; or, quite differently, one may use 'foundation' as a metaphor denoting a relationship of explanation, which is to say that one may mean by (3) precisely what is said in (5). And only if one treats (3) in these different ways in succession will one experience a temptation to pass from (2) to (5). The step in the argument to sub-conclusion (3) is spurious. It is not a distinct step at all, but either an unneeded restatement of the premiss of the argument or a premature assertion of its conclusion.

There is in short, only one inference to examine here, since to call material production the *foundation* of spiritual activity is either already to assert that the first explains the second, or it is merely to repeat the indispensability claim ((2)) in the form of an arresting architectural image. It is an image which has tended to arrest thought. For it has encouraged Marxists (for example, Engels) to suppose both that (3) is obviously true and that it clearly entails (5); whereas, in the sense in which (3) is obviously true, (3) just repeats (2), and in that sense, as opposed to another, in which (3) means what (5) does, (3) does not entail (5).

The single inference needing assessment here is from the indispensability of material production to the conclusion that the character of spiritual activity is explained by the nature of material production. The inference does not work, since the indispensability

---

[7] That is, unsupplemented by further considerations: I comment on the suggestion that such considerations might charitably be added at p. 128 below.

of material production does not guarantee for it the asserted explanatory role. (Does the fact that an organism must breathe show that its non-breathing activities are explained by the nature of its respiration?) Even the opposite explanatory relationship is compatible with material production's indispensability. People must work and must organize themselves to do so, yet it might be true that the ways they work and the forms of organization they adopt are determined by political and cultural complexes which develop autonomously and which maintain a strong grip on them.

I do not claim that the inference from (2) to (5) could not be redeemed through some sort of defensible supplementation to its premiss. That may or not be so. What I do say is that Engels is wrong to think that the argument has luminous power *just as it stands*. He thinks that all that is necessary to travel from its premiss to its conclusion is to cut away the 'overgrowth of ideology', that only misty thinking could prevent a person from feeling the otherwise manifest force of the argument. But that is a big mistake. Historical materialism may be true, but it is not a 'simple fact'.

So much for Engel's inferences. Now some further remarks on the claim that material production is indispensable to spiritual activity. The claim is impregnable, but it cannot make material production prior to spiritual activity as far as explanation is concerned. For it is also true that spiritual activity is indispensable to material production.

There are two reasons for saying that material production requires spiritual activity. The second might be contested, but a Marxist is committed to acknowledging both.

The first reason has to do with the fact that mental acts figure in the process of material production. Now, when that process gets beyond a quite primitive phase, then the capacity to perform the mental acts it requires depends on participation in a culture.[8] But the existence of a culture depends, in turn, on spiritual activity, as that was identified (by examples) on pages 126–7 above.

The second reason for saying that material production requires spiritual activity is that, in a developed society, religion and/or law and/or ideology (each of which is or involves spiritual activity) are

---

[8] Notice that I have not said that there is a form of material production which is so primitive that it does not require mental activity. That would be idiotic, since all production is an intentional process. But the mentation incident to very primitive production might not require what could properly be called culture.

essential, at least on a Marxian view, to secure order *in* the labour process (to discipline the labouring agents) and an ordering *of* the labour process (to organize production). People will not undergo the self-denial inherent in labour in the absence of legal or religio-moral sanction, and work will not proceed smoothly unless production relations enjoy a clarity of definition which only law or something like it can provide.

It might be suggested, in a last-ditch defence of Engels, that, even if material production and spiritual activity are indeed mutually indispensable, material production retains priority in that it is indispensable to life itself. But spiritual activity is also indispensable to life, since it is indispensable to material production, and indispensability is a transitive relation.

There is, finally, yet another difficulty in attempting to establish the secondary status of spiritual activity on the basis of the indispensability claim. For even if spiritual activity were not indispensable, it would remain unavoidable for beings with human attributes. Even if we absurdly supposed that it was unnecessary to survival, we could still predict that a society will express itself culturally as confidently as we can predict that it will devote energy to work. If, therefore, the indispensability of material production is thought significant *because* it renders material production unavoid-able, then its indispensability would be no argument for the dominance of the material over the spiritual, even if the spiritual were dispensable.

3. Some people will regard the foregoing discussion as a preposter-ously meticulous deconstruction of what is, after all, a passage in an obituary address. My reply to that charge is that it is widely supposed within Marxism that the indispensability of material production gives it explanatory priority, and that it is useful to display the several ways in which that is a mistake. When we take Engels at his word, and press his words hard, the mistakes emerge, so it is worth taking Engels's statement strictly, even if he did not mean it to be so taken.

I think, moreover, that Engels intended every thought which I have attributed to him. The words 'therefore' and 'consequently' do not undergo a weakening of their meaning when they are uttered in a funeral oration, and it was precisely because they did accept the sort of argument that Engels sketched at Marx's graveside that Marx and Engels became historical materialists in the first place. It is entirely implausible to suppose that they reached the theory as a result of an extensive study of past history. It came to them early, as a blazing (supposed) insight: part 1 of *The German Ideology* makes that clear.[9] Historical materialism is supposed to be quite evidently true, for those who have shuffled off the historical idealism of German ideology.[10] (I am not saying (the un-Popperian thing) that Marx and Engels should not have affirmed historical materialism in advance of protracted empirical study. I am criticizing their extraordinary confidence that every unprejudiced person could just see that it was true, without any such study.)

In a footnote in the first volume of *Capital*, Marx replies to a critic who agrees that economic life is centrally important in modern times, but denies that it played the same role in the Middle Ages, or in antiquity. Marx thinks it extremely telling to point out, in response, 'that the Middle Ages could not live on Catholicism, nor the ancient world on politics'.[11] This shows that he fell into the error that trapped Engels. And so, perhaps, did Bertolt Brecht, when he wrote 'Erst kommt das Fressen, dann kommt die Moral', which is an excellent aphorism, but which is not the good argument for historical materialism which some people, such as, maybe, Brecht, have thought it is. 'Grub comes before morality' is obviously true in some sense, and it is no doubt also true, though not so obviously, in a more important sense. Perhaps it is even true when it is used to sum up the fundamental outlook of historical materialism, but that is very far from obvious. One purpose of this chapter has been to remove the spurious self-evidence that statements like Brecht's have when they are used to formulate ambitious theses.

The Engels argument is bad, but it is beguiling, largely because of the treacherous equivocation on 'foundation'. It is only by carefully examining the fallacy which that equivocation generates that we

---

[9] As does this sentence from *The Communist Manifesto*: 'Does it require deep intuition to comprehend that man's ideas, views and conceptions, in one word, man's consciousness, changes with every change in the conditions of his material existence, in his social relations and in his social life?' (p. 503).

[10] For comment on the Marxian propensity to exaggerate what the falsehood of historical idealism proves, see the end of ch. 9 sect. 7 below.

[11] *Capital* i. 176 n. Marx goes on to make a subtler claim which I am not here criticizing.

can come to understand how intelligent Marxists could have thought that so controversial a theory as historical materialism was *obviously* true.[12]

[12] In general, a persisting tendency to view a controversial claim as obviously true requires for its explanation not only the uncovering of a motive for that mistaken view but also the exhibition of a mechanism which makes the view possible. See, further, ch. 14, pp. 290–1 below.

8

RECONSIDERING HISTORICAL MATERIALISM

1. I called my book on Karl Marx's theory of history a *defence*, because in it I defended what I took to be Karl Marx's theory of history. I believed the theory to be true before I began to write the book, and that initial conviction more or less survived the strain of writing it. More recently, however, I have come to wonder whether the theory which the book defends is true (though not whether, as I claimed, it was affirmed by Karl Marx). I do not now believe that historical materialism is false, but I am not sure how to tell whether or not it is true. Certain considerations, to be exhibited below, constitute a strong challenge to historical materialism, but while they do plainly represent a serious *challenge* to the theory, it is unclear what kind and degree of revision of it, if any, they justify.[1]

That is unclear because we still have only a rather crude conception of what sort of evidence would confirm or disconfirm historical materialism. I tried, in *KMTH*, to make the theory more determinate, and thereby to clarify its confirmation conditions, but it will be apparent from the challenge to be described in this chapter that substantial further clarification is required.

Some people may think that, in raising a challenge to historical materialism, I am letting the side down. So let me emphasize that my belated reservations about the theory do not weaken my belief that it is both desirable and possible to extinguish existing capitalist social relations and to reorganize society on a just and humane basis. The political significance of retreat from historical materialism should not be exaggerated. An appreciation of the principal evils of capitalism, which are its injustice, its hostility to the development of the faculties of the individual, and its voracious ravaging of the natural and built environment, does not depend on ambitious theses about the whole of human history. Nor does the claim that it is possible to establish a society without exploitation which is hospitable to human fulfilment require, or perhaps even follow from, those theses. So scepticism about historical materialism should leave the socialist project more or less where it would otherwise be. There are, it is true, Marxist claims about how society

[1] I propose what I think is an appropriate revision which, so I also think, preserves the spirit of the original, in the next chapter.

works whose falsehood would make supersession of capitalism and installation of socialism less likely. But one can maintain those claims without believing, as I am still sure that Marx did, that the fundamental process in history is the material one of the growth of human productive power.[2]

2. The epigraph of *KMTH* reproduces the final sentence of *The Little Boy and his House*,[3] which was my favourite book when I was a child. The sentence is as follows:

For what they all said was, 'It depends . . . It all depends . . . It all depends on where you live and what you have to build with.'

I thought that sentence was a charming way of communicating a central thesis of my book: that forms of society reflect material possibilities and constraints. But while my book was in press, or perhaps, I confess, a little earlier, I was rereading *The Little Boy and his House*, and I came to see that my use of its final sentence was to some extent exploitative. When the sentence is abstracted from its context what it seems to mean makes it a very suitable epigraph for the book. Seen in context, however, the sentence can be a point of departure for formulating the challenge to historical materialism that I want to discuss here.

Let me, then, supply the context. The story concerns an unnamed little boy, who, at the outset, has no house to live in. In winter he is

---

[2] The political applicability of historical materialism is limited, since it is a theory about *epochal* development, and the time horizon of political action necessarily falls short of the epochal. (The epochal scope of historical materialism is something which people are inclined to forget. The late Harry Braverman's *Labour and Monopoly Capital* is often invoked against the *KMTH* thesis that productive forces are explanatorily more fundamental than production relations, since Braverman claimed that the way the forces develop under capitalism is determined by the class antagonism between potentially insurgent workers and capitalists who forestall insurgency by introducing technologies which deskill and demean the workers. But Braverman would not himself have objected to the primacy thesis in this fashion, since he realized that historical materialism was about epochs: 'The treatment of the interplay between the forces and relations of production occupied Marx in almost all his historical writing, and while there is no question that he gave primacy to the forces of production in the long sweep of history, the idea that this primacy could be used in a formulistic way on a day-to-day basis would never have entered his mind' (*Labour and Monopoly Capital*, 19). It would follow that the pattern of development of productive power in relatively restricted time periods is not probative with respect to historical materialist theses.)

[3] By Stephen Bone and Mary Adshead.

too cold, in summer he is too hot, when it rains he gets wet, and when it is windy he is nearly blown away. So he goes to see his uncle, who is sympathetic. They agree that the little boy needs something to live in. His uncle then explains that there exist many different kinds of dwelling, and that it would be wise for the little boy to examine some of them before deciding what he wants for himself. There follows a world tour, in which nine types of accommodation are examined, in nine different countries. But the boy finds each kind of dwelling either inherently unappealing (for example, because it is a Romany gypsy's tent too low to stand up in, or because it is an unpleasantly damp Spanish cave) or, however appealing, unattainable in his circumstances (for example, because it is a house made of stones which lie around the Irish fields, and none lie around the fields where he lives, or because it is an igloo, and igloos would not last long in the little boy's climate). Returning to wherever they started from—the book does not say but linguistic evidence suggests that it is England—the boy sighs and says, 'What a lot of different ways of building houses!', whereupon, somewhat surprisingly, he and his uncle set about building a small red-brick bungalow. Having finished building, they invite their nine new friends to see the result, and the friends come with their wives and animals and they are so impressed that they go home determined to build houses just like the little boy's house. But when they get home they change their minds. And now I shall quote the last couple of pages of the book, which end with the sentence I used as an epigraph:

And they all went home determined to build brick houses like the Little Boy had built.

But when they all got home again, Don Estaban thought that after all it *was* very convenient to have a cave all ready made for you, and Johnnie Faa and Big Bear thought how convenient it was to have a house you could carry about wherever you wanted to go, and Wang Fu thought it was even more convenient to have a house that would carry *you* about. And E-took-a-shoo saw that where he lived he would *have* to build with ice and snow because there was nothing else, and M'popo and M'toto saw that they would *have* to build with grass and mud because they had nothing else, and Mr. Michael O'Flaherty thought that if you had a lot of stones lying about the fields it was a shame not to use them, and Lars Larsson thought the same about the trees in the forest.

> So
> what
> do
> you
> think
> they
> did?
> THEY ALL WENT ON
> BUILDING JUST AS THEY'D
> ALWAYS DONE.
> FOR
> WHAT THEY
> ALL SAID
> WAS . . .
> 'It depends . . .
> It all depends . . .
> It all depends on WHERE YOU LIVE
> and WHAT YOU HAVE TO BUILD WITH'.

3. Let us think about why the little boy's friends decide not to build red-brick bungalows. In at least most cases, they are said to change their minds for reasons which *appear* accessible to historical materialism: they reject bungalow-building after reflecting on features of their physical circumstances. But their reasons for carrying on as before could appear favourable to historical materialism without actually being so. The next to last sentence says: they all went on building just as they'd always done. And I now see that, notwithstanding their sincere materialist-sounding avowals, they went on building as they'd always done partly just *because* they *had* always built in that way, and they consequently recognized themselves in the ways of life that went with their dwellings. This is a non-materialist reason for architectural conservatism, but it can come to appear materialist, because one way that a culture consolidates itself is by misrepresenting the feasible set of material possibilities as being smaller that it is in fact. Culturally disruptive material possibilities are screened out of thought and imagination: in certain contexts people prefer to think that they have no choice but to take a course to which, in fact, there are alternatives.

Big Bear thought it convenient to have a house (i.e., a tepee) that he could carry about, whereas Wang Fu thought it more convenient to have one (i.e., a houseboat) that would carry him about, but I do not think they reached these contrasting judgements because they made different technical calculations. I think they were led to them by the potent force of familiarity, which determined where they felt at home; and 'to be at home', unlike 'to be housed', is not a materialist property. It is the dialectic of subject finding itself in object that explains, at least in part, why Big Bear and Wang Fu conceived convenience differently. (I say 'at least in part' because I need not deny that houseboats are more likely to appear in territory dense with waterway, and tepees are more likely on riverless plains. But even if their respective ancestors developed their different housings under pressure of such material determinations, it is entirely implausible to think that Big Bear and Wang Fu stuck to custom not at all because it was custom, but just because the plains remained riverless and the rivers hadn't dried up.)

If, then, it all depends on where you live and what you have to build with, the importance of where you live is not purely materialist. The way of life where you live counts, as well as what you have to build with there. And people's need for shelter is in no clear sense greater than their need for traditions which tell them who they are.

And now I shall leave the story behind, but I shall presently return to the issue which I think it raises.

4. Marx produced at least four sets of ideas: a philosophical anthropology, a theory of history, an economics, and a vision of the society of the future.

There are connections among these doctrines, but before we consider some of them, I would like to point out that, despite great differences in their domains of application, the four doctrines have something important in common. In each doctrine the major emphasis, albeit in a suitably different way, is on the *activity of production*, and each of the four is, partly for that reason, *a materialist doctrine*.

The philosophical anthropology says that humans are essentially creative beings, or, in standard sexist Marxist language: man is an essentially creative being, most at home with himself when he is developing and exercising his talents and powers.

According to the theory of history, growth in productive power is the force underlying social change.

In the economic theory magnitude of value is explained not, as in rival accounts, at least partly in terms of desire and scarcity, but wholly in terms of labour, and labour is 'essentially the expenditure of human brain, nerves, muscles and sense 'organs',[4] the using up of a certain amount of human material substance: labour time, the immediate determinant of value, is but a measure of, or a proxy for, the quantity of living matter consumed in the process of production.

Finally, the main indictment of capitalism is that it crushes people's creative potentials, and the chief good of communism is that it permits a prodigious flowering of human talent, in which the free expression of the powers inside each person harmonizes with the free expression of the powers of all. Communism is the release of individual and collective productive capacity from the confinement of oppressive social structure.

5. I now believe that the philosophical anthropology suffers severely from one-sidedness. This has evident consequences for the vision of the desirable future, since that vision comes from the anthropology (see section 8). It should have no consequences for the economic theory, which answers questions about which the anthropology should be silent. Its consequences for the theory of history are, as we shall see (in sections 9–11), hard to judge.

6. My charge against Marxist philosophical anthropology is that, in its exclusive emphasis on the creative side of human nature, it neglects a whole domain of human need and aspiration, which is prominent in the philosophy of Hegel. In *KMTH* I said that for Marx, by contrast with Hegel, 'the ruling interest and difficulty of men was relating to the *world*, not to the *self*'.[5] I would still affirm that antithesis, and I now want to add that, to put it crudely, Marx went too far in the materialist direction. In his anti-Hegelian, Feuerbachian affirmation of the radical objectivity of matter,[6]

---

[4] *Capital*, i. 164. See also p. 274.
[5] *KMTH* 22.
[6] One of Feuerbach's achievements, according to Marx, was 'his opposing to the negation of the negation, which claims to be the absolute positive, the self-supporting positive, positively based on itself'. (*Economic and Philosophic Manuscripts*, 328).

Marx focused on the relationship of the subject to an object which is in no way subject, and, as time went on,[7] he came to neglect the subject's relationship to itself, and that aspect of the subject's relationship to others which is a mediated (that is, indirect) form of relationship to itself. He rightly reacted against Hegel's extravagant representation of all reality as ultimately an expression of self, but he over-reacted, and he failed to do justice to the self's irreducible interest in a definition of itself, and to the social manifestations of that interest.

I refer to the social manifestations of the interest in self identification because I think that human groupings whose lines of demarcation are not economic, such as religious communities, and nations, are as strong and as durable as they evidently are partly because they offer satisfaction to the individual's need for self identification. In adhering to traditionally defined collectivities people retain a sense of who they are.

I do not say that Marx denied that there is a need for self definition,[8] but he failed to give the truth due emphasis, and Marxist tradition has followed his lead. The interest in defining or locating oneself is not catered for by 'the development of human powers as an end in itself',[9] which is the good Marx and Marxist emphasize. For, to begin with, the creative activity characterized by the quoted phrase need not provide a sense of self, and it is thought of as good in large part independently of any self-understanding it may afford: the perfection and employment of a person's gifts is an attractive idea apart from any grasp of himself that may result. And even when a person does gain an understanding of himself through creative activity, because, as Marxist tradition says, he recognizes himself in what he has made, then he typically understands himself

---

[7] For he is less guilty of that neglect in the 1844 *Manuscripts* and in the associated 'Comments on James Mill', where the need to affirm one's identity is interpreted as a need for a fulfilling kind of social labour in community with others: see 'Comments', 225–6.

[8] The expression 'self definition', especially, perhaps, when it is hyphenated ('self-definition'), suggests reference to a process in which the self defines itself, in which, that is, the self is not only what gets defined but also what does the defining. I shall not employ the hyphenated form, since, when I speak of the need for self definition, I mean the self's need not for the process but for the result, and I do not mean its need to define itself, but its need to be defined, whatever may, or must, do the defining. If self definition, even as I intend the phrase, is necessarily due to the activity of the self, and if the self needs that activity as well as its result, then so be it, but what especially matters here is the self's need to end up defined.

[9] *Capital*, iii. 959.

as possessed of a certain kind of capacity: he is not necessarily thereby able to locate himself as a member of a particular human community.

A person does not only need to develop and enjoy his powers. He needs to know who he is, and how his identity connects him with particular others. He must, as Hegel saw, find something outside himself which he did not create, and to which something inside himself corresponds, because of the social process that created him, or because of a remaking of self wrought by later experience. He must be able to identify himself with some part of objective social reality: spirit, as Hegel said, finds itself at home in its own otherness as such.[10]

A word about how the need for identity asserts its causal power. Whereas the need for food has causal importance because it drives people to seek to acquire food, by producing and/or by appropriating the fruits of production, the impact of the need for identity on action is more indirect. The need for identity does not, standardly, drive people to seek to achieve an identity, and that is so for two reasons. The first is that people do not usually lack an identity: they receive an identity as a by-product of the rearing process. The right thing to say, in most cases, is not that people are motivated by their *need* for identity, but that they are motivated by their *identity*, for which they have a strong need, and the motivating power of identity reflects the strength of the need identity fulfils. Quebecois do not have a need for identity which drives them to become Quebecois. Since they are raised as Quebecois, their need for identity is readily satisfied. Quebecois are motivated not to acquire an identity but to protect and celebrate the identity they are given.

Now it is true that creation and enrichment, and change, of identity can also result from a person's initiatives, from chosen engagements with which he comes to identify. But, even then, it is not usually a matter of a deliberate attempt to forge a (new) identity for oneself: apart from special cases, that would be self-defeating, since, on the whole, one's identity must be experienced as not a matter for choice—and that is the second reason why people do not set themselves the project of achieving an identity. What rather happens is that people engage themselves with people and institutions *other* than to secure an identity, and then the

[10] I quote from memory, and I am afraid that I have lost my record of where Hegel says this (or nearly this).

engagement persists when whatever its original rationale was has gone, so that it becomes an identification ungrounded in further reasons. The reason for abiding in some connections is that one has invested oneself in them and consequently finds oneself there (which does not, again, mean that the purpose of the investment was to find oneself there), and a person is incomplete without connections of that perhaps non-rational, but certainly not irrational, kind.

I claim, then, that there is a human need to which Marxist observation is commonly blind, one different from and as deep as the need to cultivate one's talents. It is the need to be able to say not what I can do but who I am, satisfaction of which has historically been found in identification with others in a shared culture based on nationality, or race, or religion, or some slice or amalgam thereof. The identifications take benign, harmless, and catastrophically malignant forms. They generate, or at least sustain, ethnic and other bonds whose strength Marxists systematically undervalue, because they neglect the need for self-identity satisfied by them.[11]

To prevent misapprehension, I enter two caveats. First, I have not said that there exists a human need for religion, or for nationalism, or for something rather like them. The need I affirm is to have a sense of who I am. I say that the forms of consciousness just mentioned have, in past history, offered to satisfy that need, and have thereby obtained much of their power, but I advance no

---

[11] I agree with Frank Parkin that what I would call divisions of identity are as deep as those of class, and that they cannot be explained in the usual Marxist way. But I think he is wrong to suppose that this weakness in Marxism casts doubt on its treatment of domination and exploitation as centring in class conflict. Parkin commits a category mistake when he maintains that domination or exploitation is predominantly racial in one society, religious in another, and of a class nature in a third. For racial exploitation and class exploitation are not two species of one genus. Racial exploitation is (largely) relegation to an exploited class because of race. And if, as Parkin thinks, Protestants exploit Catholics in Northern Ireland, then the exploitation is economic, and not in a comparable sense religious. Catholics are denied access to material values, not religious ones.

So while I think that Marxism lacks an explanation of the potency of identities as bases of allocation to classes, I do not think that it is also mistaken in refusing to put religious and racial exploitation on a par with economic exploitation. It is false that 'closure on racial grounds plays a directly equivalent role to closure on the basis of property'. Unlike racism, property is not, in the first instance, a means of protecting privilege. It *is* privilege, although, like any privilege, it offers those who have it ways of protecting what they have. (See Parkin, *Marxism and Class Theory*, esp. pp. 94, 114.)

opinion about what features a form of consciousness must have to be a possible satisfier of the need I have emphasized.[12]

And the second caveat is that, in speaking of the need for an understanding of oneself, I mean 'understanding' in the sense in which false understanding is an example of it. I do not deny that many of the self-portrayals from which people draw satisfaction display a large measure of distortion and illusion. And religion and nationalism may, of course, be cases in point: nothing said here is intended to contradict the proposition, with which I sympathize, that their more familiar forms constitute immature means of securing self identification, appropriate to a less than fully civilized stage of human development.

7. Let us turn to the vision of the future, which I discussed in *KMTH* (see chapter 5, section 7) under the heading 'Communism as the Liberation of the Content'. At the level of the individual, the liberation of the content is the release of his powers: he escapes location within a social role thought of as confining them. But I now suggest that Marx's desire to abolish social roles reflects a failure to appreciate how the very constraints of role can help to link a person with others in satisfying community.

'In a communist society', says Marx, 'there are no painters but at most people who engage in painting among other activities.'[13] I argued that this means two things: first, and obviously, that no one spends all of his active time painting. But, less obviously and more interestingly, it also means that there are not even part-time

---

[12] And I accept Alan Carling's criticism of my failure to cite gender, alongside nationality, race, and religion, as a powerful source of self-identification: 'Is it not beyond question that gender is a rather early and significant point of reference for "who I am"? Do I not share a culture with people of my gender as well as, and probably before, I share one with people in my slice of the amalgamated union of nationality, race, and religion?' ('Rational Choice Marxism', 57).

That rebuke is justified, but I cannot also endorse Carling's objections (ibid. 58–61) to my criticisms of Frank Parkin in the last footnote, which ride roughshod over nuances in my statements. Footnote 11 does not, *pace* Carling, deny that there exists in Northern Ireland something aptly called 'religious exploitation' but only that it 'plays a directly equivalent role' to economic exploitation. I allowed that, as the power of ethnicity attests, 'divisions of identity are as deep as those of class', and n. 11 is a contribution to delineating the different ways in which they are fundamental, *inter alia* with respect to exploitation.

[13] *The German Ideology*, 394. For further discussion of this sentence see ch. 10, sect. 6, subsect. ii below.

painters, where to be a painter is to be identified as, and to identify oneself as, one whose role it is to paint (even if one has other roles too). Under communism people now and then paint, but no one assumes the status painter, even from time to time.

I now wonder why roles should be abolished, and even why, ideally, people should engage in richly various activities. Why should a man or woman *not* find fulfilment in his or her work as a painter, conceived as his contribution to the society to which he belongs, and located within a nexus of expectations connecting him to other people? And what is so bad about a person dedicating himself to one or a small number of lines of activity only? There is nothing wrong with a division of labour in which each type of work has value, even though no one performs more than, say, two types of work, so that many talents in each individual perforce lie underdeveloped.[14] Marx wanted the full gamut of each person's capacity to be realized: '"free activity"', he said, 'is for the communists the creative manifestation of life arising from the free development of *all* abilities.'[15] Now, whether or not that ideal is desirable, it is certainly unrealizable, as you will see if you imagine someone trying to realize it, in a single lifetime. But it is not even desirable, in every case, to realize it as much as possible. There is often a choice between modest development of each of quite a few abilities and virtuoso development of one or very few, and there is no basis for asserting the *general* superiority of either of these choices. What constitutes the free development of the individual in a given case depends on many things, and his *free* development is never his *full* development,[16] for that is possible only for beings which are sub- or super-human. A society in which everyone is free to develop in any direction is not the same as a society in which anyone is able to develop in every direction: that kind of society will never exist, because there will never be people with that order of ability.[17]

---

[14] It also bears remarking that a single demanding speciality can call upon a wide range of powers: see Lawrence Haworth, 'Leisure, Work and Profession', 329.

[15] *The German Ideology*, 225.

[16] Marx too casually juxtaposes the two when he looks to the 'full and free development of every individual' in 'a higher form of society': see *Capital*, i. 739. See also the revealing phrase 'the free development of the individual as a whole' and its context, at *The German Ideology*, 256.

[17] It might be suggested, on Marx's behalf, that the full development of a person's power need not be, as I have supposed, the development of his full (= all of his)

Marx's ideal is properly called materialist because of its demand that the living substance within the individual be allowed to grow and emerge in, as he puts it in the phrase just quoted, a 'creative manifestation of life'. Elsewhere he says that to be free 'in the materialistic sense' is to be 'free not through the negative power to avoid this or that, but through the positive power to assert (one's) true individuality', and one's individuality, when asserted, is 'the vital manifestation of (one's) being'.[18] His ideal qualifies as materialist because it is semi-biological, and it is certainly materialist in the sense of the opposition between the material and the social defended in chapter 4 of *KMTH*. It is true that for Marx the liberation of the human material is possible only in community with others, since 'only within the community has each individual the means of cultivating his gifts in all directions',[19] but here society is required, as Marx puts it, as a *means*, to an independently specified (and, I argued, absurd) goal. It is not required, less instrumentally, as a field for that self-identification the need for which is unnoticed in Marx's vitalistic formulations.

I have criticized Marx's ideal both for being too materialist and for requiring an impossibly total development of the individual. I think these are connected excesses, but I acknowledge that I have not articulated the connection between them. The idea that the human substance within should be nourished and expressed need not, it is true, imply a demand for the *plenary* development which I claim is impossible. But I do think, even if I cannot show, that the materialism encourages the wish to draw forth everything in the individual, and I note that no corresponding error is naturally associated with an emphasis on the importance of self definition.

power, but just a development of his power than which there could not be a greater development. But this saving manœuvre cannot be sustained, since Marx so often speaks of the individual developing *all* of his powers.

[18] *The Holy Family*, 131. I believe that the ideal figured forth in the following much-quoted passage also deserves to be called materialist: 'when the limited bourgeois form is stripped away, what is wealth other than the universality of individual needs, capacities, pleasures, productive forces, etc., created through universal change? The full development of human mastery over the forces of nature, those of so-called nature as well as of humanity's own nature? The absolute working out of his creative potentialities . . . which makes this totality of development, i.e. the development of all human powers as such the end in itself, not as measured on a *pre-determined* yardstick?' (*The Grundrisse*, 488). I return to this passage at ch. 10, p. 200 below.

[19] *The German Ideology*, 78.

There is no temptation to think that one has a satisfactory identity only when one identifies with everything that can be identified with.

I argued that Marx's anthropology misses one great side of human need and aspiration, and I have now criticized an extreme version of the ideal of creativity the anthropology exalts, by urging that the *full* development of the individual is an ill-considered notion. To prevent misunderstanding I should therefore add that I do not, of course, reject the ideal of creativity as such, which remains a valuable part of the Marxist inheritance and which has, as we shall see in section 12, important political applications.

8. The vision of the future inherits the one-sidedness of the anthropology, but the limitations of the anthropology should not influence one's attitude to the labour theory of value, which should never have been defended, as it sometimes has been, on anthropological grounds. The question persists of the bearing of the anthropology on the theory of history, and it is a particularly difficult one.

Now there are phenomena, such as religion and nationalism, whose importance historical materialism *seems* to underrate, and which are intelligible in the light of the self's need for definition. But even if the theory of history really does undervalue what a more Hegelian anthropology would honour, it does not follow that it is because the theory of history depends upon an un-Hegelian anthropology that the undervaluation occurs, for, as I shall argue in section 10, *it is unclear that historical materialism is attached to the materialist anthropology I have criticized.* First, though, a brief discussion of the two phenomena just mentioned.

A certain cliché of anti-Marxist thought is probably true, namely that Marx misjudged the significance of religion and nationalism. He saw and exposed the class uses to which such ideologies are put. But he did not pursue the consequences of what he sometimes acknowledged, that they have origins far removed from class struggle. The power they have when they are used for particular class purposes is applied to those purposes, not derived from them. They might, in consequence, have a social and historical weight beyond their role within the schema of base and superstructure.

Marx's awareness that religion's source is deep in human need is evident in his statement that it is the opium of the people. He did not mean that priests devise it on behalf of exploiters and dispense it to the people to keep them in order. What priests do helps to keep the people still, but religion does not come from priests. It is, instead, 'the sigh of the oppressed creature, the soul of a heartless world, just as it is the spirit of a spiritless situation. It is the opium of the people.'[20]

Participation in religion is a form of alienation. It is a search on an illusory plane for what is unavailable in life itself. If religion is the spirit of a spiritless situation, one might expect that it will disappear only when there is spirit in life itself. It would then follow that, since there is no religion under communism, there will be a spirit in the free association of individuals. But where does Marx say anything about it?

Let us turn from religion to nationalism. Two passages in the *Communist Manifesto* warrant mention here. The first is the statement that working men have no country,[21] which expressed an expectation that the various national proletariats would rapidly transcend particularism in favour of international solidarity. It is hard to repel the suggestion that the workers refuted this when they marched to the trenches of World War I. Consider too what the *Manifesto* says about nationality and culture:

In place of the old local and national seclusion and self-sufficiency, we have intercourse in every direction, universal inter-dependence of nations. And as in material, so also in intellectual production. The intellectual creations of individual nations become common property. National one-sidedness and narrow-mindedness become more and more impossible, and from the numerous national and local literatures, there arises a world literature.[22]

Now if Marx means just that locally produced cultural objects become globally available through improved education and communication, then of course he is absolutely right. But I think his remarks go beyond that. I think they reflect a belief and hope that men and women will relate to other men and women as fellow human beings, and on a world scale, not in addition to but instead of finding special fellowship in particular cultures. Against that I would say that literatures are national, or in some other way

---

[20] Introduction to *A Contribution to the Critique of Hegel's Philosophy of Law*, 175.
[21] *The Communist Manifesto*, 502. Note how false the predictions made at this point in the *Manifesto* are.
[22] Ibid. 488.

parochial, because their makers are, as they must be, connected with particular sets of people. Like everybody else they need to, and do, participate in concrete universals. Marxist universalism suffers from the abstractness of the Enlightenment universalism criticized by Hegel. The Enlightenment was wrong because the universal can exist only in a determinate embodiment: there is no way of being human which is not *a* way of being human.

I do not deny that the literature of one nation can be appreciated by the people of another, and they need not think of it as foreign literature to do so. When people from different cultures meet, they get things they do not get at home. But I think Marx is guilty of the different idea that people can, should, and will relate to each other just as people, an idea that ignores the particularization needed for human formation and human relationship. He complained that 'in bourgeois society a general or a banker plays a great part, but man pure and simple plays a very mean part.'[22] I am not on the side of the generals and bankers, but I do not think they are unattractive because the characterizations they satisfy are too specific, and that man pure and simple is what everyone should try to be.

I have expressed a positive attitude to ties of nationality, so I had better add that I lack the Hegelian belief that the state is a good medium for the embodiment of nationality.[23] It is probably true that whenever national sentiment fixes itself, as it usually does, on the state, there results a set of preposterous illusions and infantile emotions on which manipulating political rulers opportunistically play. But even if that claim is too strong, it is evident that, unlike literature, the state is a terribly dangerous vehicle of self-expression, and it is a good thing that in our own time people are developing identifications of more local kinds, and also international ones, identifications which cut within and across the boundaries of states.[24]

9. Two questions remain, only the second of which will be pursued in this chapter (in sections 10 and 11). The discussion of the chapter

---

[22] *Capital*, i. 135.

[23] No one was keener on nationality than Johann Gottfried Herder, and yet he hated states: see Isaiah Berlin's 'Herder and the Enlightenment', 158–65, 181.

[24] Marx was not alone in his tendency to underestimate the strength of national bonds. For a brilliant account of general intellectual failure on that score, see Isaiah Berlin's essay on 'Nationalism': there is a good summary statement on p. 337.

to follow is to a large extent a response, if not precisely an answer, to the first question.

That first question is: how much damage to historical materialism is caused by the fact that the phenomenon of attachment to ways of life that give meaning to life is not materialistically explainable? Is the force of that attachment great enough to block or direct the development of the productive forces, or influence the character of economic structures, in ways and degrees which embarrass the theory of history? This is the question I said at the outset I found it hard to answer, because the confirmation conditions of the theory of history remain unclear. It may seem obvious that the human interest I have emphasized makes historical materialism unbelievable, but it is not obvious in fact. That people have goals that are as important, or even more important, to them than development of the productive forces need not contradict historical materialism, since even if 'people have other goals which are always preferred to productive development whenever they conflict with it', the conflict might never determine the direction of events at critical junctures and might therefore never assume pivotal significance.[25]

10. The second question is whether Marxism's one-sided anthropology is the source of historical materialism's lack of focus on the phenomenon referred to in the first question, however damaging or otherwise to historical materialism that lack of focus may be.

It is natural to think that the anthropology and the theory of history are closely related, since each has the activity of production at its centre. Yet they seem on further (if not, perhaps, in the final) analysis, to have little to do with one another. Hence, although I think that the anthropology is false, and also that historical materialism *may* be false because it neglects what the anthropology cannot explain, I also think that *if* historical materialism is false then we probably have parallel errors here, rather than one error giving rise to another: although historical materialism does not depend on the philosophical anthropology, considerations which

---

[25] The quotation is from Allen Wood, to whom I am here indebted, but I have modified his point, since he says that the conflict might be too infrequent to threaten historical materialism, and the crucial question is not how many times it occurs, but whether, as I have said, it assumes pivotal significance. (See Wood, *Karl Marx*, 30.)

appear to refute the anthropology might also, but independently, refute historical materialism.

Production in the philosophical anthropology is not identical with production in the theory of history. According to the anthropology, people flourish in the cultivation and exercise of their manifold powers, and they are especially productive—which in *this* instance means creative—in the condition of freedom conferred by material plenty. But, in the production of interest to the theory of history, people produce not freely but because they have to, since nature does not otherwise supply their wants; and the development in history of the productive power of *man* (that is, of man as such, of man as a species) occurs at the expense of the creative capacity of the *men* who are the agents and victims of that development. They are forced to perform repugnant labour which is a denial, not an expression, of their natures: it is not 'the free play of their own physical and mental powers'.[26] The historically necessitated production is transformation of the world into an habitable place by arduous labour, but the human essence of the anthropology is expressed in production performed as an end in itself, and such production differs not only in aim, but, typically, in form and in content, from production which has an instrumental rationale.[27]

When Marx says that 'people have history because they must *produce* their life'[28] the 'must' derives not from their creative natures but from circumstances. The necessity to produce in history is not the necessity to produce under which Marx thought Milton wrote *Paradise Lost*, for the *historical* necessity to produce is not at all a necessity to express one's being. Marx said that Milton 'produced *Paradise Lost* for the same reason that a silk worm produces silk. It was an activity of *his* nature.'[29] But the necessity

---

[26] *Capital*, i. 284. It is, in fact, 'only through the most tremendous waste of individual development that the development of humanity in general is secured and pursued', at least 'in that epoch of history that directly precedes the conscious reconstruction of human society' (ibid. iii. 182). See *Theories of Surplus Value*, ii. 118 for a similar statement; and for a very grim formulation of the point, see the remarkable climax to Marx's 'Future Results of British Rule in India', 222.

[27] I do not say that the two categories of production cannot overlap, and it may be that their potential intersection is greater than Marx allowed himself to hope: see the final pages of ch. 10 below.

[28] *The German Ideology*, 41.

[29] *Theories of Surplus Value*, i. 401.

under which people produce their lives goes against, not with, the grain of their natures.

If 'people have history *because* they must produce their life', it follows that there will be no history when they do not have to produce their life, because, for example, their natural environment is unusually hospitable. And this consequence is affirmed by Marx. He calls the earth 'too lavish' when she supplies means of survival without human assistance, for she then

'keeps man in hand, like a child in leading-strings'. She does not make his own development, a natural necessity. . . . It is the necessity of bringing a natural force under the control of society, of economizing on it, of appropriating it or subduing it on a large scale by the work of the human hand, that plays the most decisive role in the history of industry'[30]

and hence, we may add, in history *sans phrase*. Where the fruit falls from the tree into humanity's lap there is no history because there is no *need* for history. History, one might say, is a substitute for nature: it occurs only when and because nature is niggardly.

If people produce, historically, not because it belongs to their *nature* to do so, but for the almost opposite reason that it is a requirement of survival and improvement in their inclement *situation*, then it follows that the Marxist theory of human nature is, as I contend, an inappropriate basis on which to found historical materialism. The appropriate premises in an argument for historical materialism feature, instead, the situation of scarcity in which history-making humanity is placed, together with the intelligence and rationality which enables people to ameliorate, and, ultimately, to extricate themselves from, that situation.[31] The argument would not benefit from a premiss which says that humanity is by nature productive in the sense that human fulfilment lies in some kind of productive activity, for such a premiss is irrelevant to the questions how and why humanity is productive in history.

To show how easy it is, and how wrong, to elide the distinction between historical materialism and the Marxist conception of human nature, I quote and criticize Allen Wood:

Historical progress consists fundamentally in the growth of people's

---

[30] *Capital*, i. 649.
[31] See ch. 5 above for an extended defence of the argument in *KMTH* which rests on those premises.

abilities to shape and control the world about them. This is the most basic way in which they develop and express their human essence. It is the definite means by which they may in time gain a measure of freedom, of mastery over their social creations.[32]

Wood's first sentence is ambiguous, because of the phrase 'people's abilities', which may denote either abilities inherent in individuals or the Ability of Man, of humanity as such, and only under the latter interpretation is the sentence true to Marx, who thought that the growth of the productive power of humanity proceeded in tandem with confinement of the creative capacity of most humans. It follows that Wood's second sentence is false: people do not develop and express their human essence in activity which thwarts that essence. The third sentence, taken out of context, might still be true, since an essence-frustrating cause could have essence-congenial effects, but if we take it to mean that humanity engages in self-denying labour *in order* 'in time' to achieve self-fulfilment, then it is false, since it is false—it could not be true—that the whole of history has a purpose which humanity sets and pursues, and in his more sober moments Marx ridiculed just such claims.[33] (In the most ambitious of those readings of historical materialism in which humanity is an agent with a purpose, the historical production whose character is dictated by circumstance is undertaken in order to realize a conquest of nature after which production need no longer be dictated by circumstance: under communism essence-governed creativity is possible for the first time.[34] In a slightly less extravagant reading, there exists no purpose of facilitating creative expression independently of and prior to history, but, once production begins under the imperative of survival, the latent powers of humanity are roused,[35] and the project of attaining a creative existence is founded.)

[32] *Karl Marx*, 75.

[33] For an unsober moment see the passage at p. 281 of Marx's article on Friedrich List's *Nationales System*, in which he flirts with the suggestion that humanity undertakes production in history so that it can one day engage in production as an end in itself.

[34] Or possible, that is, for people in general, since it is false that essence-based creativity is never exhibited in history: one person who exhibited it was, as we have seen (see p. 148 above), John Milton. On creativity before and after the advent of communism, see *KMTH* 205. (By the way: would a communist Milton lack the historical Milton's singleness of vocation? Would he function not as a *writer* but as one who engages in writing 'among other activities' (see sect. 7 above)? The idea is neither attractive nor plausible.)

[35] It is adversity which 'spurs man on to the multiplication of his needs, his capacities, and the instruments and modes of his labour'. (*Capital*, i. 649).

Since the production of history frustrates human nature, it does not occur because it is human nature to be productive. The theory of history does not, accordingly, derive from the anthropology. But the two doctrines do not contradict one another,[36] and since, as I noted a moment ago, essence-frustrating causes can have essence-congenial effects, it is possible to conjoin the two theories: one could say that humanity is essentially creative, but that its historical creativity, this side of communism, is governed not by its essence but by its circumstances, so that there is a frustration of the human essence which only communism, the ultimate result of essence-frustrating activity, will relieve.

The feasibility of this conjunction throws no doubt on the separability of historical materialism and Marxist anthropology: what we have here is truly a conjunction, rather than, as it were, a fusion. It is the anthropology, and not historical materialism, which grounds the description of historical production as essence-frustrating, that being a notion foreign to the historical materialist vocabulary. And the independent contribution to the conjunction of the theory of history is plain from the coherence of the following fantasy: one might, at a pinch, imagine two kinds of creature, one whose essence it was to create and the other not, undergoing similarly toilsome histories because of similarly adverse circumstances. In one case, but not the other, the toil would be a self-alienating exercise of essential powers.

11. I deal here with objections to the claims of section 10.

It might be argued that the anthropology supplies *part* of the explanation of the reworking of the world in history, since, even if the thesis that humanity is by nature creative is irrelevant to the human *interest* in transforming the environment, it is needed to explain why and how people are *able* to pursue that interest. The fact that humanity is by nature productive enables it to do what intelligence and rationality induce it to do against the rigour of scarcity. That people *can* transform the world, it might be said, is an implicit premiss in the argument of chapter 6 of *KMTH*.

But this argument for the relevance of the anthropology to the theory of history is mistaken. For the relevant implicit premiss of the theory of history is not that humanity is *essentially* productive,

---

[36] A tension between the two doctrines, but one which falls short of being a contradiction between them, is explored in ch. 9, sect. 7 below.

but just that, whether or not this is an essential truth about them, human beings can produce, and perhaps, indeed, in a sense of 'produce' different from that in which, according to Marx, producing belongs to their essence.

One might, however, say that historical materialism requires the anthropology as a basis for its forecast of how human beings will occupy themselves under communism. But I have wanted here to separate the vision of the future from the theory of the past, and I have meant by 'historical materialism' the theory of the dialectic of forces and relations of production which comes to an end with the achievement of communism. Historical materialism here is the theory of what Marx called *prehistory*,[37] and the present objection is therefore out of order.

The claim that historical materialism does not contradict the anthropology could also be challenged. For, according to historical materialism, people produce because of scarcity, because they have to, while the thesis that humanity is by nature creative entails that people would produce even when they do not have to produce, when, indeed, they do not have to do anything. Yet, as I emphasized in *KMTH*, Marx represents people as not producing in the Arcadian conditions which stimulate no historical development.[38]

To deal definitively with this objection one would need to be more clear about the concept of human essence than I am at the moment. But a rather simple distinction will, I think, get us somewhere. Here are two contrasting principles about essence, neither of which is absurd:

E: If an activity is essential to a being, then the being does not *exist* (and, *a fortiori*, does not flourish) unless it performs it.

F: If an activity is essential to a being, then the being does not *flourish* (though it might exist) unless it performs it.

If our understanding of essence includes principle *E*, then the objection stated above succeeds, unless Marx thought, as perhaps, indeed, he did, that people in Arcadian conditions are, in virtue of their underdevelopment, pre-human. This last saving suggestion might seem to offer only temporary relief, since the objector could then say that non-Arcadians *are* human for Marx, and even though

---

[37] See the reference to prehistory at p. 22 of Marx's Preface to the *Critique of Political Economy*.

[38] *KMTH* 23–4; and see p. 149 above.

they do produce—so that the objection does not apply in its original form—they do not produce in a way that manifests their essence, as the *E* conception of essence would require.

But it is not pedantic to rejoin that *E* may not require that essential activity be performed in a satisfactory fashion. One might, then, silence the objector by saying that people produce because circumstances give them no other choice, but that in producing they exercise their essential powers, yet not, because of situational constraint, in a satisfactory way.[39] (Note that in such a view the theory of history and the anthropology remain substantially independent of each other, along the lines laid out in the last paragraph of section 10 above.)

Consider now principle *F*. On its different construal of essence, the objection fails, although it would follow that if Arcadians are humans, then they are not flourishing ones. Marx strongly implies, of course, that, whatever they are, they are contented; but he did not regard contentment as a sufficient condition of flourishing.[40]

12. I have been distinguishing production which flows from human nature from production which reflects adverse human circumstance, and I would like to end by quoting a politically potent commentary by Jon Elster, which relates to that distinction. In a liberating inversion of conventional wisdom about 'the problem of incentives', he claims that they are needed not in order to get people to produce, but to get them to produce in circumstances of scarcity which prevent their natural creativity from expressing itself. Having quoted Marx's statement that in the future society 'the free, unobstructed, progressive and universal development of the forces of production is itself the presupposition of society and hence of its reproduction',[41] he goes on:

[39] The view just sketched bears comparison with the following difficult passage: 'We see how the history of *industry* and the established *objective* existence of industry are the *open* book of *man's essential powers*, the perceptibly existing human *psychology*. Hitherto this was not conceived in its connection with man's essential being, but only in an external relation of utility . . . We have before us the *objectified essential powers* of man in the form of *sensuous, alien, useful* objects, in the form of estrangement, displayed in *ordinary material industry* . . . all human activity hitherto has been labour—that is, industry—activity estranged from itself' (*Economic and Philosophic Manuscripts*, 302–3).

[40] See the personal views he expressed in a 'Confession' reprinted in McLellan, *Karl Marx*, 456–7.

[41] *The Grundrisse*, 540.

According to the view of human nature worked out in the *Economic and Philosophic Manuscripts* innovative and creative activity is natural for man. Contrary to the usual approach in political economy, the problem is not one of creating incentives to innovation, but of removing the obstacles to the natural creative urge of the individual 'in whom his own realization exists as an inner necessity'.[42] Special incentives are needed only under conditions of scarcity and poverty, in which the needs of the individual are twisted and his capacities developed only in a one-sided way. In the early stages of capitalism there was indeed a great deal of scarcity and poverty . . .

so that incentives to innovation, such as the patent system, and extravagant rewards to entrepreneurship, were required. But

given the technology developed by capitalism itself, it is materially feasible to install a regime in which the level of want satisfaction is so high that innovation as a spontaneous activity comes into its own—as part of the general self-actualization of individuals. The result will be a rate of innovation far in excess of anything seen before.[43]

13. The main contentions of this chapter are as follows:

1. Marxist philosophical anthropology is one-sided. Its conception of human nature and human good overlooks the need for self identity than which nothing is more essentially human. (See sections 6 and 7.)

2. Marx and his followers have underestimated the importance of phenomena, such as religion and nationalism, which satisfy the need for self identity. (Section 8.)

3. It is unclear whether or not phenomena of that kind impinge in a damaging way on historical materialism. (Section 9.)

4. Historical materialism and Marxist philosophical anthropology are independent of, though also consistent with, each other. (Sections 10 and 11.)

5. If historical materialism is, as (3) allows it may be, false, then, in virtue of (4), it is not false because it relies on a false anthropology, but it and the anthropology are false for parallel reasons.

Is historical materialism false? Some distinctions which are relevant to the task of answering that question are provided in the following chapter.

---

[42] *Economic and Philosophic Manuscripts*, 304.
[43] *Making Sense of Marx*, 261–2.

9

RESTRICTED AND INCLUSIVE HISTORICAL MATERIALISM

1. Marxism is not one theory, but a set of more or less related theories. And two members of the set *seem* especially closely connected. I have in mind, on the one hand, the Marxist theory of history, which is also called *historical materialism*, and, on the other, the Marxist conception of human nature, which we can also call Marx's *philosophical anthropology*. Historical materialism seems to be founded on the Marxist view of what people essentially are.

The heart of historical materialism is the thesis that there is, throughout history's course, a tendency towards growth of human productive power, and that forms of society (or economic structures[1]) rise and fall when and because they enable and promote, or frustrate and impede, that growth. Human productive activity increases in potency as history unfolds, and social forms accommodate themselves to that material growth process. They flourish to the extent that they help to raise the level of development of the productive forces, and they decline when they no longer do so.

It is controversial what the various levels of productive power and associated forms of society are supposed to be. I have argued[2] that the most defensible periodization is a four-stage story.

At the first stage, productive power is too meagre to enable a class of non-producers to live off the labour of producers. The *material* position is one of absence of surplus, and the corresponding *social* (or *economic*) form is a primitive classless society.

In the second stage of material development, a surplus appears, of a size sufficient to support an exploiting class, but not large enough to sustain a capitalist accumulation process. The corresponding social form is, accordingly, a pre-capitalist class society, one, that is, in which the producers do not enter a contract to supply their labour power, as they do under capitalism, but are

---

[1] I here use 'social forms' and 'economic structures' interchangeably since 'from a Marxian viewpoint, social forms are distinguished and unified by their types of economic structure' (*KMTH* 78–9).

[2] See *KMTH* 197–201.

forced, independently of contract, to yield it in the service of slave-owner, feudal lord, or other non-capitalist superior.

At stage 3 the surplus has become generous enough to make capitalism possible. It then grows still further under the impetus of capitalist competition, until it becomes so massive that capitalism becomes untenable,[3] and the fourth and final social form, which is non-primitive communism, the modern classless society, emerges.

And that is the story of humankind, according to historical materialism, in my reading of the doctrine. It is a story which, you will have noticed, makes large and controversial claims; but, as I shall later emphasize, a number of what are commonly thought of as historical materialist theses are not entailed by what has just been said.

A word, now, about the Marxist conception of human nature. It is a conception which represents men and women as essentially creative beings, who are only truly *themselves* when they are developing and exercising their productive faculties. Marxist philosophical anthropology perhaps allows that a human being can *exist* without in some important sense being a producer, but it certainly denies that he can be fully and distinctively *human* without being productive.[4] Marxism's theory of human nature therefore appears to be (part of) the basis of Marxism's theory of history: it is natural to attribute to Marxism the thought that human history is a history of growth in productive power *because* humans are by nature productive beings.

The impression that historical materialism rests upon the Marxist conception of human nature is encouraged by a well-known passage in *The German Ideology* of 1846, which may reasonably be regarded as the founding document of historical materialism:

People can be distinguished from animals by consciousness, by religion, or by anything else you please. They themselves begin to render themselves different from animals as soon as they begin to *produce* their means of subsistence . . .[5]

---

[3] There is much disagreement within Marxism about why capitalism then becomes untenable. In my view, it is ultimately because people no longer have to labour in the traditional sense that they can no longer be made to labour for capitalists.

[4] See ch. 8, pp. 152–3 above for an elaboration of that statement.

[5] *The German Ideology*, 31. I have amended the translation to eliminate an unwanted ambiguity.

In a natural reading of that passage, it suggests that history begins when productive activity begins, and that this originating break-through also marks the beginning of humanity's acquisition of a distinctively human nature, beyond the animal. It looks as though the act of producing, which identifies people as human, is also the act repeated performances of which constitute the core of the process of human history.

2. I argued in section 10 of the foregoing chapter that the appearance described in the immediately preceding pages is a false one, and that historical materialism is not, in fact, grounded in Marxian philosophical anthropology. The idea that people are by nature productive is an inappropriate basis for representing history as the growth of human productive power, and the apparent dependence of the Marxist theory of history on the Marxist theory of human nature is an illusion.

I also said (Chapter 8, section 6) that the Marxist theory of human nature fatally overlooks a whole side of human concern, to wit, the human need for self definition, which helps to explain the power of cultural phenomena that have often been considered problems for historical materialism. But I claimed (Chapter 8, section 10) that, if a deficiency in the Marxist conception of human nature prevents Marxists from appreciating the full significance of, for example, religious and national feeling, it nevertheless does not follow that those phenomena falsify historical materialism. Not every mistake people make is a mistake in every theory they hold, and since, as I have urged, historical materialism does not depend on the Marxist view of human nature, it might be free of the errors which that view embodies.

But all that follows is that it *might* be free of them. For even if historical materialism is not committed by a theory of human nature to underestimating religion and nationalism, it might do so anyway. Historical materialism might be false because it neglects or depreciates what the anthropology cannot explain, even if, should that be so, we would then have two parallel errors, rather than one error giving rise to the other. And critics of Marxism do not, of course, believe that phenomena such as religion and nationalism pose problems for Marxists without affecting their theory of history. The critics think those phenomena defeat historical materialism itself.

3. *Does* historical materialism unduly depreciate forms of consciousness like religion and nationalism? The answer may depend on how we take historical materialism, for, to introduce a pair of terms which I shall forthwith explain, we can take it either in an *inclusive* or in a *restricted* way, and if we take it in the second way then phenomena such as religion and nationalism pose less threat to it.

Recall that historical materialism is the theory which says *that there exists, throughout history, a tendency towards growth of human productive power, and that forms of society rise and fall when and because they enable and promote, or frustrate and impede, that growth.* Now we obtain capsule formulations of inclusive and restricted historical materialism if we qualify a related statement[6] in respectively these different ways:

History is, $\dfrac{\text{centrally}}{\textit{inter alia,}}$ the systematic growth of human productive power, and forms of society rise and fall when and because they enable and promote, or frustrate and impede, that growth.

By inserting 'centrally' within the first pair of commas, we obtain a short statement of inclusive historical materialism. By inserting '*inter alia*', we obtain a short statement of restricted historical materialism. The word 'systematic', which appears in both formulations, is intended to convey the thought that the process of productive growth possesses an autonomous momentum: the master claim of historical materialism, which both of its construals share, says not that human productive power for whatever reason, and perhaps for a miscellany of them, grows, but that it is in the nature of the human situation, considered in its most general aspects, that there will be a tendency for productive power to grow.[7]

In inclusive historical materialism the process described at the beginning of this chapter is the *centre* of historical development, in

---

[6] The italicized existential statement is neutral between the two versions of historical materialism, whereas the sentence formed by omitting, rather than filling, the first pair of commas in the sentence-frame below provides an inclusive statement of historical materialism, one pretty well equivalent to the result of retaining the commas and inserting 'centrally'. I used an existential formulation on p. 155 above because I wanted restricted historical materialism to be possible. At *KMTH* 26 I used a non-existential formulation, since I had not thought of the possibility of formulating historical materialism non-inclusively when I wrote *KMTH*.

[7] See, further, ch. 5, sects. 1, 2 above.

the sense that major developments in those spheres of activity which lie beyond production and the economy are, in their large lines, explained by material and/or economic changes.[8] Important religious transformations, for example, are peripheral, not in the fatuous because question-begging sense that they are *not* economic changes, but in the more pertinent sense that their principal features, or most of them,[9] are explained by the process here called central *because* of its privileged explanatory position.

Restricted historical materialism is more modest in reach. It is primarily a theory about the course of material development itself, rather than about the relationship *between* that development and other developments. To be sure, it has implications for processes outside the economy, but they are not the extensive ones definitive of inclusive historical materialism. Restricted historical materialism does not say that the principal features of spiritual existence are materially or economically explained. It requires of spiritual phenomena only that they do not disrupt the independently determined material and economic sequence plotted out in section 1 of this chapter (or whatever alternative sequence is the best one to propose), and also that they do not so contribute to that sequence that it loses the autonomy which any historical materialism must assign to it. In short, while spiritual phenomena may have material and economic effects, they must neither profoundly disturb nor be ultimately responsible for material progress.

[8] *Material* changes are changes in production or in productive forces, considered in abstraction from the social or economic forms, that is, relations of production, in which they occur. *Economic* changes are changes in relations of production proper. I mean the distinction between the material and the economic as it is explained in *KMTH*, ch. 6: see the entry 'Economic (vs. material)' in *KMTH*'s index.

In what follows I sometimes use the phrase 'materially explained' as an abbreviation of 'materially and/or economically explained', a device which receives some justification from the fact that in historical materialism as I conceive it the material explains the economic. In any case, the line between the material and the economic, which was drawn in ch. 4 of *KMTH*, is of reduced interest in this chapter, where what matters, instead, is the line between the material and economic on the one hand, and what is neither material nor economic on the other.

These explications leave much to be desired, and I apologize for that. I also apologize for using the word 'spiritual' in what follows as a comprehensive vague term to denote social and cultural phenomena which are neither material nor economic. All this terminological looseness conceals theoretical problems, which I do not here try to solve.

[9] Some such qualifying phrase is needed, but it is hard to find a truly felicitous one. The problem of what should count as a 'principal' feature is addressed in sect. 8 below.

Restricted historical materialism thus allows spiritual life to develop in freedom from material life, under the proviso that it may not interfere in specified ways with the latter. Restricted historical materialism only asserts that the material determines the spiritual to the extent necessary to prevent the spiritual from determining the material. It does not deny further influence, but it has no commitment to it. It does not seek to explain the main lines of spiritual development: explanation of spiritual phenomena is promised only when they impinge in threatening ways on the material sphere. For restricted historical materialism *does* need to provide materialist explanations of spiritual phenomena which have a considerable economic effect: that point will be illustrated in the next section.

Inclusive historical materialism affirms the claims of restricted historical materialism, and adds further ones. It affirms the claims of restricted historical materialism since they follow from the thesis italicized at the beginning of this section, which both doctrines share. But it undertakes, in addition, to explain the principal features of spiritual phenomena, whatever they turn out to be, and whether or not the italicized thesis requires those explanations. There is, by contrast, no commitment in the very logic of restricted historical materialism to explaining spiritual life to any particular extent. The shape and size of restricted historical materialism's explanatory burden depend on the data. It is logically possible for that burden to be identical with what inclusive historical materialism shoulders, but it is also utterly unlikely.

Restricted and inclusive historical materialism could also be called defensive and offensive historical materialism, and that nomenclature might be more informative, but I have avoided it because it has misleading associations. Restricted historical materialism is defensive, since it is content to protect the story of material progress from undue spiritual intrusion, and inclusive historical materialism is offensive, since it seeks explanatory conquest of the spiritual other than for self-protective reasons.

I hope that the distinction I have tried to construct will become more clear through discussion of a familiar challenge to historical materialism, to which section 4 is devoted.

4. The challenge is Max Weber's account of the Protestant Reformation and its aftermath, or, to be fair, a version of Weber's account which takes it at its starkest and ignores his qualifying disclaimers.[10] In the present reading of Weber he comes close to saying that the character of European religious development explains why capitalism arose in Europe and not elsewhere: Protestantism, and, more particularly, Calvinism, was, to use R. H. Tawney's description of Weber's thesis, 'the parent of capitalism'.[11] I adopt what may be an exaggerated reading of Weber because it suits my methodological purposes. I am trying to determine not whether historical materialism is true, but *how* to judge, on given evidence, whether it is true, and that exercise justifies a measure of simplification.

In the present account the Reformation is understood as a reaction to corruption and other excess in the practice of the Roman Catholic Church. In revulsion against the luxury indulged by that Church, the new religious teaching preaches asceticism, and, more specifically, an asceticism of the sort Weber called 'worldly', to contrast it with the cloistered asceticism of the monastery. In reaction against Roman Catholic abuse of priestly, episcopal, and papal power, the new religious teaching supports individualism in the relationship between the worshipper and his God: that relationship is no longer to be mediated by authoritative third parties.

Because of its individualism and its worldly asceticism, the new religion is a great encouragement to capitalist enterprise. The link between individualism and capitalism is easy to see. But the worldly asceticism also favours capitalism, since its ascetic component forbids extravagant consumption and its worldly component enjoins dedication to productive market-oriented work, and a zealously productive individual who consumes little cannot but accumulate a lot, and is therefore a capitalist—or so Weber argued.[12] Good Protestant conduct thereby becomes synonymous with good business practice, and success in that practice is an

---

[10] The final paragraph of *The Protestant Ethic* (p. 183) contains Weber's strongest disclaimer, and one which, in my view, contradicts the tenor of many statements in the body of the book. (See, too, ibid. 90–2, 193 n. 6, 277–8 n. 84). I here ignore not only Weber's disclaimers, but also, if Gordon Marshall is right, his severe confusion about what he was trying to explain: see *In Search of the Spirit of Capitalism*, 55 ff.

[11] *Religion and the Rise of Capitalism*, 212.

[12] I add that clause because I have never understood how it would have been inconsistent with Protestantism to work hard, consume little, and devote the resulting surplus to charity, instead of investing it. This lacuna in Weber's reasoning weakens his argument at, for example, *The Protestant Ethic*, 172.

especially potent outward sign of spiritual salvation. So when
Christian asceticism 'slammed the door of the monastery behind it'
and 'strode into the marketplace' it generated capitalist results, by
fashioning for its adherents 'a life *in* the world' which was 'neither
of nor for this world'.[13]

That sketch says something about the causes of Protestantism
and something about its effects. Imagine that the sketch has been
expanded in similar vein, so that it embodies the following
assertions:

1. Protestantism took hold and persisted for non-economic
   reasons.

2. Protestantism had important consequences for European
   religious life.

3. Protestantism had important consequences for European
   economic life.

Now this trio of statements constitutes a challenge to historical
materialism, but the nature and weight of the challenge depend on
how historical materialism is construed. The conjunction of (1) and
(2) threatens inclusive historical materialism, since that theory
promises an economic explanation of religiously important religious changes, and (1) says of this religious change, which (2) says
is important, that it lacked an economic explanation. Restricted
historical materialism makes no predictions about the course of
religious life considered just as such, and it is therefore unem-
barrassed by the conjunction of (1) and (2). It is, however, in
common with inclusive historical materialism, challenged, though
not, I think, refuted, by the addition of (3), since (3) *suggests* that
Protestantism substantially changed the trajectory of economic
development, and restricted historical materialism does deny that
religion can do that.

I now want to indicate how (3)'s challenge to both historical
materialisms might be neutralized, so that the rise and career of
Protestantism would embarrass only inclusive and not also restricted historical materialism. To this end, I shall expound some claims
of the British historian H. M. Robertson, whose *Aspects of the Rise
of Economic Individualism* was an extended polemic against
Weber's *Protestant Ethic*.

[13] Ibid. 154 (my emphasis); see also p. 181.

Robertson's critique of Weber bears on (3) in at least two ways. In some parts of his book he expresses doubt that Protestantism ever had the impact on economic life that Weber said it did. That part of Robertson's polemic, which tends towards a denial of (3), does not interest me here. I want, instead, to draw attention to passages in which he more or less accepts (3), but contrives to neutralize its anti-materialist power. He does so particularly effectively by arguing that Weber committed an important procedural error when he assembled evidence for his claim that the Reformation generated the spirit of capitalism. According to Robertson, Weber's more impressive textual citations came not from early Protestant doctrine but, as Weber himself often failed to remark, from late writings which differed significantly from the early ones, *for the amount of commerce-favouring injunction in a text tended to be greater the later was its date.* In one instructive instance, the original edition of a text had had little capitalist spirit, and a rather later edition much more, and Weber had used the later edition only, without noting its differences from the earlier one.[14]

Now since the economy was, of course, becoming more capitalist as time went on, and since it would be implausible to suppose that it was becoming more capitalist *because* religion was—for independent reasons—becoming more favourable to capitalism, Robertson was able to conclude that it was only because religion was adapting itself to a climate of capitalist enterprise that it, in turn, encouraged such enterprise. 'The doctrine of the "calling"', which was central to Weber's case, 'did not breed a spirit of capitalism. The spirit of capitalism was responsible for a gradual modification and attrition of [that] doctrine'.[15] And Robertson also made the (3)-neutralizing claim that not all Protestantism, and not even all Calvinism, favoured capitalism, and that not all non-Protestantism, that is, Catholicism, disfavoured it. On the whole, each variant of Christianity favoured capitalism where capitalism was for other reasons strong, and not otherwise.

Now Robertson's critique does not touch our propositions (1) and (2), and it therefore does not counter the full Weberian

---

[14] See *Aspects*, 15 ff. for Robertson's comparison of *The Whole Duty of Man* of 1657, and *The New Whole Duty of Man*, which appeared nearly one hundred years later.

[15] *Aspects*, 27; cf. ibid. 32: 'The Protestant Ethic changed as the result of the influence of a rising capitalistically-minded middle class. . . . From being a hindrance to enterprise it became a spur.'

challenge to inclusive historical materialism. It does, however, reduce the force of (3) as a counter-example to both historical materialisms. For, even if we continue to accept (3), we can now hypothesize, in the light of Robertson,[16] that, if Protestant teaching indeed had substantial economic effects, then the features of Protestantism in virtue of which it had those effects appeared in Protestantism because the religion was adapting itself to the economy. We can plead that, even if the commerce-favouring religious changes were *essential* to continued capitalist development, restricted historical materialism is as yet undefeated, since it is a credible hypothesis that those changes occurred *because* they favoured the development of commerce.

Someone might say that it is unnecessary, in order to save restricted historical materialism, to neutralize (3) in any such way. For in our Weberian sketch spiritual phenomena do not impede or divert, but encourage, the course of material and economic development which historical materialism postulates. But this suggestion embodies a misunderstanding of the master claim of historical materialism which, as I indicated in section 3, lays down that it is a result of extremely general material features of the human situation that there is a persistent tendency for productive power to grow. If, therefore, the rise of capitalism, and the growth of productive power it promoted, were assignable to the Protestant influence, then the master claim of historical materialism would, in its required reading, be false. The consequences mentioned in proposition (3), do, therefore, challenge historical materialism, despite the fact that they were materially progressive in bearing.

A neutralizing explanation of spiritual phenomena which have such substantial economic effects is required to meet the challenge they pose. And that challenge is not met by assigning to the economically consequential spiritual phenomena just any economic cause, no matter what it may be. The relevant spiritual phenomena must, instead, be seen to occur *because* of their tendency to have the economic effects they do. Economic explanations of them which lack that property—which are not, that is, functional explan-

---

[16] The debate in response to Weber's *Protestant Ethic* did not, of course, end with the contribution of Robertson, whose views I am not endorsing, but adopting for the merely methodological purpose of explicating restricted historical materialism. For a recent critical survey of the debate, see Marshall's *In Search of the Spirit of Capitalism*. Marshall comments on the rejection of Robertson's criticism by others at pp. 87–8.

ations[17]—are consistent with a merely interactionist view of the relationship between the economic and the spiritual, and on such a view there is no reason to suppose that the prescribed line of material and economic advance will be maintained: it would be an accident if it was. To preserve that line we must say that, in virtue of the existing economic situation, the religious change to be explained would stimulate economic progress, and that it occurred because it would do so.

When we explain spiritual phenomena in this fashion, we can, if need be, concede that they are necessary and sufficient, in the circumstances, to keep material development on its theoretically mandated course. The concession does not contradict historical materialism, as long as the state of the economy was itself sufficient for the emergence and/or persistence of the given spiritual phenomena. But—to repeat the point made above—if it were sufficient for their persistence, but did not also functionally explain them, then it would be an accident that their impact on the economy kept it on course, and that is something which could not be an accident for historical materialism.

I think that many Marxists would, in practice, be content with the Robertson 'refutation' of Weber. They would not be disturbed by propositions (1) and (2) (see page 162 above) until proposition (3) had been added to them. And, if that is so, then many Marxists are in practice restricted historical materialists, even if, when offering a brief statement of their Marxism, they are disposed to utter inclusivist formulations.

5. Having distinguished between restricted and inclusive historical materialism, I now ask: in which of these two ways did Karl Marx construe his doctrine? Part of the answer is that he never contemplated the distinction which I have tried to draw, and he therefore never *knowingly* chose between the two theories. But one may nevertheless also say that he did commit himself, and, in my view, regrettably, to the inclusive variant. One proof of his commitment to it is the *German Ideology*, which abounds in

---

[17] For a brief account of the nature of functional explanation, see ch. 1, sect. 1 above. More extended discussions are available in *KMTH* chs. 9, 10, and in the four articles by me in the bibliography to this book which have 'functional' or 'functionalism' in their titles.

inclusivist formulations.[18] But possibly more revealing still of his inclusivist leaning is the argument for historical materialism at which he hints in various places.[19] It is an argument which he never himself expressly stated, but it was propounded forthrightly and lucidly by Frederick Engels, in his speech at Marx's graveside (see Chapter 7 above). The conclusion of that argument is that the nature of (what I have here called) spiritual existence is to be explained by the character of material production, 'instead of vice-versa'. That is a claim which restricted historical materialism does not make. It is an inclusivist claim, since the explanatory priority which it assigns to the material side of life means that spiritual life is, on the whole, to be materialistically explained. The argument's conclusion is consonant with the following inclusivist formulation, which is due to Engels, but which there is every reason to think that Marx would have endorsed:

I hope even British respectability will not be overshocked if I use, in English, as well as in so many other languages, the term 'historical materialism', to designate that view of the course of history which seeks the ultimate cause and the great moving power of *all* important historic events in the economic development of society . . . [20]

My own argument for historical materialism,[21] by contrast with that of Marx and Engels, accords with a restricted construal of the doctrine, and provides no reason for affirming an inclusivist one. For my argument, whatever may be its value, is supposed to show only that there exists a tendency for productive power to grow, and for forms of society consequently to adjust themselves accordingly. The implications of that contention for the non-economic domain are just those of restricted historical materialism.

6. Now, although Marx and Engels thought inclusively about historical materialism, it does not *quite* follow that the theory itself must be taken in that way. In this section I argue that it need not be so taken, and in the next I argue that Marx and Engels had no good reason to be inclusivist, and some good reason to adopt the restricted interpretation.

[18] For some of them, see *The German Ideology*, 32, 36–7, 43, 53–4, 59.
[19] e.g., ibid. 41–2; *Capital*, i. 176 n.
[20] Introduction to the English edition of *Socialism, Utopian and Scientific*, 102 (my emphases).
[21] See *KMTH*, ch. 6, sect. 4 and also ch. 5 above.

The German Ideology certainly cannot be recovered for restricted historical materialism, but the more precise and circumspect statement of the theory in the Preface of 1859[22] (which, like so many other commentators on Marx, I have always regarded as canonical) *nearly* can be. The apparent obstacle to a restricted construal of the Preface is its set of statements about ideology and the superstructure. Because of their presence, the Preface seems, on an initial reading, to assert a more extensive control of society by economic reality than restricted historical materialism requires. The Preface seems to support the judgment that, while what Marx says about the dialectic of forces and relations of production may admit of restricted construal when it is considered apart from the rest of what he says, restricted construal is impossible when one examines the connections he asserts *between* the forces/relations dialectic and the domains of politics, law, religion, culture, and social consciousness in general.

Before I respond to that contention, a word about the boundaries of the superstructure, and of ideology. I take ideology to consist of forms of consciousness, and I take the superstructure to be institutional. I therefore regard neither as including the other, which is a mildly controversial view. Since I do hold that view, I treat the problems posed by ideology and the superstructure separately, but nothing of substance for our purposes turns on this method of treatment.

There is, I shall argue in a moment, no statement in the Preface about the superstructure which resists restricted construal, but the document does, I concede, contain one unambiguously inclusivist sentence about consciousness, which says that 'it is not the consciousness of men that determines their being, but, on the contrary, their social being that determines their consciousness'.[23] If that sentence is removed, what remains is, I would claim, open to restricted construal. I regard the quoted sentence as a flourish, Marx's own inclusivist comment on the doctrine he is setting out, and not a comment which that doctrine, as otherwise set out, requires. I do not contend that he did not mean what he said when

---

[22] *Critique of Political Economy*, 20–2.

[23] I am supposing, somewhat contentiously, that 'social being' here refers to specifically economic social being, and that the phrase is not being used with such width of reference that a person's political activity, for example, would be part of his social being. The quoted sentence is not inclusivist when it is interpreted in the second way.

he wrote the quoted sentence, and I accept that its presence colours the rest of the Preface. My claim is that the rest of the Preface may be seen as having a different colour when the quoted sentence is removed.[24] The result of such excising surgery can be read as a statement of restricted historical materialism, the theory which, so I claim, many Marxists have in practice[25] favoured.

Even when its inclusivist sentence has been deleted, the Preface does, of course, offer economic explanations of spiritual developments, and notably of the 'ideological forms in which men become conscious of [the conflict between forces and relations of production] and fight it out'. But such explanations leave unanswered the question *how much* of social consciousness is controlled by material and economic existence, and they are therefore consistent with restricted historical materialism.

I turn from consciousness to the superstructure. In *KMTH* I distinguished between two ways of using the term 'superstructure', and I expressed a preference for one of them. The term could be used, as it commonly is,[26] to denote all non-economic institutions, or, instead, as I recommended, to denote just those non-economic institutions whose character is explained by the economic structure. I argued that the second and less usual characterization was preferable, and that it did not prevent one from asserting what I *then* took to be the principal Marxist theoretical claim about non-economic institutions, namely, that their character is largely explained by the nature of the economic structure. On the definition of 'superstructure' which I favoured, that inclusivist claim could be put by saying that non-economic institutions are largely superstructural, rather than by saying, as one must on the more usual definition, which I disfavoured, that the character of the superstructure is largely explained by the nature of the economic structure.

I think that I was more or less[27] right to insist that the superstructure be thought of as composed, by definition, of

[24] The sentence displays Marx's commitment to the 'sociology' described in sect. 10 below, and the fact that it can be removed without rendering what remains incoherent confirms the separability of that sociology from the Marxist theory of history.

[25] See the remarks at the end of sect. 4 above.

[26] And with no textual justification whatsoever. For a protest against the common practice of inflating the superstructure see my review of Rader's *Marx's Interpretaion of History*, 221–2.

[27] I enter this qualification for reasons given in the Addendum to this chapter.

institutions explained by the economic structure, but it now seems to me unnecessary to add the inclusivist claim that most non-economic institutional reality is superstructural. The Preface says that '*a* legal and political superstructure' rises on the real basis of the economic structure. The use of 'a', rather than 'the', allows the interpretation that what is said to rise on the economic basis is not all legal and political reality, as that is antecedently understood, but just such legal and political reality as is specially relevant economically, and there is no need to add that *most* legal and political reality does have special economic relevance.

7. In the contention of section 6, the historical materialism of the 1859 Preface is open to a restricted construal, after one imposing sentence in it has been set aside. I do not say that an inclusivist reading of what then remains is impossible, and it is, of course, the reading which Marx himself favoured. But I now want to argue that he should not have favoured it, since some of his own views tell strongly against it.

Though inclining towards inclusivism, Marx never maintained—what even inclusivism does not entail—that *all* spiritual phenomena are ideological or superstructural, and he thought of part of culture as expressing something other than the material needs of humanity and the interests of particular classes. This part he calls, in *The Theories of Surplus Value*, 'the free spiritual production of [a] particular social formation', and he contrasts it with the formation's 'ideological component parts'. I believe he calls it *free* not only because it does not serve immediate material needs, but also for the more interesting reason that it has aspects (of its content, or its form, or its themes and emphases) which are neither superstructural on anything nor an ideological reflection of a class point of view.[28]

Free spiritual production presumably appears within, among other places, the folklore, song, dance, and handiwork of popular culture, but in its higher forms it proceeds largely inside the precincts of the ruling class, prior to the socialist revolution. It is

[28] *Theories of Surplus Value*, i. 285. I grant that the paragraph from which the quotation comes sounds inclusivist, but that does not spoil my point, which is not that Marx *recognized* the anti-inclusivist significance of 'free spiritual production', but that he *ought* to have.

only within that class that 'human capacities can develop freely', and in that development 'the working class serves merely as a basis'.[29] So there is, in class history, a limited prefiguration of the general liberation of essential human creativity which is promised for the communist future. It would, indeed, be absurd to think that there is *no* pre-communist anticipation of the human flourishing which becomes unconstrained after it.

Now if culture is not, even on this side of communism, *entirely* constrained by material and economic circumstance, then what reason might there be for saying, as inclusivism does, that it is *on the whole*, or *in its main lines*, so constrained? One might well claim that since, in pre-communist history, the mass of humanity are engulfed in material concern, the realm of creative culture must perforce be small, and much smaller than the realm of material production. One might hope to attach sense to that statement about the sizes of the two 'realms' by using something like the distribution of people's time and energy as a measure. But no estimate of the relative sizes of the material and the creative domains entails anything about whether or not the principal features of the latter are materially or economically *explained*, and creative culture's meagre size does not, therefore, support the claims of inclusive historical materialism.

It is the creative side of human nature, the side emphasized by Marxist philosophical anthropology, which finds fulfilment in free cultural activity both before and after the communist revolution. Before distinguishing between inclusive and restricted historical materialism, I argued that the Marxist conception of human nature is so disconnected from historical materialism that it neither supports it nor condemns it.[30] I must now add that, whereas the anthropology does indeed dictate no commitment to historical materialism, it favours a restricted rather than an inclusive historical materialism if, for whatever reason, one wants to be an

---

[29] *Theories of Surplus Value*, iii, 97–8. Cf. *The German Ideology*, 78; *Capital*, i. 667; *The Grundrisse*, 634, 705–6; *Critique of the Gotha Programme*, 20; and Engels, *The Housing Question*, 565. See, further *KMTH* 205, where some of those texts are quoted and discussed.

[30] Since Marxist philosophical anthropology is explanatory not of the production imposed by necessity around which historical materialism revolves but of the production which goes beyond the economic sphere, one might say that, while historical materialism is a theory of *prehistory* (in the sense of the 1859 Preface: see ch. 8, p. 152 above), Marxist anthropology is the theory of fully human history and its pre-communist anticipation.

historical materialist at all. And that is because the anthropology predicts the appearance of free spiritual production. To be sure, the existence of free spiritual production in history is logically consistent with inclusive historical materialism, but, once an independent human interest in creativity has been acknowledged, there seems to be no reason to expect the activity which it generates to be pervasively dominated, as inclusivism requires, by material and economic conditions. One might well think that the human interest in conquering scarcity is so overwhelming that it would not yield to the impulsions of creativity at critical junctures, but that thought supports only restricted historical materialism, the theory that nothing outside material development substantially disturbs its course.

In Chapter 8 I contrasted the Marxist theories of history and human nature, and I said that the theory of human nature neglected an essential human feature, to wit, the need for self identification, which certain historically powerful forms of consciousness fulfil. I also said that it was unclear that historical materialism may be charged with similar neglect, and I have argued, in this chapter, that such a charge is less likely to apply if historical materialism is taken in what I have called a restricted way. So phenomena associated with an aspect of human nature which Marxist anthropology fails to honour encourage a restricted construal of historical material-ism. And I am now adding that the said construal is also encouraged by phenomena associated with the aspect of human nature which Marxist anthropology *does* emphasize, to wit, the creative side of human personality. I am invoking the Marxist conception of human nature against inclusive historical material-ism.

If Marx and Engels had good theoretical reason not to be inclusivist why did they nevertheless lean in that direction? Did they, perhaps, have good political reasons for doing so? I cannot think of any. Marxism's politically important claims about exploitation and the necessity of revolutionary opposition to it do not mandate a reductive attitude to culture as a whole and to non-economic institutions in general, but only to those forms of consciousness and those institutions which serve to defend or to mask exploitation, or to impede the struggle against it, however large or small is the place of such ideas and institutions within the non-economic domain as a whole. Reactionary ideas and institutions do fall within the explanatory ambition of restricted historical materialism. What political reason could increase that ambition? Why should a theory which is inspired by a practical interest in the liberation of humanity from economic oppression encumber itself with very bold hypotheses about things which have nothing to do with economic oppression?

I suggest that Marx and Engels were inclusivist neither for good theoretical reasons, nor for good or bad political ones, but for bad theoretical reasons. Some of their bad theoretical reasons were examined in Chapter 7, where I criticized a famous faulty argument for (inclusive) historical materialism. But such arguments were not what drew them to inclusivism in the first place. To understand the genesis of their inclusivist bias, we must recall the intellectual circumstances of origin of historical materialism.

Historical materialism was forged in combat against the Hegelian idealist view of history, which is ridiculed in *The German Ideology*, and which was not only idealist but inclusively so, since, in the Hegelian view, essential features of material and economic life are understood only when they are grasped as manifestations of (human?) self-consciousness at a certain stage of its progressive unfolding. Marx and Engels had no difficulty in demolishing this extravaganza in *The German Ideology*, but there is, alas, little room for doubt that they supposed that the considerations which refuted it also served to establish its mirror opposite. It is possible for Hegelianism to be false without its opposite being true, but there is not much recognition of that possibility in Marx. Hence, when he replaced Hegelian idealism by his own materialism, he retained the inclusivism of the rejected doctrine. Perhaps, instead of turning him upside down, or right side up, Marx would have done better, after toppling Hegel, to leave him lying there, on a horizontal plane. The really important things that Marx had to say, about both the history and liberation of humanity, did not require him to turn the arrow between consciousness and being the other way round.[31]

---

[31] Marx tended to commit the following fallacious inference: since ideas are produced by materially situated people, the material situation of people explains the ideas they produce. Hegel denied both the premiss and the conclusion of that argument, and he rejected its conclusion on the basis of his rejection of its premiss. Hegel's inference from the falsehood of the premiss to the falsehood of the conclusion was sound. That may help to explain why Marx committed his own, unsound, inference.

8. The distinction between restricted and inclusive historical materialism clarifies a problem about how to formulate historical materialism which has preoccupied me for more than twenty-five years.

I was always aware that no one could suppose, and that no sane Marxist had ever really supposed, that *every* feature of, for example, a religious institution had an economic explanation. Historical materialism could not be committed to explaining why Anglicans subscribe to exactly Thirty-Nine Articles, why the Jewish minion requires ten males, rather than nine or twelve, or why Rastafarians favour dread-locked hair. I do not say that it is obvious that such things lack economic explanations. But it is obvious that there need not be economic explanations of them for historical materialism to be true.

Having realized that historical materialism could not pretend to explain everything, I felt it necessary to say, in general terms, what it must claim to explain. And I concluded, thus espousing inclusivism, that it must claim to explain the *principal* or *important* features of non-economic phenomena, for I sloppily supposed that the italicized adjectives could be used interchangeably in this context.

I then asked myself what was the appropriate criterion of importance, and I found myself tempted by the thought that the important features of, for example, a religion, are just those in virtue of which the religion has some sort of economic impact. But I did not yield to that tempting thought, for I recognized that the standard of importance it recommends is question-begging: the economically important features of a religion need not be important as religious features, or in any other further sense. Thus, even if one were to succeed in providing an economic explanation of the economically important features of a religion, one would not be entitled to conclude that one had thereby explained its important features, *tout court*. I nevertheless remained tempted to embrace the stated criterion of importance, out of what I now see was an obscure awareness that historical materialism need not occupy itself with economically inconsequential religious features.

The move to restricted historical materialism is an articulation of that obscure awareness. Restricted historical materialism is called *restricted* because it restricts itself to explaining those non-economic phenomena which possess economic relevance, but there

is in restricted historical materialism no suggestion that a phenomenon is in some general sense important if and only if it is
economically important, and, for a restricted historical materialist,
there is no obligation to formulate a criterion of importance in
general. Unlike inclusive historical materialism, the restricted
doctrine says nothing about economically irrelevant phenomena.

The restricted construal commits historical materialism to
explaining only those non-economic phenomena which have
substantial material or economic consequences, since they pose a
challenge which must be neutralized. And the appropriately
neutralizing way of explaining them (see the end of section 4 above)
is by recourse to functional explanation. Hence my predilection for
functional explanation in *KMTH* confirms that when I wrote it I
was already, implicitly or incipiently, a restricted historical materialist, even though I often reproduced the traditional inclusivist
formulations (and—see section 5 above—the argument for historical materialism which I favoured is further confirmation of the
same thing, since it could not be thought to support an inclusive
version of the theory).

I claim not that all historical materialist explanations are
functional explanations, but that the non-economic phenomena
which a theory *must* explain to count as an historical materialist
theory are to be explained functionally. That conclusion is a
deduction from a thesis about the minimal scope of historical
materialist explanation to a thesis about its nature.

Now someone might say that, whatever may be the interest and
merit of the theory I have recommended to historical materialists, it
has no right to be called a *materialist* theory of history. In inclusive
historical materialism there is the considerable asymmetry that
spiritual life is largely explained by material life, whereas the
converse is denied. Restricted historical materialism has in it the
much smaller asymmetry that it forbids spiritual phenomena to
affect material ones in certain decisive ways but puts no prohibition
on material phenomena affecting spiritual ones. And it might be
claimed that that lesser asymmetry is not enough to qualify
restricted historical materialism as a *materialist* theory of history,
as opposed to a theory of material history.

My entirely tentative response to this difficulty (if, indeed, it is a
difficulty), is as follows. Restricted historical materialism assigns a
certain direction to material development, which it forbids spiritual

phenomena to upset. To decide whether the restricted doctrine is truly a materialism we have to ask whether it is compatible with a claim that spiritual life too has an inherent direction with which material phenomena cannot interfere. If that compatibility obtains, then there is indeed no reason to call restricted historical materialism a *materialism*. But the extent and nature of the interaction between material and spiritual phenomena make it likely that prohibiting spiritual life from redirecting material life is, in the end, incompatible with an opposite prohibition forbidding material life from redirecting spiritual. The interaction between the two ensures that material life would have to redirect spiritual in crucial ways in order not to be redirected by it. That being so, restricted historical materialism does assign to material life a kind of priority, and one which justifies its designation as a *materialism*.

9. I summarize here the main claims of the foregoing sections of this chapter.

1. The Marxist theory of history seems to be founded on the Marxist conception of human nature: it is plausible to say that Marxism sees history as a process of growth in human productive power because it regards humans as by nature productive beings.

2. But historical materialism does not *in fact* rest upon the Marxist philosophical anthropology since, although both theories emphasize production, they do so for different reasons, and the productions they emphasize consequently differ in character. Marxist philosophical anthropology is, moreover, vitiatingly one-sided. Its conception of human nature and human good overlooks the need for self definition, than which nothing is more essentially human. And that need is part of the explanation of the peculiar strength of national and other self identifications, which Marxists tend to undervalue.

3. Does historical materialism proper undervalue what Marxists undervalue? The answer is less likely to be positive if historical materialism is construed in a restricted, instead of in the traditional inclusive, way. In inclusive historical materialism material and economic development explains the principal features of other, non-economic or spiritual, developments. But restricted historical materialism says of spiritual phenomena only that they do not govern material development, and it commits itself to materialist

explanation of spiritual phenomena only when, were they not so explained, they would be seen to control material development.

4. Inclusive historical materialism is challenged both by the claim that the Protestant Reformation lacked economic causes and by the claim that it had extensive economic effects, whereas restricted historical materialism is challenged by the second claim only. That challenge collapses if the features of Protestantism in virtue of which it had economic effects arose because of their tendency to have such effects.

5. It is evident from the way Marx and Engels formulated, and argued for, historical materialism that they favoured an inclusive construal of it.

6. Even so, the theory stated in the 1859 Preface is open to a restricted construal, once a certain inclusivist flourish has been excised from it.

7. Both features of human nature which Marxists neglect (see 2) and features which they emphasize (see 1) tell against inclusive historical materialism. Marx and Engels may have tended towards inclusivism because Hegel was an inclusive historical idealist and they wrongly thought that refutation of inclusive historical idealism established inclusive historical materialism.

8. Restricted historical materialism arises naturally out of reflection on the question which features of non-economic pheno-mena historical materialism is committed to explaining, and the appropriate way of explaining such features is by recourse to functional explanation.

10. So far, this chapter differs extensively in detail, but not in substance, from the article of the same title out of which I have constructed it. But here, in a kind of epilogue, I shall say something substantially new.

Erik Wright has helped me to see that the distinction between restricted and inclusive historical materialism is better understood in the light of a prior distinction between Marxist theory of history and Marxist sociology.

In this different and, as it now seems to me, superior approach to the issues of the chapter, the Marxist theory of history is identified with what I considered a merely restricted variant of it, and the familiar Marxist theses which that doctrine refrains from asserting are allocated to Marxist sociology. Marxist sociology is a set of theses not about how social formations succeed one another, but about how the elements within a given social formation are related. Its central claim is, if you like, that social being determines consciousness, or, in the language of the present chapter, that material and economic existence explains the main lines of spiritual existence.

The central claim of the sociology is not—or so, in effect, I have argued at length above—required by the central claim of the theory of history, which is that changes in relations of production comply with and serve an autonomous development of the productive forces across history. The latter claim does not entail that non-economic structures and modes of consciousness are, in their broad lines, to be explained in material and economic terms. Nor does the converse entailment hold: the central sociological claim, that is, the being/consciousness doctrine, does not entail that the productive forces tend to develop. The sociology may have entailments, and it certainly has likely implications, for historical dynamics, but it does not require the interaction of forces and relations of production which the theory of history describes.

A good illustration of the different claims and liabilities of the two theories is the problem of the Asiatic Mode of production, which has always bothered Marxists. The difficulty with the Asiatic Mode, in the classical Marxist perception of it, is that it appears to contain within itself no principle of forward development, but, on the contrary, a strong tendency to reproduce itself incessantly in the same form. It is therefore a counter-example to a theory of history which posits a tendency for forces of production to develop and for relations of production to follow suit. But the feature of the Asiatic Mode which creates trouble for the theory of history in no way threatens Marxist sociology, since it is the character of the productive forces (e.g., the needs of irrigation) which are thought to give Asiatic society its stubbornly unchanging character. The classical description of the Asiatic Mode disconfirms the Marxist theory of history precisely because of the particular way in which it confirms the Marxist sociology.

In the Wright approach to the problems of this chapter, inclusive historical materialism is best seen, not as a rival theory of history, but as a conjunction of the Marxist theory of history, which *is* restricted historical materialism, and the Marxist sociology. I do not think that the distinction between restricted and inclusive historical materialism artificially bisects received doctrine, but that, on the contrary, inclusive historical materialism is a fusion of theories whose domains are sufficiently separate that the theories should be subjected to independent assessment. I conjecture, moreover, that the reason why some people resist the idea that the restricted doctrine can qualify as even *a* construal of historical materialism is that they have never properly separated—and neither did I in *KMTH*—questions about how the elements within a society are related from questions about how social forms succeed one another.

Addendum: On the Superstructure

I now believe that, when we think about the superstructure, our fundamental concept should be of a superstructural fact or phenomenon, rather than of a superstructural institution, the latter idea being insufficiently general and insufficiently abstract. (A superstructural fact or phenomenon is one which is not economic but which is in a certain way economically explained.) This move is motivated by a desire to avoid the unnecessary puzzlement that comes of asking questions like: do universities belong to the superstructure? I think that some of what goes on in them is clearly superstructural, and some is not, so that universities are not, as such, either superstructural or non-superstructural institutions. Again: suppose we say that the Soviet state runs the Soviet economy. Does it follow that the base/superstructure distinction fails to apply in the USSR? I think not. I do not think application of the distinction requires concrete institutional differentiation between what it distinguishes.

I think, on the contrary, that the distinction applies wherever one can establish that non-economic functions are carried out for the sake of economic ones, and that is possible without institutional differentiation. To illustrate this point in an extreme way, I tell a simple sequential story:

a. We begin with a stateless condition in which exploiting landowners who are considered demigods by exploited peasants manage to prevail without coercive backing: there is ideology, but no superstructure.

b. The ideology collapses, and this leads the landowners to appoint bureaucrats to keep the peasants in order.

c. The bureaucrats perform badly, so the landowners fire them and take over the state functions themselves, on a part-time basis. They travel back and forth between Economic Structure Street and Superstructure Boulevard.

d. Having tired of travelling, they begin to perform both functions in the same office, at different times.

e. They call in organization and methods experts, who enable them to rationalize their work. Henceforth they carry out their basic and superstructural work by means of the very same actions, perhaps as follows: Their basic work is to issue instructions about ploughing etc. to peasants, and their superstructural work is to issue instructions about ploughing peasants to policemen. The peasants and policemen speak different languages, and this enables the landowners to issue both sets of instructions in one and the same breath: they utter phonemes which, as it happens, have suitably different semantic interpretations in the two languages.

Now the distinction between base and superstructure is here sustained, since the landowners produce social order in order to keep the economic wheels turning, but there is not only no institutional manifestation of the distinction, but also no realization of the distinction in what we should intuitively call separate actions. The distinction requires no more than distinguishable upshots of actions, with one upshot being subordinated to the other. (Compare 'joint production' (in the economist's sense) of steel and a rustproofing liquid. The jointness of their production would not mean that the second is not produced for the sake of the first.)

3
Capitalism, Labour, and Freedom

10

THE DIALECTIC OF LABOUR IN MARX

> Begin not with the good old things but with
> the bad new ones.
>
> > Bertolt Brecht

The *Communist Manifesto* lampooned those who fought capitalism on behalf of the traditional values it was corroding.[1] Their conservative response was not only futile, but blind—to the new possibilities capitalism creates and indeed partly realizes. Marx's celebration of capitalism is the main theme of the present chapter. It locates, amid the evils of capitalist society, goods to be preserved and developed in freedom from their capitalist integument in a socialist future.

In the first part of the chapter I accumulate materials later used to exhibit capitalism's progressive character. In particular, I construct (section 1) a modest concept of dialectic, which leads to a description (section 2) or one form or aspect of freedom. It emerges (section 3) that labour under capitalism, although it is alienated, and, indeed, just because it is alienated, shows the seeds and some of the growth of this freedom, and that it is lacking in earlier, much romanticized, craft labour. The contrast is strengthened (section 4) by attention to different kinds of division of labour, and set within a wider context (section 5) which invites homage to capitalism. Section 6 adumbrates a discussion of the fate of labour under communism.

1.   DIALECTIC

In Hegel's theory of knowledge, there is an epistemological ascent in three stages. The point of departure is *sensuous consciousness* the summit is *reason*, and *understanding* lies along the route between them. The initial position is the most primitive encounter between mind and the world, predating any form of reflection. The mind does not experience itself as separate from the world, and it is incapable of distinguishing things and aspects in what lies before it. The elements of the object are merged, and the subject merges with

---

[1] pp. 507–10.

them. Understanding is the sphere of analysis. The subject asserts an absolute distinction between itself and the object, and it is able to discriminate parts and features of the object. Understanding is a necessary phase in the acquisition of knowledge, but it must be surpassed by reason, which accepts understanding's distinctions, but does not maintain them intact, since reason recognizes deeper unities that are beyond understanding's competence. It recaptures the integration understanding suspended, without renouncing the achievements premised on that suspension.

Epistemology is not the only area Hegel trisected in the manner just sketched. While I do not seek endorsement of his procedure in epistemology or in general, I do submit that the rhythm realized in the progress exhibited above sometimes occurs in a person's development. With respect to categorially various items to which a person may be related—his spouse, his family, his country, his job, his role, his body, his desires—it seems possible for him to sustain something like each of the three attitudes we have separated. He may fail in significant ways to distinguish himself and what he is from the other to which he is related; he may possess a strong sense of its otherness, so that it seems alien to him; or he may have that sense, yet find it compatible with close engagement. What is more, it sometimes happens that he occupies the three positions successively, in the order Hegel thought canonical in epistemology and elsewhere.

A domain offering examples of the sequence Hegel favoured is that of marriage. In its early stages a person may feel his interests and purposes to be identical with those of his spouse. Both may feel that way, and thus combine their lives to an extent which from outside looks artificial or moronic. But then one or both may revolt against fusion, and become hostile to continued connection. Finally, a new harmony may supervene, not through relapse into complete mutual absorption, but by discovery of a unity which is not antagonistic to the individuality of each.

Referring to this sequence in intimate relations, Hegel wrote in his fragment 'On Love' that 'the process is: unity, separated opposites, reunion.'[2] He thought the course of true love always has this structure, but we need not agree when we acknowledge that there is such a structure, and that it deserves attention. The term 'dialectical' will hereafter be applied to processes of the envisaged

[2] 'On Love', 308.

kind. I shall say that a subject undergoes a dialectical process if it passes from a stage where it is undivided from some object, through a stage where it divides itself from it in a manner which creates disunity, to a stage where distinction persists but unity is restored. I shall label the successive stages 'undifferentiated unity', 'different-iated disunity', and 'differentiated unity'. Finally, a process may be deemed dialectical, but incompletely so, if it passes from the first to the second stage without achieving the third, or from the second to the third without originating in the first.

I shall be meaning nothing more than this by the term 'dialectical' here. Some of the things to which so using the term does not commit me are worth noting.

First, I do not maintain that *all* processes of spiritual growth are dialectical in the specified sense.

Second, I do not claim that mine is the only defensible use of the term, where a use of 'dialectical' is defensible if it is both well defined and appropriately related to some Hegelian or Marxian use.

Finally, I do not affirm any dialectical laws. Processes displaying the required structure count as dialectical whether or not their stages *generate* one another: it is enough that they *follow* one another, for whatever reason. In seeing dialectic in a process, we discern its contour in an intellectually satisfying manner, but the explanation of why it unfolds as it does is not thereby disclosed to us. I am not asserting that there is something necessary or natural about dialectical sequence, not claiming that subjectivity merged with an object tends in time to propel itself away from the object, and then tends to reunite with it, the independence it has gained being preserved. But I do think that many processes in which subject and object are implicated in changing relation are well conceived as transitions from undifferentiated unity, through differentiated disunity, to differentiated unity.

This concept of dialectic is the descriptive residue of a concept which Hegel certainly, and Marx perhaps, thought had explanatory import as well. Whether it admits of explantory construal is a question which I shall not here pursue.[3]

---

[3] I do not myself think that Marx himself used dialectic with explanatory pretension in his mature work. I agree with Engels (*Anti-Dühring* 185 ff.) and Lenin ('What "The Friends of the People" Are', 443–4) that Marx's invocation of 'the negation of the negation' in his dramatic discussion of 'The Historical Tendency of Capitalist Accumulation' (*Capital*, i, ch. 32) was without explanatory ambition.

Hegel constructs dialectical sequences in all his major works. A particularly clear one is his presentation of 'Ethical Life', the name he gave to the object of philosophical sociology. Ethical Life begins with the *family*, a sphere of merger, the members being immediately concerned in one another's welfare, not externally bound by calculated ties of advantage. The weal and woe of any member of the family is experienced as such by each. Counterposed to the family is *civil society*, a collection of autonomous individuals released from the family cocoon, engaged in economic competition and co-operation. Independence and separation predominate, and partnerships depend on unfeeling contract. But civil society is subordinate to the *state*, that is, not the political institutions merely, but the entire national community, which sustains the independence at work in economic life but complements it by providing collective identity and culture, without which an economy is impossible, for at the very least a common language is required for the expression of contractual agreements. The family shows undifferentiated unity, civil society differentiation and disunion and the state differentiated unity.

Turning to Marxism, we may cite the legendary development from primitive communism, a collective structure and consciousness inhibiting individuation, through the divisions of class society, which stimulate an assertion of selfhood, to modern communism, which preserves individuality in a context of regained collectivity.

The sequence primitive communism/class society/modern communism is more prominent in Soviet and kindred doctrine than in the thought of Marx, which is dominated by a different triad: from pre-capitalist society, through capitalism, to the communism of the future. Whereas pre-capitalist society, even in its class-divided forms, displays the appearance of community in a society integrated with nature, capitalism sets individuals against one another, and society against nature. Communism preserves the inherited individuation, but restores community, and equilibrium between humanity and its environment. ' "The association of the future" will combine the sober reasonableness of the bourgeois era with the "care for the common social welfare" which characterized previous societies'.[4] The Marxian historical epochs thus correspond to Hegel's triadic division of Ethical Life.

---

[4] Hal Draper, 'The Death of the State', 305, quoting an unpublished 1884 Engels fragment. For an interesting meditation on communism's many syntheses, see Goldmann's 'Socialism and Humanism', especially pp. 41, 49.

The dialectic of labour is one strand in the pre-capitalism/ capitalism/communism transformation. It will be introduced following a preparatory discussion of freedom.

2. THE FREEDOM OF DETACHMENT

In the second stage of dialectical process the subject breaks free of the object (which may be another subject) to which he has been attached, and experiences himself as detached from it.[5] I shall call what he experiences 'the freedom of detachment', and the absence of that freedom will be called 'engulfment'.

This experience of freedom is not an experience of freedom from constraint. For whatever engulfed the now detached subject may now limit and pressure his choices, and the subject may be aware that it does. That he has placed a distance between it and himself does not mean it cannot by action at a distance constrain him.

Detachment from X is, then, compatible with experiencing X as constraining. Indeed, it is entailed by experiencing X as constraining: I can feel constrained by X only if I feel myself to be independent of X. This holds even if X is an impulse or desire, for I cannot sense constraint by it unless it impinges upon me as though from without.

I do not assert that detachment from X is entailed by *being* (as opposed to *feeling*) constrained by X. The question whether engulfment by X is compatible with constraint by X can be answered only by probing deeper than is to my purpose.

An agent aware of constraint has a desire or project which he and we can identify as his own and whose fulfilment is made impossible or difficult by something felt as outside him. He may act against his will, but his will is his own, not captured by the constraining agency. But a person lacking the freedom of detachment does not treat himself as separate from whatever compromises that freedom in a way that would enable him to think of it as impeding him, or dictating to him. He does not experience it as in opposition to his will, for it envelops his will.

A young child is in the thrall of his parents' ideas and values. They enter his being, and control him more directly than do the punishments and rewards which are required once his identity is

---

[5] I here take '*A* experiences *B*' to entail that *B* exists. Thus the experience of constraint entails constraint, that of freedom from constraint entails freedom from constraint, and that of detachment entails detachment.

more developed. In Hegel's language, the immature person's will is (in part) immediately identical with that of his seniors. But the identity is not symmetrical. Though the child's world is the world of his parents, theirs is not the world of the child. One might even say that he knows them to be separate from him, yet does not know himself to be separate from them.

To the extent that such a child is engulfed, he does not feel constrained. But no engulfment is total. The self is never effaced by environing circumstances or other selves, and engulfment in *X* is compatible with feeling constrained by *Y*, where *X* and *Y* are distinct: a person lacking the freedom of detachment may also experience obstacles to, and pressures upon, his will. It is necessary to identify finely the values *X* and *Y* take here. The child may be engulfed by his parents in some of their manifestations and not others.

Engulfment in *X* involves lack of awareness of oneself as capable of independence from *X*. This includes the case of the child, who is not in fact so capable, and the case of the spouse, who is but does not grasp the fact. In either instance, engulfment does not survive a lucid recognition of the nature of one's relation to the engulfing agency. When that relation becomes perspicuous, it is broken. It may then be true that the unfreedom of engulfment is replaced by an experience of constraint. 'I was unaware how much I fell in with *X*'s desires and intentions, how much my life was immersed in his. But I became aware, and I now experience *X* and his plans as an obstacle to me.' One could not be aware of that immersion. (It does not follow that the idea of a feeling of engulfment is self-contradictory, though it does follow that any such feeling will include at most a confused awareness of engulfment.)

The characterization of engulfment ventured above is incomplete. I have, for example, left it open whether engulfment by *X* is compatible with constraint by *X*. This suggests a reductive manœuvre which would eliminate the interest of the concept. Someone who is hostile to my attempt to find in engulfment the absence of a freedom which is not freedom from constraint might contend that, if I have any phenomenon in view, it is just that of an agent who is constrained without realizing it. But the contention is mistaken: this will not suffice for engulfment. For a person may know himself to be independent of *X*, yet not know that *X* promises the failure of a project he has. He may not know that someone of his acquaintance by whom he is in no sense enthralled has ensured that he will have to act against his wishes. Or he may not know that a door through which he wants to pass is locked, and so is forcing him to remain in the room.

Here there is ignorance of constraint without engulfment. What must be added—*added* if engulfment is indeed compatible with constraint—is that the subject does not experience himself as independent of X. That conception requires further clarification, but the latter is not supplied by the clear idea of a constrained person's not knowing that he is constrained.

3. TRADITIONAL AND MODERN LABOUR

Many observers of the emerging factory civilization pictured the ancestral work scene as a garden from which capitalist development expelled the producers, to deposit them in an industrial hell. The artistic work of the handicraftsman, performed for its own sake, not merely for the living it yields, appeared in favourable contrast to the alienated toils of working-class life. Traces of this outlook may be found in Marx's writings. But he does not finally accept the romantic attitude that the new society disrupted a pre-industrial idyll.[6]

For Marx thinks that the very values of traditional artisanship reveal the engulfment of the artificer. His contentment with, and absorption in, his own narrow trade compose what Marx deemed a 'servile relationship'.[7] He identifies with his work and his role, but his mind is subjected to his occupation, whereas the modern proletarian does not care about the job he performs, or what kind of job it is.[8] The wage-worker's indifference manifests his alienation. But it also betokens a birth of freedom. The artisan using his own means of production, typically handed down by his father, is caught like a 'snail inside its shell';[9] but the fact that the nineteenth-century worker is propertyless, which explains his misery, signifies an independence, a detachment from this particular machine and this particular job, a disengagement the guildsman does not know.

Engels is not just thinking of the future when he finds such disengagement appealing:

---

[6] For an idealized conception of pre-industrial life, with which Marx and Engels were to break, see the opening pages of Engels's *Condition of the Working Class*.

[7] *The German Ideology*, 66.

[8] *Ibid.*; see also *The Grundrisse*, 296–7, and 'Comments on Mill', 221.

[9] *Capital*, i. 480.

it was absolutely necessary to cut the umbilical cord which still bound the worker of the past to the land. The hand weaver who had his little house, garden and field along with his loom was a quiet, contented man, 'godly and honourable', despite all misery and despite all political pressure; he doffed his cap to the rich, to the priest and to the officials of the state and inwardly was altogether a slave. It is precisely modern large-scale industry which has turned the worker, formerly chained to the land, into a completely propertyless proletarian, liberated from all traditional fetters, *a free outlaw*.[10]

The person here called 'free' is typically forced to spend the best part of his time and energy doing what he has no inclination to do, in factory labour. That he does not doff his cap to the rich is compatible with their extensive control over him. He has not escaped constraint: he has won the freedom of detachment. By contrast, the 'worker of the past' could not so much as 'conceive the idea'[11] of rejecting his conditions of life. He understood himself only as part of them, whereas in the 'society of free competition, the individual appears detached from the natural bonds etc. which in earlier historical periods make him the accessory of a definite and limited human conglomerate'.[12]

The transition is from engulfment in nature, one's work, and one's role in a society itself engulfed in nature; a passage from what Marx called '*naturwüchsig* conditions of existence', to alienation, abstract[13] individuality, and the freedom of detachment. At one point Marx states the difference cryptically: only wage-workers stand in a *relation* to their conditions of labour and life.[14] He means that one can be related to something only if one is suitably independent of it, whereas medieval workers are, he says, 'merged' with their instruments of labour.[15]

This merger was not a useless misfortune, for 'the subjection of the producer to one branch exclusively . . . is a necessary step in the development' of the human productive faculty. The enclosure of the worker inside a definite locale within the material and social conditions of production ensure that

---

[10] *The Housing Question*, 563.
[11] Ibid. 564.
[12] *The Grundrisse*, 84; see also pp. 161, 226.
[13] This term is discussed in sect. 4 below.
[14] *The Grundrisse*, 489; see also *The German Ideology*, 44.
[15] *The Grundrisse*, 505.

each separate branch of production acquires the form that is technically suited to it, slowly perfects it, and, so soon as a given degree of maturity has been reached, rapidly crystallises that form.

Even the shape of the instruments of labour

once definitely settled by experience, petrifies, as is proved by their being in many cases handed down in the same form by one generation to another during thousands of years.

Thereby the worker and the tools come to fit one another. But capitalist industry violates this happy accommodation. The 'new modern science of technology' resolves each production 'process into its constituent movements, *without any regard to their possible execution by the hand of man*'[16] The inhumane disregard breaks the snail's shell.

The resultant transition is dialectical in the sense specified in section 1. In the first stage the craftsman is fastened to his work facilities and surroundings, absorbed into a particular cell within the body social, which is at peace with nature. The proletarian is free of such encumbrance, but also bereft of the solace and security it confers. He enjoys an independence but loses the possession the craftsman knew. To complete the dialectic, the communist producer would have to establish some new form of unity with his situation, without sacrificing the acquired autonomy.

The respective experiences of craftsman and proletarian, the contrasting phenomenologies of their everyday lives, reflect and consolidate similarly antithetical ownership positions, or production relations. The pre-proletarian labourer has the right and the duty to work with particular means of production in a particular place. He is both endowed with and bound to particular means of production. The proletarian lacks the right and the duty to work in any particular factory. A labour contract, which neither he nor his employer need renew, is required for him to engage in production.

For Marx, the central episode in the genesis of capitalism is a dual severance of the labourer from his means of production. Gone are his intimate control of and by them, and his rights over, and duties to, them. The prelude to capitalism is

---

[16] All the quotations in this paragraph are from *Capital*, 616 (my emphases).

a series of historical processes, resulting in a *Decomposition of the Original Union* existing between the Labouring Man and his Instruments of Labour. . . . The Separation between the Man of Labour and the Instruments of Labour once established, such a state of things will maintain itself and reproduce itself upon a constantly increasing scale, until a new and fundamental revolution in the mode of production should again overturn it, and restore the original union in a new historical form.[17]

So we again encounter: undifferentiated unity, differentiation without unity, differentiated unity.

Marx's dialectic of labour draws upon Hegel's dialectic of consciousness and nature, but adds emphasis on the technological aspect. The craftsman is sunk in the object, nature, means of production, land, the immediate environment. The son succeeds his father as one season gives way to the next: it is his natural destiny.[18] The conflict between consciousness and nature is undeveloped. It explodes under capitalism, as humanity splits itself off from nature, and splits it apart, exercising a destructive freedom. Capitalism is spirit in its negative form, assaulting nature and hallowed *naturwüchsig* social conditions. A freely realized unity is established under socialism. Nature is returned to spirit, but it is now a spiritualized nature.

The materialist elaboration of these formulae stresses that craft production keeps humanity attached to nature by blocking the further development of the productive faculty it once advanced, since it hinders the collectivization of labour, which is a premiss of increasing productivity. In handicraft the worker manages a total process of production. He employs his own instruments in his own shop and fashions a complete article, which he can call his own work. He does not serve up a fragment to be joined to other fragments made by other men, or merely add a contribution to an ensemble travelling along the factory floor. Capitalism socializes labour and insults craft pride, but because it makes the labourer co-operate 'systematically with others, he strips off the fetters of his individuality and develops the capabilities of his species'.[19]

---

[17] 'Wages, Price and Profit', 425. Cf. *The Grundrisse*, 505, 890–1; *Capital*, i, pt. 8; *Theories of Surplus Value*, iii. 314–15, 422–3.

[18] See the quotation from Hegel's *Realphilosophie* in Avineri, *Hegel's Theory of the Modern State*, 106 n. 66.

[19] *Capital*, i. 447, see also pp. 927–8.

A human being transcends his limitations by working with others, and submission to the capitalist division of labour enables the stupendous productive feats of which the race is capable. The Promethean virtues listed in Marx's characterization of specifically human labour[20] are realized as properties of the factory or industry as a whole.[21] But under capitalism these values make only an alienated appearance. The power of the species is not suffused through its members. It confronts them as something foreign,[22] as the possession of the capitalist, who monopolizes intention and knowledge. The capitalist may be personally ignorant, but he is the social repository of science, since those who know are in his hire.[23] Knowledge and skill are applied in the productive process, but not by the producers themselves.[24] Their action is imposed on them, by supervisor and machine. As social production grows in sophistication, less talent is required of each operative. In future society the theory governing industry will be shared, and the achievement of the species will no longer face its members as an alien power, but will enter their lives as production is democratically planned and understood by all. Socialism will provide for *men* the creative existence achieved under capitalism by *man*.

So persons sunk variously in nature but also at home in it lose that integration to gain abstract freedom and collective power dissociated from individuals—a step on the road to concrete freedom and disalienation of that power.

4. MODES OF THE DIVISION OF LABOUR

The opposition abstract/concrete pervades the work of Hegel, and was used in the last paragraph to sum up a train of thought recovered from Marx. He did not himself use the terms with Hegelian frequency, but they figure in the construction of a

---

[20] See *Economic and Philosophic Manuscripts*, 276–7; *Capital*, 283–4. For Marx human labour, by contrast with the animal's, is in its higher forms characterized by intentionality, limitless scope, etc.

[21] 'The first definition given above of productive labour [on pp. 283 ff.], a definition deduced from the very nature of the production of material objects, still remains correct for the collective labourer, considered as a whole. But it no longer holds good for each member taken individually'. (*Capital*, 644; see also pp. 482–3, 643).

[22] *Capital* iii. 179; *Theories of Surplus Value*, iii. 443.

[23] *Capital*, i. 508–9.

[24] See *The Grundrisse*, 692–5; *Theories of Surplus Value*, ii. 234.

distinction basic to his economics. In this section I begin with that distinction and attempt to show its conceptual continuity with the Hegelian opposition it verbally reproduces.

For Marx all labour is both concrete and abstract. It is concrete in so far as it employs specific facilities in a specific way and issues in a product of determinate physical properties, capable of satisfying some human desires and not others, namely a use-value. It is abstract in so far as it is a quantity of total social labour, measurable by the amount of time absorbed in its performance, and issuing, in market economies, in an exchange-value, and in all economies in a proportion of social wealth, however that is to be reckoned. Now under capitalism the abstract moment gains ascendancy. For it matters neither to the labourer nor to his employer what concrete labour is performed. Each care only about how much exchange-value he will obtain from its performance. Each contrasts with the feudal serf and lord, since they consumed, and so were interested in the concrete character of, the immediate result of the serf's labour. Under capitalism the abstract aspect takes precedence in fact and in consciousness.

But labour becomes abstract under capitalism in a further sense. Concrete differences between different kinds of labour not only matter less, as explained above: they are also reduced in extent. I shall elucidate by noticing the different forms the division of labour takes in medieval and modern times.

Capitalism increases the number of distinct jobs involved in the production of a given product, but at the same time it decreases the specialization of the worker. Pre-capitalist weavers and tanners participated in several stages of the respective production processes, and weaving operations differed significantly in kind from tanning operations, and among themselves. But mechanized textile and leather factories demand similar simple movements from their operatives.[25] The products of the factories differ because of diversity in raw materials and machines on which, and at which,

---

[25] '[A]s the *division of labour* increases, labour is *simplified*. The special skill of the worker becomes worthless. He is transformed into a simple, monotonous productive force that does not have to use intense bodily or intellectual faculties. His labour becomes a labour that anyone can perform'. ('Wage-Labour and Capital', 225). '[I]n place of the hierarchy of specialized workers that characterizes manufacture, there appears, in the automatic factory, a tendency to equalize and reduce to one and the same level every kind of work that has to be done by the minders of the machines'. (*Capital*, i. 545).

like labour is spent. Capitalism's ideal is to homogenize tasks across and within all branches of production, so that workers may move from job to job doing much the same simple thing in a variety of settings.

To recapitulate. Under the sway of capital the immediate interest in labour is for its abstract quality of producing wealth in general, exchange-value, the particular embodiment of which ceases to matter; and the concrete differences between kinds of labour are diminished. Labour is then abstract 'not only as a category but in reality':

> The fact that the particular kind of labour employed is immaterial is appropriate to a form of society in which individuals easily pass from one type of labour to another, the particular type of labour being accidental to them and therefore irrelevant. Labour, not only as a category but in reality, has become a means to create wealth in general, *and has ceased to be tied as an attribute to a particular individual.*[26]

The last clause may be taken to imply that the transformation has a liberating aspect: it enables escape from engulfment. Since the abstract labour of capitalism lacks a definite shape, the person who performs it is not stamped by any concrete work process and he becomes aware of his capacity and his need for a full and unspecialized life:

> What characterizes the division of labour in the automatic workshop is that labour has there completely lost its specialized character. But the moment every special development stops, the need for universality, the tendency towards an integral development of the individual begins to be felt.[27]

The proletarian has become labour in general, though only in general, and he therefore aspires to develop his abilities generally. The artisan lacks that aspiration just because some few of his abilities are developed and fused with conditions of labour and life he cannot conceive transcending. 'The automatic workshop wipes out specialists and craft idiocy.'[28] This 'idiocy' is the same as that referred to rural life in *The Communist Manifesto.*[29] It is not feeble

---

[26] *Critique of Political Economy*, 210 (my emphases). Cf. *The Poverty of Philosophy*, 127; 'Results of the Immediate Process of Production', 1013–14, 1033–4; *Theories of Surplus Value*, iii. 444.

[27] *The Poverty of Philosophy*, 190.

[28] Ibid.

[29] p. 488.

intelligence, for it is compatible with demanding craftsmanship. It is rather 'narrow parochialism',[30] an uncomplaining acceptance of a restricted life, not perceived as restricted.

Marx's contrast between medieval and modern labour moves in an Hegelian orbit. The proletarian's freedom is the kind Hegel called 'abstract' and 'negative', the 'freedom of the void', 'freedom as the understanding conceives it', for the understanding[31] knows only distinction and separation, and therefore conceives freedom as the lack of 'every restriction and every content'.[32] It is a freedom from everything particular, directed upon nothing in particular.

Nevertheless, this freedom abstract and negative, 'fettered to no determinate existence', 'not bound at all by particularity',[33] is an 'essential factor'[34] in the formation of full and concrete freedom, which would appropriate its circumstances, not flee them.[35]

Medieval work for Marx is concrete but not universal. It has a definite contour with the result that the labourer is defined and limited by it. Modern work is universal but abstract. The labourer is not confined but his activity has lost shape and sense. It has been 'robbed . . . of all real life-content' and is performed by 'abstract individuals'.[36] Activity under communism is to be both universal and concrete, an unrestricted engagement with something particular and definite, no longer a freedom suspended in a vacuum (the proletarian), nor an unfreedom with content (the craftsman).

5. THE PROGRESSIVE CHARACTER OF CAPITALISM

Those who see in engulfment only integration and a sense of belonging oppose the disengagement capitalism brings. A representative complaint is Lewis Mumford's: 'What was . . . the boasted 'mobility of labour' but the breakdown of stable social relations and the disorganization of family life?'[37] Capitalism tramples upon communal values, and it is fair to counter its boasts by recalling them. But it does not merely destroy. Mumford forgets

[30] *Theories of Surplus Value*, ii. 475.
[31] See p. 184 above.
[32] *The Philosophy of Right*, 21–2.
[33] *The Phenomenology of Mind*, 232.
[34] *The Philosophy of Right*, 227.
[35] *The Phenomenology of Mind*, 234.
[36] *The German Ideology*, 87.
[37] *Technics and Civilisation*, 195. That Mumford's views were not normally conservative testifies to the attractiveness of the conservative position he adopts here.

that mobility of labour is also mobility of human beings, who escape confining perspectives and visit different *milieux*. I do not say that the gain outweighs the loss, for I do not know how to measure either. But I do think that to admire stability and the pastoral and to notice nothing good emerging in their collapse is to appreciate but one side of human potential and need. People want belonging *and* freedom, integration *and* independence, community *and* individuality, and when capitalism sacrifices the first member of these and like pairs, it concurrently enfranchises the second.

Labour mobility entails release from economic bonds forged by political and ideological authority. The impermanent ties replacing them derive from what Marx called 'callous cash payment'.[38] But this did not prevent him from correcting 'romantics' who saw 'the substitution of a monetary system, cold and hard, for picturesque relations between men', and neglected the attendant liberation.[39]

That Marx was aware of the destructive side of capitalism needs no proof. On countless occasions he emphasized that nothing is so exalted as to be immune to exploitation in the drive for profit; that all natural endowments, all skill, all science, all passion, are prey to capital's cupidity. Less familiar is what he often went on to say, for example:

Hence the great civilizing influence of capital, its production of a stage of society compared with which all earlier stages appear to be merely *local developments* of humanity and idolatry of nature.[40]

Its destructiveness is

permanently revolutionary, tearing down all obstacles that impede the development of the productive forces, the expansion of needs, the diversity of production and the exploitation and exchange of natural and intellectual forces.

It does away with

national boundaries and prejudices . . . the inherited self-sufficient satisfaction of existing needs confined within well-defined bounds, and the reproduction of the traditional way of life'.[41]

[38] *The Communist Manifesto*, 487.
[39] 'Fragment des Urtextes', 874.
[40] *The Grundrisse*, 409–10 (my emphasis on 'Hence').
[41] Ibid. 410. Here is how *The Communist Manifesto*, in similar vein, describes 'the bourgeois epoch': 'All fixed, fast-frozen relations, with their train of ancient and venerable prejudices and opinions, are swept away, all new-formed ones become

Alienation is the cost of rescue from envelopment in the natural and social environment which is the human condition before capitalism. Capital steals and shrinks each person's labouring power, but it promotes an unprecedented increase in the power of humankind. Its enormous production within the frame of a global market transforms a collection of isolated groups of parochial people into a wondrously creative universal humanity. There flourishes in parallel with alienation a magnificent assertion of sovereignty over the physical world. A utilitarian attitude, in theory and in practice, supplants the 'idolatry of nature'. There is, to be sure, no wisdom in the exercise of this sovereignty. It threatens to mangle nature irreparably, and communism will not perpetuate it in its uncontrolled form. On the other hand, it will in some respects extend it, since not all humanly desirable transformations of nature are compatible with the constraints of the market.[42]

Marx holds not only that capitalism as a matter of fact develops a cosmopolitan civilization of production but also that it must do so and that it alone can do so. This *'most extreme form of alienation'* 'in which the worker . . . is opposed to his own conditions and to his own product is a necessary transitional stage'.[43] Why is it necessary? Why must capitalism give rise to the asserted result? And why can capitalism alone do it, and a pre-capitalist economy not? Marx answers these questions by economic reasoning which will not be discussed here.[44] To the question why capitalist, and not pre-capitalist, arrangements are capable of sponsoring great advances in production, he suggests an additional answer on the level of philosophical anthropology, which I shall now examine.

Under capitalism people are restless and unfulfilled. The identity they once borrowed from their circumstances is gone, and no new

antiquated before they can ossify. All that is solid melts into air, all that is holy is profaned, and man is at last compelled to face, with sober senses, his real conditions of life, and his relations with his kind' (p. 487). For a profound discussion of this theme in Marx see Marshall Berman's *All That is Solid Melts Into Air*, ch. 2—and, indeed, the rest of that magnificent book.

[42] *The Grundrisse*, 410.

[43] Ibid. 515.

[44] See *KMTH*, ch. 11 for an attempt to show that capitalism and capitalism alone fosters unlimited production. There is also the point made above (p. 192) that pre-capitalist economies fetter production by preventing the collectivization of labour. Technical progress requires the latter, but it presupposes a mobility of labour which pre-capitalist rules forbid.

one has appeared. Pre-capitalist people are at peace with themselves and at home in the world, unfrustrated and possessed of 'plenitude'. It is Marx's idea that they enjoy fulfilment only because their powers and wants are limited, their human nature stunted. Prodigious power develops explosively under capitalism, dissociated from individuals, by virtue of an economic system which presupposes their alienation from that power. Only such a system can advance that power, only a system in which it is not directed to serving their needs. For those needs, inherited from past society, are narrow in range. If the point of production were to fulfil them, it would fail to be prodigious. It is only once production is out of gear with limited human needs that they will be caused to lose their limited character; their development will be stimulated by the development of production itself. The contentment and order of the ancient world must be forfeited if human nature is to grow:

At early stages of development the single individual appears to be more complete, since he has not yet elaborated the abundance of his relationships, and has not established them as powers that are opposed to himself. It is as ridiculous to wish to return to that primitive abundance as it is to believe in the continuing necessity of its complete depletion. The bourgeois view has never got beyond opposition to this romantic outlook and thus will be accompanied by it, as a legitimate antithesis, right up to its blessed end.[45]

The second sentence rebukes both those who would retreat to bygone tranquillity and those who think that people are by nature unsatisfiable and doomed to endless quest. The latter bourgeois view is fittingly resisted by the former romantic one. Neither understands the nature of human potential.

The theme is elaborated in a text worth quoting at length:

the ancient conception, in which man always appears (in however narrowly national, religious, or political a definition) as the aim of production, seems very much more exalted than the modern world, in which production is the aim of man and wealth the aim of production.[46]

The parenthesis implies that the man of antiquity is man in confinement. Forgetting that, we find antiquity superior to modernity, which consumes individuals on the altar of productivity. Yet if we look through the alienation to what is being achieved within it

[45] *The Grundrisse*, 162.
[46] *The Grundrisse*, 488.

and distorted by it, we find that to be the basis of true wealth and a larger fulfilment. For

> what is wealth, if not the universality of needs, capacities, enjoyments, productive powers, etc., of individuals, produced in universal exchange? What, if not the full development of human control over the forces of nature—those of his own nature as well as those of so-called 'nature'? What, if not the absolute elaboration of his creative dispositions, without any preconditions other than antecedent historical evolution which makes the totality of this evolution—i.e. the evolution of all human powers as such, unmeasured by any previously established yardstick—an end in itself?[47]

It is a familiar socialist criticism of capitalism that it fosters production for production's sake, not for the satisfaction of human need. Yet it is an equally familiar socialist ideal that labour should be performed as an end in itself, not as a mere means to acquiring goods external to it. What socialists despise in capitalism is thus an anticipation, on an alienated plane, of what they value. Under capitalism's production for production's sake, people produce only for rewards enjoyed outside the production process. Under communism's production servicing human needs, they find productive activity itself rewarding.[48]

The passage concludes:

> In bourgeois political economy—and in the epoch of production to which it corresponds—this complete elaboration of what lies within man appears as his total alienation, and the destruction of all fixed, one-sided purposes as the sacrifice of the end in itself to a wholly external compulsion. Hence in one way the childlike world of the ancients appears to be superior; and this is so, as long as we seek closed shape, form and established limitation. The ancients provide a narrow satisfaction, where the modern world leaves us unsatisfied, or, where it appears to be satisfied with itself, is *vulgar*.[49]

Hannah Arendt's *Human Condition* is a contemporary paradigm of the search for 'closed shape, form and established limitation'. She is revolted by current agitation and restlessness, by the fearful

---

[47] Ibid.

[48] Capitalism 'produces the complete material conditions of the entire and universal development of the productive forces of the individual' (*The Grundrisse*, 515). But what it makes possible for future individuals it makes already actual for humankind, the latter being the foundation of the former. Cf. *Theories of Surplus Value*, 117–18.

[49] *The Grundrisse*, 488; see also 157–8.

laceration of man's natural and historical home by man. But she is not a socialist, for she discerns no good in the evils of capitalism, and so expects socialism to perpetuate and magnify the evils, whereas it promises to develop the goods.

For Marx the goods can be brought forth only in the train of the evils. The process of inversion, in which people serve production instead of production serving them, is necessary, though it

is obviously merely a historical necessity, a necessity for the development of productive forces from a definite historical starting point, or basis, but in no way an *absolute* necessity of production; it is, rather, ephemeral. The result and the immanent aim of the process is to destroy and transform the basis itself, as well as this form of the process.[50]

The definite starting-point is one of engulfment, rendering the inversion necessary if production is to advance. The inversion advances production, cancels engulfment, and, in the self-wrought collapse of capitalism, cancels itself. What is the human condition in the society which lies beyond?

6. PROSPECTS

To determine Marx's reply we must recall his thesis that the dialectic spanning pre-capitalist society and capitalism is appropriately completed in a communist future.[51] The separations forced by capitalism will be maintained in a society enjoying the integration once but no longer purchased at the price of merger.

But to assert that communism consummates the dialectic is not to reveal in what manner it does so. What sort of activity preserves the producer's transcendence of his job while restoring the engagement missing in proletarian labour? A thorough review of the possibilities will not be attempted. I limit myself to tentative comments on Marxian pronouncements about future society which touch the theme of unengulfed integration.

[50] Ibid. 831–2. In the following similar statement the analogy with Feuerbach's idea of the inversion inherent in religion is explicit: 'From the historical point of view, this inversion appears as a transitional stage that is necessary in order to obtain, by force and at the expense of the majority, the creation of wealth as such, i.e. the unlimited productivity of social labour which alone is able to constitute the material basis of a free human society. It is necessary to traverse this antagonistic form just as it is inevitable that man begin by giving his spiritual forces a religious form by erecting them opposite himself as autonomous powers' ('Results of the Immediate Process of Production', 990).

[51] See pp. 186, 192, 196 above.

Before addressing myself to them, I want to consider an activity which it may seem Marx must banish from future society: handicraft. Its restoration is favoured by that trend in socialist thought which descends from William Morris, and by some enthusiasts of 'communal living'. Since Marx thought craft labour engulfing, and since labour under communism is to exhibit engagement without engulfment, must craft labour not be omitted from the repertoire of future activity? Since, moreover, Marxian communism is based on advanced technology, must it not for this second reason exclude craftsmanship, whose technology is elementary? Yet if Marx's positions commit him against craft labour, are they not in undesirable conflict with an attractive form of human endeavour?

The tension between craft labour and high technology will be dealt with later. Here I develop an answer which Marx could have given to the first question.

Recall that the medieval artisan was engulfed not only in the labour process proper, but also in the society environing it, and that it was in connection with that environment that his labour was engulfing. If we consider craft labour in physical terms, characterized by the nature of its techniques and products, then it becomes clear that craft labour need not appear within something like the craftsman's role in medieval society, and so we may hold that, although craft labour *was* engulfing, it need not be so in the future.

This is not to say that the engulfing effect of craft labour was *entirely* due to the society in which it was placed. The circumstances surrounding it were a necessary condition of its engulfing quality, but its physical properties also mattered. Indeed, they contributed to the social engulfment which made craft labour engulfing, by facilitating the craftsman's intense identification with his role.

For the labourer to escape a 'servile relationship'[52] to his work, it was necessary that artisanship be replaced by a labour of repellent material character, but it does not follow that a return to the earlier physical form betokens a renewal of the engulfment which attended it. Craft labour *can* be unengulfing, but if engulfed craft labour is the point of departure, transition to craft labour without engulfment requires the demise of craft labour and the rise of proletarian.

[52] See p. 189 above.

Proletarian labour effects a break with the engulfment craft labour promoted, but it thereby enables craft labour to reappear free of its original 'idiocy'.[53]

The passage from engulfment to integration without engulfment is impossible without an intervening phase of fragmented, alienated labour. Craft labour cannot be fragmented: therefore proletarian labour is an historical prerequisite of unengulfed craft labour. We saw above that production for developed human needs cannot succeed production for undeveloped human needs.[54] A stage of production undirected to human needs must first be traversed. Similarly, a meaningful work process which is also enslaving cannot just lose its enslaving quality, but can appear without it after a phase during which the work process lacks meaning.

I have not said that Marx's communism favours craft labour. I have argued only that such favour would be compatible with his doctrine of the engulfment inherent in historical craft labour. Whether craft labour is supposed to flourish under communism is another matter. To the question what does happen under communism I now turn.

Three familiar motifs in Marx's unfinished prognosis will occupy my attention: (i) The conquest of nature by humanity, (ii) the abolition of the division of labour, and (iii) the persistence of the realm of necessity.

i. The pre-capitalist unity of humanity and nature rested on the fact that humanity had not escaped nature's dominance. The unity of the future reverses the original one, since it is based on the human subjugation of nature. Sometimes this appears to mean that nature is worked by labour possessed of science and technology. But some of Marx's less restrained forecasts raise the question whether his communism is compatible with labour, in any economist's sense. He presents the conquest of nature in extremely radical terms, foreseeing it as so transformed by past scientific industry that technology is no longer applied to nature but integrated with it:

Labour does not seem any more to be an essential part of the process of production. The human factor is restricted to watching and supervising the production process. . . .

[53] See p. 195 above.
[54] See p. 199 above.

The worker no longer inserts transformed natural objects[55] as intermediaries between the material and himself; he now inserts the natural process that he has transformed into an industrial one between himself and inorganic nature, over which he has achieved mastery. He is no longer the principal agent of the production process: he exists alongside it.[56]

The world has been wrought into a system which by its own action produces the environment and objects which people need. Marx calls the beneficiaries 'workers', but the designation is inappropriate. They do not wield tools or work at machines, but rule over an industrialized nature the line between which and machinery is invisible. The writ of the Curse of Adam lapses: there is no exploitation of labour because there is no labour to be exploited, no toilers to be governed but only physical process to be administered. Town and country are united because industry and nature are one. The ravages of class society give way to freedom in an industrial Eden. And since the need to supervise cannot consume much time, there is full range for 'that development of human energy which is an end in itself',[57] for activity which is not labour because it lacks an economic end—but which may none the less resemble activity which once was labour. Those who want craftsmanship to recapture its status as means of material existence must reject the picture, but the picture does not reject widespread performance, 'alongside the production process', of something like the creative activity they prize. I have in mind advanced forms of highly specialized activity which are inherently rewarding and which do not produce the accoutrements of survival but which do cater to more refined human needs. The activities fall outside 'the production process', narrowly conceived, but they do not face the spectre of meaninglessness which threatens craft production of goods that machines could make just as well.[58]

ii. If labour is abolished, so too is the division of labour. Marx prophesied the latter's disappearance in *The German Ideology*, a decade before he wrote the *Grundrisse* text just discussed. I do not know whether the early prophecy was already accompanied by a

---

[55] i.e., tools and machines.
[56] *The Grundrisse*, 705.
[57] See p. 207 below.
[58] For a development of that idea see Lawrence Haworth, 'Leisure, Work and Profession', 328–30.

belief in the withering away of labour itself, as activity geared to economic ends. It is unclear whether the attractively varied activity sketched below was supposed to constitute production, or take place outside it. Let us waive that question. The passage bears on the theme of integration without engulfment whatever the answer to it may be:

as soon as the distribution of labour comes into being, each man has a particular, exclusive sphere of activity, which is forced upon him, and from which he cannot escape. He is a hunter, a fisherman, a shepherd, or a critical critic, and must remain so if he does not want to lose his means of livelihood; while in communist society, where nobody has one exclusive sphere of activity but each can become accomplished in any branch he wishes, society regulates the general production and thus makes it possible for me to do one thing today and another tomorrow, to hunt in the morning, fish in the afternoon, rear cattle in the evening, criticize after dinner, just as I have a mind, without ever becoming hunter, fisherman, shepherd, or critic.[59]

Marx here attributes three desirable qualities to activity—be it labour or not—in future society. First, and most obviously, a person does not give himself up to one activity only. Second, he does not relate to any of his several activities as to a role in a fixed social structure. And third, what he does is something he wishes to do. The last feature raises issues far from the centre of this chapter, but I shall look at it briefly after considering the second, which is relevant to our theme.

Communist man hunts, fishes, herds sheep, and criticizes 'without ever becoming hunter, fisherman, shepherd, or critic'. I believe that the quoted phrase adds to the initial assertion of variation in activity. This man is not even successively a hunter, fisherman, and critic, though he does hunt, fish, and criticize. For he is in none of these activities entering a position in a structure of roles, in such a way that he could identify himself, if only for the time being, as a hunter, etc. He is nevertheless thoroughly engaged by what he is doing. The sum of which is that he enjoys integration without engulfment. Perhaps the thought I have tried to elicit is present more clearly here:

[59] *The German Ideology*, 57. In a deleted sentence, communist man is also said to go in for shoemaking, gardening, and acting. His interests (with the exception of shoemaking) are curiously similar to those of a cultured gentleman farmer. But the meaning is clearly allegorical—which is not to say that the allegory is easy to decode.

with a communist organisation of society, there disappears the subordination of the artist to local and national narrowness, which arises entirely
from the division of labour, and also the subordination of the artist to some
definite art, thanks to which he is exclusively a painter, sculptor, etc., *the
very name of his activity adequately expressing the narrowness of his
professional development* and his dependence on division of labour. In a
communist society there are no painters but at most people who engage in
painting among other activities.[60]

I am claiming that the last sentence does not say 'in a communist
society there are no full-time painters but at most part-time
painters'. People paint, but the status 'painter' is not assumed even
from time to time.

The abolition of roles may be conceptual or sociological
nonsense, but it is an idea we find in Marx. The reproach that he
sought a complete absorption of the individual by society states the
reverse of his aim. Having complained that in modern times 'a
general or a banker plays a great part, but mere man . . . a very
shabby part',[61] he would not be impressed by a jack-of-all-roles,
who is other than mere man, whatever he took that to be. He
wanted individuals to face one another and themselves without
mediation of institutions. For they represent 'fixation of social
activity, consolidation of what we ourselves produce into an
objective power above us'.[62] It is no great exaggeration to say that
Marx's freely associated individuals constitute an alternative to,
not a form of, society.[63]

iii. The third desideratum is that a person's activity suits his
wishes, since 'society regulates the general production and thus
makes it possible for me to do one thing today and another
tomorrow . . . just as I have a mind'.

Recall the question we postponed: does the variegated activity
subserve economic ends? Is it part of 'general production', or
divorced from it? On the first interpretation, something like this
must be meant: we draw up a budget of tasks, and each of us
undertakes whichever ones appeal most to him, subject to there
being reasonably harmonious order in the resulting array of
activities. I may not be able to do everything I want to do, but

---

[60] Ibid. 394 (my emphases).
[61] *Capital*, i. 135.
[62] *The German Ideology*, 47.
[63] For criticism of Marx's hostility to roles, see ch. 8, sect. 7 above.

whatever I do will be something I like, and that is a significant recommendation.

This reading is compatible with the phrase 'just as I have a mind' only if economically productive activities can be generally appealing. If they cannot, then the variegated activity must proceed outside the economic sphere. Now at least sometimes Marx did view work tasks as bound always to be unsatisfying. There was probably a deep pessimism on that score underlying his programme for a nature which produces by itself, with minimal human input.[64] A somewhat gloomy perception of the labour that remains under communism informs this famous passage:

the realm of freedom actually begins only where labour which is determined by necessity and mundane considerations ceases; thus in the very nature of things it lies beyond the sphere of actual material production. Just as the savage must wrestle with nature to satisfy his wants, to maintain and reproduce life, so must civilised man, and he must do so in all social formations and under all possible modes of production. With his development this realm of physical necessity expands as a result of his wants; but, at the same time, the forces of production which satisfy these wants also increase. Freedom in this field can only consist in socialized man, the associated producers, rationally regulating their interchange with nature, bringing it under their common control, instead of being ruled by it as by a blind power; and achieving this with the least expenditure of energy and under conditions most favourable to, and worthy of, their human nature. But it nonetheless still remains a realm of necessity. Beyond it begins that development of human energy which is an end in itself, the true realm of freedom, which, however, can blossom forth only with this realm of necessity as its basis. The shortening of the working-day is its basic prerequisite.[65]

On this account, freedom inside communist industry is regrettably limited, and Marx looks for what he calls *true* freedom beyond the economic zone. His idea is not that 'labour has become not only a means of life but life's prime want',[66] but that, being a means of life, it cannot be wanted, and will be replaced by desired activity as the working day contracts.

This negative appraisal of future working conditions, however warranted it may be on other grounds, here rests on a fallacious

---

[64] See p. 204 above.
[65] *Capital*, iii. 958–9.
[66] *Critique of the Gotha Programme*, 24.

conflation of distinct ideas. Granted, there will always be a set of operations on whose completion the provisioning of the race depends. But it does not follow, and it is not equally undeniable, that there will always be tasks which people perform against their inclinations because they have to. That a task must be and is fulfilled does not imply that the motive for its performance is that its performance is necessary. (Some eating is enjoyable.) But Marx asserts this implication when he says that the 'realm of freedom', first glossed as activity not *determined* by mundane requirements, must 'in the very nature of things' lie beyond the sphere servicing those requirements. Up to now the level of the productive forces has imposed on economic activity the property of not being performed for its own sake. Whether it must retain that property in future is a complex question of technology and psychology, not a matter of the manifest 'very nature of things'.

The possibility Marx swiftly excludes is that economic necessities might be met, at least partly, by 'that development of human energy which is an end in itself'. One cannot decide *a priori* the extent of compatibility between economically valuable labour and creative fulfilment. Marx thought that he knew that their compatibility would always be small. Hence his need to forecast a virtual disappearance of labour.[67]

[67] For thoughtful but, in my view, unsuccessful criticism of part iii of this section see James Klagge's 'Marx's Realms of "Freedom" and "Necessity"'.

II

THE LABOUR THEORY OF VALUE AND THE
CONCEPT OF EXPLOITATION

It is we who ploughed the prairies, built the cities where they trade,
Dug the mines and built the workshops, endless miles of railroad laid,
Now we stand outcast and starving, 'mid the wonders we have made . . .
'Solidarity'. by Ralph Chaplin (to the tune of 'Battle Hymn of the Republic').

This chapter shows that the relationship between the labour theory of value and the concept of exploitation is one of mutual irrelevance. The labour theory of value is not a suitable basis for the charge of exploitation directed by Marxists against capitalism, and the real foundation of that charge is something much simpler which, for reasons to be stated, is widely confused with the labour theory of value.

1. I begin with a summary presentation of the labour theory of value, as we find it in the first volume of *Capital*.[1] I define the term 'value', and then I indicate what the labour theory says about what it denotes. What follows is one way of organizing the ideas laid out in the first few pages of Marx's *magnum opus*. Having completed my own presentation of those ideas, I shall describe a different way of presenting them, which I do not think is right.

It is convenient to define value by reference to exchange-value, with which I therefore begin.

Exchange-value is a property of things which are desired; in Marxian language, then, it is a property of use-values.[2] It is, however, a property, not of all use-values, but of those use-values which are bought and sold, which undergo market transactions. Such use-values Marxism calls 'commodities'. Exchange-value, then, is a property of commodities.

What property is it? The exchange-value of a commodity is its power of exchanging against quantities of other commodities. It is

---

[1] A less summary and more sequential—and more critical—presentation of the same material will be found in sect. 7 below, where I also have occasion to remark on some famous differences between vol. i and other parts of *Capital*.
[2] Fuller definitions of the technical terms introduced here will be found in App. ii of *KMTH*.

measured by the number of commodities of any other kind for which it will exchange under equilibrium conditions. Thus the exchange-value of a coat might be eight shirts, and also three hats, and also eighty pounds sterling.

Exchange-value is a relative magnitude. Underlying the exchange-value of a commodity is its value, an absolute magnitude. A commodity a has n units of commodity b as its exchange-value just in case the ratio between the values of a and b is $n : 1$. The exchange-values relative to one another of two commodities will remain the same when each changes in value if the changes are identical in direction and proportion.

The central claim of the labour theory of value is that magnitude of value is determined by socially necessary labour time. To be more precise: the exchange-value of a commodity varies directly and uniformly with the quantity of labour time required to produce it under standard conditions of productivity, and inversely and uniformly with the quantity of labour time standardly required to produce other commodities, and with no further circumstance. The condition alone states the mode of determination of value *tout court*.

The labour theory of value is not true by the very definition of value, as value was defined above. In alternative presentations of the opening pages of volume i, value is *defined* as socially necessary labour time. But a stipulative definition of a technical term is not a theory, and when value is defined as socially necessary labour time, it cannot also be a central theoretical claim of the labour theory that socially necessary labour time determines value. Still, those who favour the alternative definition sometimes do proceed to a substantive theoretical thesis, to wit, that value determines equilibrium price: in equilibrium price equals value, the latter being defined in terms of socially necessary labour time.

The size of this dispute can be exaggerated. We have two propositions:

1. Socially necessary labour time determines value.

2. Value determines equilibrium price.

I say that (2) is true by definition. Others say that (1) is.[3] But whoever is right, the conjunction of (1) and (2) entails that

---

[3] For example, Ronald Meek, in *Smith, Ricardo and Marx*, 95. Meek treats (1) as true by definition and (2) as the substantive thesis. He acknowledges on p. 127 that the issue is contestable.

3. Socially necessary labour time determines equilibrium price,

and (3) is not true by definition, on any reckoning. As long as it is agreed that the labour theory of value, in its volume i version, says (3), and that (3) is not true by definition, I do not wish to insist on my view that the definitional truth is (2) rather than (1). Almost all of what follows could be restated so as to accommodate the other definition. (One bad reason why the other definition finds favour will be presented in section 7, which also offers a textual defence of my treatment of (2) as true by definition.)

We now turn to a supposed[4] corollary of the labour theory of value, the labour theory of surplus value.

The labour theory of surplus value is intended to explain the origin of non-wage income under capitalism. Call the energies and faculties the worker uses when labouring his *labour power*. Now note that under capitalism labour power is a commodity. It is sold in daily or weekly packets by the worker to the capitalist. Being a commodity, it has a value, and, like any commodity, its value is, according to (1), determined by the amount of time required to produce it. But the amount of time required to produce it is identical with the amount of time required to produce the means of subsistence of the worker, since a person's labour power is produced if and only if he is produced. Thus 'the value of labour power is the value of the means of subsistence necessary for the maintenance of its owner.'[5] The origin of non-wage income is, then, the difference between the value of labour power and the value produced by him in whom it inheres. When capitalists profit, they do so because the amount of time it takes to produce what is needed to keep producers in being for a certain period is less than the amount of time the latter spend producing during that period.

The capital paid out as wages is normally equal to the value of the producer's labour power. It is known as *variable capital*. The value produced by the worker over and above that represented by variable capital is called *surplus value*. The ratio of surplus value to variable capital is called *the rate of exploitation*:

---

[4] The labour theory of surplus value is not, in my view, validly derived from the labour theory of value, but there is no need to explain and defend that claim here.

[5] Marx, *Capital*, i. 284. Strictly speaking, the value of labour power is, according to Marx, the value of the means of subsistence needed to reproduce the labour supply, and it therefore includes the value of the means of raising children. This complication, which does not benefit the theory, will be ignored here.

The rate of
exploitation =

$$\frac{\text{surplus value}}{\text{variable capital}}$$

$$= \frac{\text{surplus value}}{\text{value of labour power}}$$

$$= \frac{\text{time worked} - \text{time required to produce the worker}}{\text{time required to produce the worker}}$$

2. Why is the term 'exploitation' used for what the rate of exploitation is a rate of? Is it because the term, as used in that phrase, denotes a kind of injustice? It is hard to think of any other good reason for using such a term.

Yet many Marxists say that the Marxian concept of exploitation is a *purely* scientific one, with no moral content. They say that to assert, in the language of Marxism, that *A* exploits *B*, is to offer no condemnation or criticism of *A*, or of the arrangements under which *A* operates. For them, (4) is false:

4. One reason for overthrowing capitalism is that it is a regime of exploitation (and exploitation is unjust).

Two kinds of Marxist deny (4). The first kind does so because he denies that there is *any* reason to do with values for overthrowing capitalism. People seek to overthrow it because of their class situation, or because of their morally ungrounded identification with the class situation of other people.

The second kind of Marxist (4)–denier believes that there are indeed values which should lead people to struggle against capitalism, but that justice is not one of them, since justice, he says, is not a Marxian value. What is wrong with capitalism is not that it is unjust, but that it crushes human potential, destroys fraternity, encourages the inhumane treatment of man by man, and has other grave defects generically different from injustice.

Now I am certain that many Marxists have held (4), and that Karl Marx was one of them. But I shall not here defend that claim. Marxists who reject it will find this chapter less challenging, but I hope that they will read it anyway. For while my main topic is the relationship between (4) and the labour theory of value, in pursuing it I uncover deep and neglected (or, at least, underplayed) ambiguities in the labour theory of value itself, and no Marxist will deny that many Marxists do affirm the theory of value.

3. I begin with an argument which is based on the labour theory of value, and whose conclusion is that the worker is exploited, where that is taken to entail an injustice. We can call it the Traditional Marxian Argument. It may be attributed to those believers in (4) who hold that the labour theory of value supports (4):

    5. Labour and labour alone creates value.

    6. The labourer receives the value of his labour power.

    7. The value of the product is greater than the value of his labour power.

∴ 8. The labourer receives less value than he creates.

∴ 9. The capitalist appropriates the remaining value.

  10. The labourer is exploited by the capitalist.

Premiss (5) comes from the labour theory of value, and the labour theory of surplus value supplies premisses (6), (7), and (9).

In the foregoing statement of the Traditional Argument, and elsewhere in this chapter, I speak of '*the* labourer' and '*the* capitalist': I thereby depict a relationship between social classes as a relationship between individuals who represent them. Anyone who finds that device objectionable can mentally pluralize 'labourer' and 'capitalist' throughout, but even an orthodox zealot *should* not object to the device, since, in individualizing the class relationship, I am imitating Marx's *Capital* practice.[6]

The Traditional Marxian Argument, as formulated above, derives a conclusion imputing injustice from a set of factual-*cum*-theoretical premisses. The Argument needs to have some premisses about injustice added to it in order not to be, as it is in its formulation above, elliptical or incomplete (and the same holds for the Simpler Marxian Argument and the Plain Argument, which are introduced below). Some reflections on what the needed further premisses should say are offered in section 11 below.

4. The Traditional Argument employs the labour theory of surplus value, which yields premisses (6), (7), and (9). But they can be replaced by a truism, which will contribute as much as they do to securing the conclusion that the labourer is exploited. The result is this simpler Marxian argument (statement (11) is the truism):

---

[6] See, for example, the superb and moving final paragraph of part 2 *Capital*, i (p. 280).

   5. Labour and labour alone creates value.

  11. The capitalist appropriates some of the value of the product.

∴ 8. The labourer receives less value than he creates, and

  12. The capitalist appropriates some of the value the labourer creates.

∴ 10. The labourer is exploited by the capitalist.

The labour theory of *surplus* value is, then, unnecessary to the moral claim Marxists make when they say that capitalism is exploitative. It does not matter what *explains* the difference between the value the worker produces and the value he receives.[7] What matters is just that there *is* that difference. (Note that, although the Simpler Marxian Argument drops the labour theory of surplus value, there is still a recognizable concept of surplus value in it, namely, the difference between the value the worker produces and the value he receives; and the value he receives can still be called variable capital.)[8]

5. We began with the labour theory of value, the thesis that the value of a commodity is determined by the socially necessary labour time required to produce it. We have arrived at an argument whose conclusion is that the labourer is exploited by the capitalist, and which supposedly draws one of its controversial premises from the labour theory of value. That is premiss 5, that labour and labour alone creates value. But we shall now show that the labour theory does not entail (5). It entails, moreover, that (5) is false.[9]

Suppose that a commodity has a certain value at a time t. then that value, says the labour theory, is determined by the socially

[7] It does not, that is, matter to the moral claim about exploitation, even if it is interesting from other points of view.

[8] It is the concept of variable capital, and not that of the value of labour power, which is crucial in the key theoretical applications of the labour theory of value—for example, in the reproduction schemas, in the transformation of values into prices, and in the doctrine of the tendency of the rate of profit to fall. *Capital* allows at least short-term divergences between the value of labour power and variable capital per labourer; and, wherever there is such a divergence, it is the second, not the first, which must be inscribed in the relevant equations.

[9] In the traditional sense of (5), according to which part of what is claimed in saying that labour creates value is that quantity of value is a function of quantity of labour. Other possible senses, such as that dealt with in sect. 10 below, are irrelevant here.

necessary labour time required to produce a commodity of that kind. Let us now ask: required to produce it *when*? The answer is: at *t*, the time when it has the value to be explained. The amount of time required to produce it in the past, and, *a fortiori*, the amount of time actually spent producing it are magnitudes strictly irrelevant to its value, if the labour theory is true.

Extreme cases make the point clear. (*a*) Suppose that there is a use-value *a*, which was produced in the past, when things such as *a* could come into being only through labour, but that labour is no longer required for things such as *a* to appear (perhaps *a* is a quantity of manna, produced by people at a time before God started what we can imagine is His now usual practice of dropping it). Then, according to the labour theory of value, *a* is valueless, despite the labour 'embodied' in it. (*b*) Contrariwise, suppose that there is a commodity *b* now on the market, and that *b* was not produced by labour, but that a great deal of labour is now required for *b*–like things to appear (*b* might be a quantity of clean air bottled before it became necessary to manufacture clean air). Then *b* has a value, even though no labour is 'embodied' in it.[10]

These statements follow from the labour theory of value. The theory entails that past labour is irrelevant to how much value a commodity now has.[11] But past labour would not be irrelevant if it created the value of the commodity. It follows that *labour does not create value, if the labour theory of value is true.*

Let us call the thesis that value is determined by socially necessary labour time—that is, the labour theory of value—*the strict doctrine*, and let us say that such sentences as (5), or ones which speak of value as embodied or congealed labour, belong to the *popular doctrine*. Strict and popular doctrine are commonly confused with one another, for several reasons. The least interesting

---

[10] It might be objected that *b* cannot have a value for Marx, since he defines value for products of labour only. The textual point is probably correct (see *Capital*, i. 129 for support), but no wise defender of Marx will want to urge in his defence the unfortunate lack of generality of the labour theory. Still, if anyone is impressed by the objection, let him imagine that *very little* labour went into *b*. The crucial point, which the extreme examples are only meant to dramatize, is that there is, according to the labour theory, 'continuous change in value-relations', since the amount of labour required to produce something of a certain kind is subject to variation. See *Capital*, ii. 153.

[11] Despite the misleading terminology in which it is cast, this is true even of Piero Sraffa's 'dated quantities of labour' analysis. See *Production of Commodities by Means of Commodities*, ch. 6; Ian Steedman, *Marx After Sraffa*, 70 n. 3.

reason—more interesting ones will be mentioned later—is that Marx often set formulations from the two doctrines side by side. Examples:

The value of a commodity is to the value of any other commodity as the labour-time necessary for the production of the one is related to the labour-time necessary for the production of the other. 'As exchange-values, all commodities are merely definite quantities of congealed labour time'.

So far as the *quantity of value* of a commodity is determined, according to my account, through the *quantity of labour-time contained in it* etc., then [it is determined] through the normal amount of labour which the production of an object costs etc.[12]

I am not saying that Marx was unaware of the difference between the strict and the popular doctrine. This sentence proves otherwise:

What determines value is not the amount of labour time incorporated in products, but rather the amount of labour time currently necessary.[13]

'Currently necessary': at the time, that is, when the commodity has the given value. The relevant socially necessary labour time is that required now, not that required when it was produced:

The value of any commodity . . . is determined not by the necessary labour-time that it itself contains, but by the *socially* necessary labour-time required for its reproduction.[14]

So I do not say that Marx was ignorant of the difference between the two doctrines. But I do say that the difference is damaging to key Marxian theses. It has grave implications, which are widely

---

[12] The first passage comes from *Capital*, i. 130 (Marx is quoting from his earlier *Critique of Political Economy*). The second comes from the 'Notes on Adolph Wagner', 184.

[13] *The Grundrisse*, 135. I have replaced the translator's 'at a given moment' by 'currently', which gives a more literal rendering.

[14] *Capital*, iii. 238. (To reproduce a commodity is to produce another just like it.) Compare *The Poverty of Philosophy*: 'It is important to emphasize the point that what determines value is not the time taken to produce a thing, but the *minimum* time it could possibly be produced in' (p. 136).
Now despite his express and theoretically mandated preference for the strict doctrine, Marx's presentation is replete with popular formulations (and so, too, is the Marxist tradition). See, for example, these pages of *Capital*, i, which are the harvest of a pretty random search: 128–30, 135–6, 141–2, 155, 190, 202, 260, 294–6, 303, 307, 323, 325–6, 430, 433, 675–6, 680. In many cases, the popular formulations in question cannot be translated into strict ones without significant loss.

unnoticed and which were not noticed by Marx. Our chief concern is with implications for the idea of exploitation. There are also implications for pure economic theory, some of which will occupy me in a subsequent digression (see section 7). But first let us look more carefully at the differences between the two formulations.

There are two reasons why the amount of labour which was actually spent on a particular product might differ from the amount now standardly required to produce that kind of product. The first is a non-standard level of efficiency in the actual labour process, which can be more or less efficient than the social norm. The second is technological change, which alters that norm.

Consider the case of inefficient labour. Marxists have always regarded it as a particularly inept criticism of the labour theory of value to object that it entails that an inefficiently produced product has more value than one produced efficiently and therefore in less time. And the asserted consequence does indeed fail to follow from the strict doctrine. But why should it not follow from the popular doctrine? If labour creates value by, as it were, congealing in the product, then if more labour is spent, must not more labour congeal, and will there not then be more value in the product?

The case of inefficient labour shows the incompatibility between the strict and popular doctrines. Marxists know about that case, but they are nevertheless reluctant to reject the popular doctrine. After all, the reason why both doctrines exist in Marxist culture, why neither one is enough, is that each has intellectual or political functions (or both) of its own to fulfil.[15] Accordingly, faced with problems such as that of inefficient labour, many Marxists propose a mixed formulation, the purpose of which is so to modify the popular doctrine that it is brought into line with the strict doctrine. And so it is said, in response to the case of inefficient labour, that

13. The worker creates value *if, and only in so far as,* his labour is socially necessary.

To the extent that actual labour time exceeds what is standardly required, labour is not value-creating. The formulation is obviously intended to preserve the popular idea of creation, without

[15] Despite their mutual incompatibility, one function of each doctrine is that it may be used, or, rather, misused, to support the other: see the last paragraph of sect. 7 below.

contradicting the strict doctrine. But I shall show that this cannot be done. The strict doctrine allows no such mixed formulations.[16]

The strict doctrine certainly rules out (13), since (13) cites the wrong amount of socially necessary labour time, namely that which is required when the commodity is being created,[17] rather than that which is required when the commodity is on the market. To have any prospect of being faithful to the strict doctrine, a mixed formulation must say not (13) but some such thing as this:

> 14. The worker creates value *if, and only in so far as*, the amount of labour he performs *will be* socially necessary when the product is marketed.

Marxists think that (14) follows from the strict doctrine because they mistakenly suppose that (14) follows from something the strict doctrine does indeed entail, but which is of no relevant interest, namely,

> 15. Value is determined by (that is, *is inferable from*) expended labour time when the amount expended is what will be socially necessary when the product is marketed.

Statement (15) does follow from the strict doctrine, just as (16) follows from the true doctrine about barometers:

> 16. The height of a mercury column on day 2 is determined by (that is, *is inferable from*) the atmospheric pressure on day 1 when day 1's atmospheric pressure is what day 2's atmospheric pressure will be.

Statement (16) is entailed by the truth that day 2's atmospheric pressure makes the height of the mercury column on day 2 what it is. But (16) does not entail that day 1's atmospheric pressure makes the height of the mercury column on day 2 what it is. And (15), similarly, gives no support to (14).

The general point is that if a magnitude m causally depends upon a magnitude m', and it is given that a magnitude m'' is equal to m', then whatever m'' is a magnitude of, magnitude m will be inferable from magnitude m''. There could then be an illusion that magnitude m'' *explains* magnitude m. Just that illusion, I claim, seizes anyone who supposes that (14) is consistent with the strict doctrine.

[16] Marx frequently had recourse to mixed formulations: see, e.g., *Capital*, i. 295, 303.

[17] There may, of course, be no such unique quantity: so much the worse for (13).

An additional problem for the mixed formulation is a case of abnormally efficient labour, or of labour which used means of production superior to those now available, where in each instance *less* labour than is now socially necessary was expended. One cannot begin to claim in such a case that value is created by labour subject to the constraint that the amount expended will be socially necessary, since here not enough labour is expended. When there is *inefficiency*, there is a chance of pretending that some of the labour which occurred did not create value. Where there is special *efficiency*, there can be no similar pretence that labour which did not occur did create value.

We conclude that attempts to salvage the popular idea of creation by recourse to mixed formulations will not succeed.

6. The strict and popular doctrines differ because of the difference between a present counterfactual magnitude (the amount of labour that would now be required to produce something) and a past actual magnitude (the amount of labour that was actually spent producing something). In the last section I cited cases where the two magnitudes differ in size (because of deviations from standard efficiency, and technical change) to prove that they are magnitudes of different things. But even if people never worked (or even could not work) other than at standard efficiency, and even if technical change never occurred (or even could not occur), so that labour actually spent was always equal to socially necessary labour time, labour actually spent would not (because it could not) be socially necessary labour time, and the strict and popular doctrines would remain incompatible. The concept of the amount of time required to produce a commodity is not the same as the concept of the amount of time actually spent producing it, and the two remain different even under the assumption that the relevant amounts are identical. Some Marxist economists were bored by this chapter when it appeared as an article, because of their practice of assuming that the labour time that is actually spent neither exceeds nor falls short of that which is socially necessary. But, while that assumption might have a methodological justification in certain contexts, it cannot imply that the things whose amounts are here assumed to be the same are *themselves* the very same thing; no assumption whatsoever can set aside the conceptual difference between actual and counterfactual labour.

What was required in the past, and still more what happened in the past—these facts are constitutively irrelevant to how much value a commodity has, if the labour theory of value is true. But they are not epistemically irrelevant. For, since technical conditions change relatively slowly, socially necessary labour time in the recent past is usually a good guide to socially necessary labour time now. Typical past actual labour time is, moreover, the best guide to how much labour time was necessary in the past. Thereby what did occur, the labour actually spent, becomes a good index of the labour that is now required, and, therefore, a good index of the value of the commodity, if the labour theory of value is true. But it does not follow that labour (actually spent) creates the value of commodities.

On the contrary: I have shown that, if the labour theory of value is true, then it follows that labour does *not* create value. And we can now also draw a stronger conclusion. For it would be quixotic to seek a basis *other than* the labour theory of value for the proposition that labour creates value.[18] We may therefore conclude that labour does not create value, whether or not the labour theory of value is true.

Some will be disposed to ask: if labour does not create value, what does? But it is a prejudice to suppose that value must be *created*. Something must, of course, explain value and its magnitudes, but not all explainers are creators. One putative explanation of value magnitudes is the labour theory of value, the strict doctrine. But it identifies no creator of value, unless we suppose that explaining is creating. *What would now be needed to produce a commodity of a certain kind*—that is not a creator in any literal sense.

Why is the popular doctrine popular? One reason is that it appears more appropriate than the strict doctrine as a basis for a charge of exploitation. We shall see (section 8 and 9) that neither doctrine in fact supports such a charge, but it is clear that the popular doctrine *seems* better suited to do so, just because it alone says that labour *creates* value. But a partly distinct reason for the popularity of the popular doctrine is that certain arguments against the strict doctrine tend to be met by an illicit shift to popular

---

[18] In, that is, the traditional sense of 'labour creates value', which is the relevant sense here: see n. 9 above.

formulations. This will be explained in the next section, where the theme of exploitation is in abeyance, and where I argue that the strict doctrine is false. The discussion of exploitation is completed in sections 8–11, which do not presuppose the next one.

7. I want here to expose, in some detail, how Marx arrived at the popular and strict doctrines in the opening pages of *Capital*.

Capital begins with what Marx rightly regards as the elementary phenomenon of capitalism, which is the commodity. A commodity is an object which 'satisfies human wants'[19] (and is therefore, in Marxian language, a *use-value*), and which undergoes market exchange with other such objects, the ratios in which it exchanges with them constituting its *exchange-value*. So a commodity is a use-value which is a 'bearer of exchange-value'.[20]

Focus on the commodity leads to the first *explanandum* of *Capital*, which is the fact that commodities exchange against one another not haphazardly but, within given limits of time and place, in definite proportions.[21] It is required to explain why they exchange in the ratios they do, or, in more modern terms, their equilibrium prices. Why, for example, is one quarter of corn worth x hundredweight of iron?

Marx replies that if, as he puts it, '1 quarter corn = x cwt. iron', then in each 'there exists in equal quantities something common to both . . . Each of them, so far as it is exchange-value, must therefore be reducible to this third', which is its value, and of which exchange-value is but 'the mode of expression'.[22] Value, then, is the absolute magnitude which the relative magnitude exchange-value reflects: the value of a given commodity is that property of it, whatever it may be, which, together with the value of other commodities, determines the given commodity's exchange-value. *Note that the way in which Marx introduces the concept of value ensures that it is true by definition that value determines equilibrium price.*

Marx's question is: what determines value, so defined? His first step towards an answer is to deny, on obscure and indefensible grounds, that use-value plays a role in determining magnitude of

[19] *Capital*, i. 125.   [21] Ibid. 127.
[20] Ibid. 126.   [22] Ibid.

value.[23] Having thus set aside use-value, he then claims that commodities 'have only one common property left, that of being products of labour', and that labour must therefore be 'the value-creating substance'; and from that he infers that the magnitude of a commodity's value depends on how much labour 'is objectified or materialized in it'.[24]

It is in this fashion that Marx arrives at the popular doctrine, the thesis that labour creates value. He reaches the popular thesis on the basis of premises none of which formulate propositions about how markets operate. But, having arrived at the stated popular conclusion, Marx now enters an observation, for which he gives no reason, but which is in fact justified by the way markets work. The observation is that the product of 'unskilful and lazy' labour is not worth more.[25] That is so because no buyer in a competitive market will pay over the odds just because an undue amount of labour has been spent producing what he buys. But Marx does not give that or any other argument for his remark, which is quite unmotivated on the premises he has employed heretofore.[26]

The point about inefficient labour leads Marx to the conclusion that value is determined not, as the popular doctrine says, by the amount of time spent producing the commodity, or the labour embodied in it, but by the amount of time required to produce it under average conditions of productivity, which Marx calls 'socially necessary labour time'.[27] This is the strict doctrine, or the labour theory of value properly so called, and, as I have tirelessly insisted, it entails that the amount of time which was actually spent producing a commodity has absolutely no effect on its value.

The strict doctrine is the bastard issue of a union between premises which have nothing to do with markets and from which

[23] 'This common element cannot be a geometrical, physical, chemical or other natural property of commodities. Such properties come into consideration only to the extent that they make the commodities useful, i.e. turn them into use-values. But clearly, the exchange relation of commodities is characterized precisely by its abstraction from their use-values. Within the exchange relation, one use-value is worth just as much as another, provided only that it is present in the appropriate quantity.... As use-values, commodities differ above all in quality, while as exchange-values they can only differ in quantity, and therefore do not contain an atom of use-value'. (Ibid. 127–8).

[24] Ibid. 129.

[25] Ibid.

[26] See the questions about inefficient labour and the popular doctrine which are posed at p. 217 above.

[27] *Capital*, i. 129.

Marx derives the popular doctrine, and one truth (the one about inefficient labour) which reflects how markets operate. Now, *had Marx addressed his original* explanandum (see page 221) *from the point of view of market facts in the first place*, he might have noticed that circumstances other than socially necessary labour time contribute to explaining it, since socially necessary labour time is demonstrably not the only determinant of equilibrium price. One such further determinant is the pattern of ownership of means of production, which can affect values, through the distribution of bargaining power to which it gives rise. Products of means of production on which there is some degree of monopoly are likely for that reason to command a higher price in equilibrium than they otherwise would, and therefore to have a higher value, under the definition of value with which Marx began.

But if value is something the explanation of which must literally create it, then, since ownership of means of production literally creates nothing, it would follow that, despite appearances, the pattern of that ownership cannot affect value formation. And that is what a Marxist says. He says that labour alone creates *value*: the pattern of ownership can affect price, and hence how much value various owners *get*. But no part of what they get is created by ownership.

But this line of defence depends essentially on the idea that labour *creates* value. If we stay with the strict doctrine, which rightly does not require that anything *creates* value, it has no motivation whatsoever.

To make this more clear, I return to the three propositions in my initial presentation of the labour theory of value (see section 1):

1. Socially necessary labour time determines value.

2. Value determines equilibrium price.

3. Socially necessary labour time determines equilibrium price.

Recall my view that the definitional statement is (2), and that (1) is the substantive theory. (1) and (2) entail (3). I said that I would say why some prefer to see (1) as true by definition. Here is one reason why.

Counter-examples to (3) abound, such as the one I noted about the pattern of ownership of means of production, or the cases of divergences in period of production and organic composition of capital.[28] Statement (3) is false, and much of the second and third volumes of *Capital* is an attempt to cope with that fact.

Now, if (3) is false, one *at least* of (1) and (2) must be false. But, if (2) is true by definition, then (1) is false, and the labour theory of value is sunk. What Marxists therefore do is to treat (1) as true by definition—so that counter-examples to (3) cannot touch it—and then simply drop (2). They redefine value, which was supposed to be whatever underlies equilibrium price, *as* socially necessary labour time, and they mask from themselves the consequent triviality of the claim that socially necessary labour time determines value by resorting to popular discourse. Their manœuvre with (1) and (2) in fact deprives the labour theory of all substance, but they conceal that consequence by construing (1) in a popular fashion, by (mis)reading it as though it says that labour *creates* value, which does not sound trivial, and they plead that the circumstances thought to be counter-examples to the labour theory do affect price but clearly have no power to bring value into being. They say that, whatever determines market ratios, and thereby who gets what amounts of value, labour alone creates what value there is to get. For how, they ask, could anything but labour, actual production, produce anything, and *how*, therefore, *could anything but labour produce value?* I reply that, once the trivializing shift has been made, one can no longer identify anything called 'value' which labour could be said to produce.[29]

The popular doctrine supplies an appearance of substance when, under pressure of counter-examples, (1) is treated as true by definition, (2) is dropped, and the labour theory is, in reality, drained of all substance. Because of its simplifying assumptions, volume i of *Capital* can proceed under definition (2) of value. When the assumptions are relaxed, (1) and (2) cannot both be true. Hence, in volume ii and iii, statement (2) is abandoned.

At this point, it is instructive to look at a central part of Marx's critique of Ricardo. If I am right, it depends on popular formulations.

---

[28] There is no originality in my invocation of these counter-examples, which have dogged the labour theory of value from its inception. I claim originality only for my diagnosis of how Marx and Marxists enable themselves to cleave to the labour theory in the face of the well-known counter-examples to it.

[29] The italicized question reflects conflation of the confused idea that labour creates value with the correct idea that it creates what has it, to wit, the use-valuable product: see sect. 8 below.

Ricardo defined value as Marx does at the beginning of *Capital*, as the absolute magnitude, whatever it may be, which underlies the relativities of equilibrium price. He then provisionally hypothesized that socially necessary labour time was that magnitude, and that it therefore determined equilibrium price. He went on to acknowledge, however, that variations in periods of production falsify his provisional hypothesis, and he consequently allowed that equilibrium price and, therefore, value, deviate from socially necessary labour time.[30]

According to Marx, Ricardo was here misled by appearances; the real deviation is not of value from socially necessary labour time, but of equilibrium price from value (which *is* socially necessary labour time).[31]

Now, both Ricardo and Marx say that equilibrium price deviates from socially necessary labour time. What then is the theoretical difference between them? I believe that there is none, or, what comes to the same thing, that the difference can be stated only in popular discourse, to which Marx therefore here resorts. He says that variations in period of production and organic composition do not affect how much value is *created*, but only how much is *appropriated* at the various sites of its creation. But if one asks, 'Exactly what is it that labour is here said to create?', then, I contend, there can be no answer, once value is no longer, as now it cannot be, defined as the absolute underlying equilibrium price.[32] Marx's quarrel with Ricardo is merely verbal, with a cover of metaphor concealing its emptiness.

The labour theory of value comes in two versions, strict and popular. The two contradict one another. But the labour theorist cannot, by way of remedy, simply drop the popular version. For despite their mutual inconsistency, each version can appear true only when it is thought to receive support from the other: 'Labour creates value' seems (but is not) a simple consequence of the thesis that value is determined by socially necessary labour time, and that

---

[30] See Ricardo's *Principles of Political Economy*, ch. 1; and see Mark Blaug, *Economic Theory in Retrospect*, 96 ff. for a brief accessible exposition.

[31] See *Theories of Surplus Value*, ii. 106, 174–80; *The Grundrisse*, 562–3; *Selected Correspondence*, 122.

[32] Hence, if I am right, the transformation problem is a strictly incoherent problem, whether or not it has a mathematical 'solution'.

thesis appears to survive refutation only when it is treated as interchangeable with the idea that labour creates value.

8. In this section I shall identify the real basis of the Marxian imputation of exploitation to the capitalist production process, the proposition which really animates Marxists, whatever they may think and say. The real basis is not the commonly stated one, sentence (5), but a fairly obvious truth which owes nothing to the labour theory of value, and which is widely confused with (5). And since (5) is itself confused with the labour theory of value, the latter is confused with the fairly obvious truth to be stated.[33]

A by-product of my discussion, then, will be an explanation why the labour theory of value, which ought to be controversial, is considered even by very intelligent Marxists to be a fairly obvious truth. When Marxists think obviously true what others think not obvious at all, one side at least is very wrong, and an explanation of the error in terms of class position or ideological standpoint is not enough, because it does not show how the error is possible, by what intellectual mechanism it can occur. What follows will help to explain how it is possible for very intelligent Marxists to be utterly wrong.

Recall what has been shown. We have seen that if the labour theory of value is true, then labour does not create value. For if labour creates value, past labour creates value; and if past labour creates value, then past labour determines the value of the product. But the labour theory of value says that value magnitudes are determined by currently necessary labour time. It follows that past labour does not create value, if the labour theory of value is true. There is, moreover, no plausible alternative basis on which to assert that labour creates value. Hence it is false that labour creates value. And I shall show in section 9 that, even if it were true, it would not be a sound basis for a charge of exploitation.

Nor does the labour theory of value itself, strictly formulated, form such a basis. Any such impression disappears once we see that it does not entail that the workers create value. In fact, the labour theory of value does not entail that the workers create anything.

Yet the workers manifestly do create something. They create the product. They do not create *value*, but they create *what has value*.

---

[33] 'Is confused with' is not a transitive relation, but the above statement is none the less true.

The small difference of phrasing covers an enormous difference of conception. What raises a charge of exploitation is not that the capitalist appropriates some of the value the worker produces, but that he appropriates some of the value of *what* the worker produces. Whether or not workers produce value, they produce the product, that which has value.

And no one else does. Or, to speak with greater care, producers are the only persons who produce what has value: it is true by definition that no human activity other than production produces what has value. This does not answer the difficult question, Who is a producer? But whatever the answer to it may be, only those whom it identifies can be said to produce what has value. And we know before we have the full answer that owners of capital, considered as such, cannot be said to do so.

Note that I am not saying that whatever has value was produced by labour, for I have not said that whatever has value was produced. I also do not deny that tools and raw materials are usually needed to produce what has value. The assertion is that labourers, in the broadest possible sense, are the only persons who produce anything which has value, and that capitalists are not labourers in that sense. If they were, capital and labour would not be distinct 'factors of production':[34] the capitalist supplies capital, which is not a kind of labour.

Some will question the claim that owners of capital, considered as such, do not produce anything. An owner of capital can, of course, *also* do some producing, for example, by carrying out a task which would otherwise fall to someone in his hire. Then he is a producer, but not *as* an owner of capital. More pertinent is the objection that owners of capital, in their very capacity as such, fulfil significant productive functions, in risking capital, making investment decisions, and so forth. But whether or not that is true, it does not entail that they produce anything in the importantly distinct sense in issue here. It does not entail, to put it one way, that they engage in the activity of producing.

[34] I use scare-quotes because there are good Marxian objections to the classification of capital and labour as distinct but comparable factors of production: note that in a sense all that is required for production is capital, since capital buys not only means of production but also labour. That only hints at the objections, which are given in *Capital* iii, ch. 48, and which do not affect the point made in the text above.

To act productively it is enough that one does something which helps to bring it about that a thing is produced, and that does not entail participating in producing it. You cannot cut without a knife, but it does not follow that, if you lack one and I lend you one, thereby enabling you to cut, then I am a cutter, or any other sort of producer. The distinction is between productive activities and producing activities. Capitalists arguably engage in the former, but once the distinction is clear, it is evident that they do not (unless they are not only capitalists) engage in the latter.

To be sure, *if*—what I here neither assert nor deny—the capitalist is a *productive* non-producer, that will have a bearing on the thesis that he is an exploiter. It will be a challenge to a charge of exploitation whose premiss is that he produces nothing. But it would be wrong to direct the challenge against the *premiss* of that charge, that he produces nothing. As that is generally intended, it cannot be denied.

And it is this fairly obvious truth which, I contend, lies at the heart of the Marxist charge of exploitation. The real basis of that charge is not that only workers produce value, but that only they produce what has it. The real Marxian argument for (10) is not the Simpler Marxian Argument (see section 4), but this different one (the Plain Argument):

17. The labourer is the person who creates the product, that which has value.

11. The capitalist appropriates some of the value of the product.

18. The labourer receives less value than the value of what he creates,

and

19. The capitalist appropriates some of the value of what the labourer creates.

10. The labourer is exploited by the capitalist.

The Plain Argument is constructed in analogy with the Simpler Marxian Argument, under the constraint that premiss (17) replaces premiss (5). The arguments are totally different, but very easy to confuse with one another.

The Plain Argument is not a (distinctively) Marxian argument: it owes nothing to any version of the labour theory of value. Hence, in calling it the *real* Marxian argument for (10), I do not mean that it is a really *Marxian* argument, for it is not. I mean, rather, that it is the argument which really moves Marxists politically, and with which, as I shall show in the following section, they confuse the arguments that they officially propound.

9. I here defend my claim that it is labour's creation of what has value, not its (supposed) creation of value, which lies at the root of the Marxist charge that capitalism is a system of exploitation.

We have seen that labour does not create value. I now argue that, even if it did, that would have no bearing on the question of exploitation.

The proposition that labour creates value is, to begin with, unnecessary to the thesis that labour is exploited. For, if we suppose that something else creates value, the impression that labour is exploited, if it was there before, will sturdily persist. Thus, imagine that the magnitude of a commodity's value is wholly determined by the extent and intensity of desire for it, and that we can therefore say that desire, not labour, creates value.[35] But imagine, too, that labour creates the product itself, out of in all senses worthless raw materials, or—the product being a pure service—out of none. Do we now lose our inclination (supposing, of course, that a belief in the labour theory of value induced one in us) to sympathize with the labourer's claim to the product, and, hence, to its value, even though we are no longer supposing that labour creates that value? I do not think that we do. The worker continues to look exploited if he creates the valuable thing and does not get all the value of the thing he creates. What matters, normatively, is what creates that thing, or so transforms it that it has (more) value,[36] not what makes things of its sort have the amount of value they do, which is what the labour theory of value is really supposed to explain.

[35] That may sound like an insane supposition, but it is not when, as here, it is the supposition that facts about desire, and not facts about labour time, determine exchange-value ratios. The reader who finds absurd the idea that desire creates value is probably himself confusing value creation with product creation, and therefore confusing the idea that desire creates value with the magical idea that it creates the desired product. Recall that value is not the same thing as use-value. Desire could not, except through magic, create use-value: it could not bring it about that something has the power to satisfy it. But bourgeois economists who think that desire contributes to the creation of value, by generating a willingness to pay for what is desired, are not believers in magic.

[36] Whatever creates (or enhances the value of) a valuable thing in *that* sense creates (some of) its value, but that is not the sense of 'creates value' in which labour is supposed to create value in the labour theory of value: see sect. 10 below.

But the claim that labour creates value is not only unnecessary to the charge of exploitation. It is no reason whatever for laying such a charge. Once again, I make the point by imagining that desire creates value. If labour's creation of value would give the labourer a claim to value *because* he had created it, then so would the desirer's creation of value give him a claim on that basis. Yet would we say that desirers are exploited because they create the value of the product, and the capitalist receives part of that value? The suggestion is absurd.[37] It must then be equally absurd to think that labourers are exploited *because* they create value which others receive.

It is absurd, but it does not seem absurd, and the explanation of the discrepancy is that it is impossible to forget that labour creates what has value. Creating value, when we suppose that workers do that, seems to matter, because we naturally think that they could create value only by creating what has it, and the relevance of the latter is mistakenly transmitted to the former. Part of the case for saying that (17) is the real basis of the charge of exploitation is that (5) cannot be yet seems to be, and the relationship between (17) and (5) explains the illusion.

But there is also a more direct reason for thinking that the essential thing is labour's creation of what has value. Look at the excerpt from 'Solidarity', which forms the epigraph of this chapter. It says nothing about value, and the labour theory is not required to appreciate its point, which is that 'we' are exploited. It does say that 'we' have made all these valuable things.

It is, then, neither the labour theory of value (that socially necessary labour time determines value), nor its popular surrogate

---

[37] Note that I am not saying that a person's desire for something is no reason why he should receive it. Of course it is a reason, albeit one singularly capable of being overridden. But a person's desire for something cannot be a reason for his receiving it *on the ground* that his desire for it enhances its value, even if his desire for it does enhance its value. That ground is surely unintelligible.

1) One more caveat. I do not suppose in the above paragraphs or anywhere else that the correct principle of reward is according to productive contribution. One can hold that the capitalist exploits the worker by appropriating part of the value of what the worker produces without holding that all of that value should go to the worker. One can affirm a principle of distribution according to need, and add that the capitalist exploits the worker because need is not the basis on which he receives part of the value of what the worker produces. Compare Jon Elster: 'a person is exploited if (i) he does not enjoy the fruits of his own labour and (ii) the difference between what he makes and what he gets cannot be justified by redistribution according to need'. ('Exploring Exploitation' 3).

(that labour creates value), but the fairly obvious truth (that labour creates what has value) rehearsed in the song, which is the real basis of the Marxist imputation of exploitation.

I have been discussing the exploitation of the propertyless wage-worker under capitalism. But if anything is the *paradigm* of exploitation for Marx, it is the exploitation of the feudal serf, who does not, according to Marx, produce value, since his product is not marketed and is therefore not a commodity. The serf's exploitation is, according to Marx, entirely manifest. The proletarian's is more covert, and it is by arguing that his position may in fact be assimilated to the serf's that Marx seeks to show that he too is exploited.

The exploitation of the serf is manifest, because nothing is more clear than that part of what he produces redounds not to him but to his feudal superior. This is not so in the same plain sense under capitalism, where the product itself is not divided between capitalist and worker, but marketed.[38]

Now Marxists contend that the labour theory of value is required to uncover the exploitation of the wage-worker, but I disagree. What is needed is not the false and irrelevant labour theory, but the mere concept of value, as defined, independently of the labour theory, in our sentence 2. It enables us to say that, whatever may be responsible for magnitudes of value, the worker does not receive all of the value of his product.

Marxists say that

20. The serf produces the whole product, but the feudal lord appropriates part of the product;

and

21. The proletarian produces all of the value of the product, but the capitalist appropriates part of the value of the product.

I accept (20), but I modify the first part of (21) so that it resembles the first part of (20), with this result:

22. The proletarian produces the whole product, but the capitalist appropriates part of the value of the product.

[38] For further discussion and textual references, see *KMTH* 333–4.

The exploitation of the proletarian is, on my account, more similar to the exploitation of the serf than traditional Marxism says. There remains the difference that in (22), by contrast with (20), there is an exercise of the concept of value (though not, of course, of the labour theory of value). That exercise is essential, since it is false that

> 23. The proletarian produces the whole product, but the capitalist appropriates part of the product.

(23) is false, since in one sense the capitalist appropriates all of what the proletarian produces and in another sense he almost always appropriates none of it. He appropriates all of it in that the whole of the product belongs to him before he sells it. But we can also say that he almost always appropriates none of it, in that he almost always sells all of it. Hence, at the level of the individual capitalist, a reference to value in characterizing his exploitative appropriation is ineliminable.

If we now shift to the relationship between the capitalist and working *classes*, we can describe capitalist exploitation without exercising the concept of value at all, and we can thereby assimilate the exploitations of serfs and wage-workers even more thoroughly. The following analogy holds:

> 24. Serfs produce all the products in feudal society, but feudal lords appropriate some of them;

and

> 25. Proletarians produce all of the products in capitalist society, but capitalists appropriate some of them.

The means of subsistence consumed by capitalists and the means of production which they use productively are all produced by workers. And there we have the essential fact of capitalist exploitation, in a formulation which involves no use of the concept of value.[39]

10. In the last two sections I have insisted that labour creates that which has value, and I have continued to deny that labour creates

---

[39] For more in the same vein, see my 'More on Exploitation and the Labour Theory of Value', 318–19.

value itself. Yet it might be objected that the insistence contradicts the denial, that, in short, (26) is true:

26. Since labour creates what has value, labour creates value.

But the objection is misguided. For *if* there is a sense of 'labour creates value' in which (26) is true, it is not the relevant traditional sense, that intended by Marxists when they assert (5). 'Labour creates what has value' could not entail 'labour creates value' where the latter is a contribution to explaining the magnitude of the value of commodities, as (5) is supposed to be. How could it follow from the fact that labour creates what has value that the *amount* of value in what it creates varies directly and uniformly with the amount of labour expended?[40]

Is there a sense, distinct from that of (5), in which 'labour creates value' does follow from 'labour creates what has value'? Probably there is. If an artist creates a beautiful object out of something which was less beautiful, then we find it natural to say that he creates beauty. And it would be similarly natural to say of a worker who creates a valuable object out of something less valuable that he creates value. But that would not support the popular version of the labour theory of value, though it would, of course, help to explain why so many Marxists mistakenly adhere to it.

11. I have argued that the essential non-normative claim in the argument that capitalism is a regime of exploitation is that the capitalist appropriates part of the value of the worker's product. That appropriation undeniably occurs, but, for it to constitute exploitation, it needs to be shown (see section 3 above) that it is an injustice, that the relevant transfer of value is unfair. In what follows I do not attempt to prove the unfairness charge, but only to lay out what needs to be shown for the charge to stick.

I believe that the crucial lacuna in the Plain Argument is a statement about the distributive background. against which the labour contract is concluded.[41] Capitalists obtain some of the value of what workers produce because capitalists do and workers do not

---

[40] And if it did follow, then the labour theory of value, the strict doctrine, would be false.
[41] It is the crucial lacuna in that it is the only *controversial* claim that needs to be added.

own means of production: that is why workers accept wage offers which generate profit for capitalists. The crucial question for exploitation is, therefore, whether or not it is fair that capitalists have the bargaining power they do. If it is morally all right that capitalists do and workers do not own means of production, then capitalist profit need not be the fruit of exploitation; and, if the pre-contractual distributive position is morally wrong, then the case for exploitation is made. The question of exploitation therefore resolves itself into the question of the moral status of capitalist private property. When apologists for capitalism deny that capital-ists are exploiters on the ground that they contribute to the creation of the product by providing its means of production, the appropri-ate Marxist reply is not merely that workers alone produce, which the apologist can (and must) concede, nor that workers produce the value, which is false and irrelevant, but that the capitalist's 'contribution' does not establish absence of exploitation, since capitalist property in means of production is theft, and the capitalist is therefore 'providing' what morally ought not to be his to provide. Exploiting is a kind of taking without giving. The capitalist does not really give, because what he appears to give was unjustly taken in the first place. Again, capitalists may well qualify as productive in certain ways (see section 8 above), but so, too, may slaveowners. But, unless their ownership of slaves is morally defensible, slaveowners nevertheless exploit, and so, too, do capitalists, unless their ownership of capital is morally defensible.

A flow of value, in either the popular or the plain sense, from the worker to the capitalist, constitutes exploitation only if the contract it fulfils arises out of an unfair bargaining situation, and regardless, moreover, of whether or not that situation precisely *forces* the worker to sell his labour to the capitalist.[42] Once the truisms of the Plain Argument are to hand, the crucial question for exploitation concerns the justice of the distribution of the means of produc-tion.[43] And that would be the crucial question even if (contrary to what I have argued) the thesis that workers create value were both true and relevant to the charge of exploitation. For, even so,

---

[42] *Is* the worker forced to work for the capitalist? The answer to that question is rather complicated: see chs. 12, 13 below.

[43] I believe that Marx, too, thought that this was the crucial question, and that a widespread failure to realize that he did is a result of a mistaken reading of an important passage in his *Critique of the Gotha Programme*: see pp. 299–300 of ch. 14 below.

workers could not create value without means of production, and if capitalists were morally entitled to those means, then they would surely be entitled to set terms for their use under which they receive some return for allowing them to be used.[44] So the thesis that labour creates value requires the same supplementation as the Plain Argument when it is used as a basis for arguing that workers are exploited.

In my view, the worker is indeed exploited by the capitalist, since the latter secures profit through private ownership of means of production, and private ownership of means of production is morally illegitimate. I shall not here try to establish its moral illegitimacy, but note that the foregoing statement is consistent with the claim, which some Marxists might wish to make, that private ownership of capital is unjust precisely *because* it enables capitalists to extract value from what workers produce. That would be one way of impugning the moral status of private ownership of capital, but there are also other ways, which I prefer, and which I have explored elsewhere.[45]

12. Table 2 sets out my theses about three propositons which have figured centrally in this chapter. The phrase 'is a suitable basis for a charge of exploitation', which heads the table's fourth column does not here mean 'establishes that capitalists exploit workers', but 'is the essential non-normative ingredient in a sound argument for the conclusion that capitalists exploit workers'.

I now summarize my arguments for the tables twelve theses:

T1: *The labour theory of value is false.* Standard counter-examples prove that socially necessary labour time is not the only determinant of equilibrium, price. The strict doctrine is, therefore, false. Marxists nevertheless maintain that the labour theory of value is true by insisting, in face of the counter-examples, that, whatever determines equilibrium price, only labour creates value. But that defence of the labour theory is cast in terms of the illicit popular doctrine. It also

---

[44] It does not follow that they are entitled to set any terms whatever for their use: one can believe that capitalists are legitimate owners of means of production but that offering wages below a certain level is nevertheless an attempt to exploit. But if, as Marxists believe, *all* profit, of whatever dimensions, is exploitation, then there can be no legitimate entitlement to private ownership of capital.

[45] In my two articles on 'Self-Ownership, World-Ownership and Equality'.

TABLE 2

	is true	follows from (1)	contra-dicts (1)	is a suitable basis for a charge of exploitation
(1) = the labour theory of value = value is determined socially necessary labour time = the strict doctrine	T1: No	T2: Yes	T3: No	T4: No
(5) = labour creates value = the popular doctrine	T5: No	T6: No	T7: Yes	T8: No
(17) = labour creates the product, that which has value	T9: Yes	T10: No	T11: No	T12: Yes

unjustifiably divorces values from price, by reference to which value was initially defined. (see section 7 above.)

T2 and T3 are entered here merely to complete the table. They record the self-evident truths that the labour theory of value follows from and does not contradict itself.

T4: *The labour theory of value is not a suitable basis for a charge of exploitation.* Workers are exploited only if they produce something. But the strict doctrine does not entail that they produce anything: it merely specifies how to determine the value of commodities, without saying anything about how commodities come into being. Commodities are, of course, produced by labour, and that, as T12 says, *is* a suitable basis on which to found a charge of exploitation. But the plain fact that labour produces commodities is, though obvious, not entailed by the labour theory of value. (See section 8 above).

T5: *Labour does not create value.* As T7 says, the labour theory of value (i.e., the strict doctrine) entails that labour does not create value. But no one asserts that labour creates value on any basis other than the labour theory of value. One may safely conclude that labour does not create value. (See pages 220, 226 above).

T6: *The labour theory of value does not entail that labour creates value.* This follows from T7 (together with the fact that the labour theory of value is not self-contradictory).

T7: *The labour theory of value entails that labour does not create value.* If labour created value, it would determine its magnitude (when, that is, 'labour creates value' is endowed with the sense that Marxists give it: for a different and irrelevant sense of 'labour creates value' see section 10 above). But the labour theory of value says that socially necessary labour time determines value magnitudes, and socially necessary labour time, the amount of time required to produce a given commodity, is not the same thing as the amount of time actually spent producing it. If, accordingly, the first determines the commodity's value, the second does not. (See sections 5 and 6 above).

T8: *The claim that labour creates value is not a suitable basis for a charge of exploitation.* Suppose that labour's (alleged) creation of value were a suitable basis for saying that workers are exploited. It would follow, by parity of reasoning, that, if desire created value, then desirers would be exploited if they did not receive, *gratis*, the product whose value is due to their desire. Yet if one supposes that value is entirely due to demand, which reflects desire, one need not then believe that those who produce what is demanded lose their claim to it, even if they do not desire it. (The producers might want it even though they do not, in the relevant sense, desire it, in order to exchange it for something they do desire). Whatever creates value is irrelevant to claims about exploitation, and it can seem relevant only when the idea of creating value is confused with the distinct idea of creating use-value, or the product itself. (See section 9 above).

T9: *Labour creates what has value.* This fairly obvious truth needs defence only against the ideological claim that capitalists too create what has value. But, if that claim were true, then capital and labour would not be distinct factors of production: *qua* capitalists, capitalists supply capital, which is not a kind of labour. Capitalists may, of course, also labour, and thereby participate in the creation of what has value, as they do when, for example, they happen to manage their own enterprises. But that is an illustration of, not a counter-example to, T9. The putatively exploitative element in capitalists' income is what they get as a result of owning capital, not the additional amount some get as a result of engaging in labour themselves. (See section 8 above).

T10 and T11 record the self-evident truths that *the labour theory of value neither entails nor contradicts the plain truth that labour creates what has value.*

T12: *That labour creates what has value is a suitable basis for a charge of exploitation.* Before arguing for T12, let me argue for an associated thesis, T12': *that labour creates what has value is the real basis of the Marxist charge of exploitation*, whatever Marxists may avow. For, as we saw, the labour theory of value (see T4) provides no basis for that charge, and that is why Marxists usually formulate the charge in popular terms, since the claim that labour *creates* value *seems* to support it. Reflection shows, however, that the popular doctrine *only seems* to provide a basis for the charge of exploitation (See T8). T12' then explains why it seems to provide such a basis: Marxists confuse 'labour creates what has value' with 'labour creates value', even though the small difference of phrasing covers an enormous difference of conception. (The same confusion helps to explain why Marxists persist in thinking that so controversial a doctrine as the labour theory of value is *obviously* true: they confuse (1) with (5) and (5) with (17), and, thereby, (1) with (17): see page 226 above).

Another argument for T12', and this one is also an argument for T12, is that the lines from 'Solidarity' which head up this chapter evidently raise a charge of exploitation, even though they say nothing above the creation of value. They speak only about the creation of what has value, and they imply that workers are exploited because they are deprived of so much of the value of the wonders they have made by those who did not labour to make them (see section 8 above).

I have prosecuted my critique of the labour theory of value with consummate intransigence because I believe that it is a terrible incubus on progressive reflection about exploitation. Instead of desperately shifting about for some or other way of defending the labour theory,[46] Marxists and quasi-Marxists should address themselves to the crucial question, which is whether or not private ownership of capital is morally legitimate.

[46] For a representative example of such desperation, see Holmstrom's 'Marx and Cohen on Exploitation and the Labour Theory of Value', 299–302, to which I reply at 'More on Exploitation and the Labour Theory of Value', 326–8, an article some parts of which (but not that one) have been incorporated into the present chapter.

12

ARE DISADVANTAGED WORKERS WHO TAKE HAZARDOUS JOBS FORCED TO TAKE HAZARDOUS JOBS?

1. We might define *ideology* as thinking which is not just incorrect but which is systematically deflected from truth because of its conformity to the limited vision and sectional interests of a particular social class. We could then say that *bourgeois* ideology is thinking deflected from truth because of the service it performs for owners and managers of capital.

Now, according to a theory I reject,[1] the ordinary language spoken in bourgeois society, by bourgeois and non-bourgeois alike, is permeated by bourgeois ideology; and ordinary language philosophy, because it respects our ordinary use of words, is, therefore, a bourgeois philosophy. And so, for example, to treat the ordinary language of force and freedom as substantially unrevisable, as an ordinary language philosopher would, is to subscribe in advance to a bourgeois point of view.

In my opinion, this theory is wrong about the relationship between ideology and ordinary language, and its proponents fail to notice the contribution ordinary language philosophy can make to ideologically infested dispute. I think ideology runs deep, but not as deep as they think. If the theory I oppose were correct, it would be almost impossible for reason and evidence to prevail against ideology, since the very language in which ideologically sensitive questions are phrased would dictate their answers. But I think it manifest that reason and evidence often defeat ideology quite handily.

My different opinion is that, in so far as there is a connection between ideology and ordinary language, then ideological distortion is not so much *in* ordinary language as *of* ordinary language: our ordinary language misleads us not because it is deformed, but because we fail to achieve a perspicuous view of its complex nature. I do not think philosophy is generated by

---

[1] The theory is affirmed by some of those who call themselves Marxists, and a passage in Marx might be thought to support it, but I would not read it that way: see *The German Ideology*, 231.

misunderstanding of language, but I do think much ideology promotes and feeds on such misunderstanding, and that ideological discourse about force and freedom is a case in point. Our ordinary language of force and freedom has unexpected logical properties of which it is easy to be unaware, and neglect of which facilitates ideological legerdemain.

Against Marxists who think that the ordinary language of force and freedom is bound itself to be bourgeois, I say that the concepts of force and freedom are so fundamental that in their ordinary employment they are secure against ideological take-over: we simply would not know what we were talking about if ideology governed their use. But in our fallible *reflection* on the same concepts, which goes beyond our *use* of them, ideology does lead us astray, and part of the remedy is to pay close attention to what we ordinarily say.

In sections 3–7[2] of this chapter, I use techniques of ordinary language philosophy in an attempt to defeat a number of ideological illusions. If I fail to achieve the effect I intend, that will not, I think, be due to fault in the method I have commended, but to my unfaultless use of it.[3]

2. I now turn to the question in this chapter's title.

It is surely uncontroversial that disadvantaged workers in hazardous industry have less attractive life options than many of the rest of us do. The main controversial questions are, respectively, factual, conceptual, and moral: i. Exactly what are the options facing typical disadvantaged workers, and what causes them to be restricted as they are? ii. How do the concepts of force and freedom apply to such workers, in the light of the answer to (i)? iii. Is it morally acceptable that they find themselves situated as they are?

I have nothing distinctive to say about (i). I shall devote most of my attention to (ii), some to (iii), and some to the relationship between (ii) and (iii).

To fix ideas, let us focus on an imaginary worker in an unimaginary situation, namely one of the 7,000 unemployed people

---

[2] The normative questions addressed in sect 8 do not lend themselves to the treatment appropriate to the conceptual questions discussed in sections 3–7.

[3] For further defence (and illustration) of the use of ordinary language philosophy in the battle against bourgeois ideology see pp. 290 ff. of ch. 14 below.

in the town of Hazelton, Pennsylvania (population: 33,000), to which the Beryllium Corporation came in 1956, offering hazardous jobs.[4] Our worker, whom I shall call *John*, took one. He was confronted with a choice between employment and health,[5] and he chose the former. Was he forced to take the health-endangering job? Did he, in taking it, contract freely? I shall deal with these questions in sections 3–7.

3. Leftists will urge that he *was* forced to enter the relevant contract, while Rightists will contend that, in entering it, he exercised his market freedom. I shall argue that, although both tend to think that they thereby contradict one another, they do not in fact, and, moreover, that if the Leftists are right, then so are the Rightists, because of a surprising general truth about force and freedom, which I shall call *T*: *if a person is forced to do something, then he is free to do that thing.* Hence, if the Leftist is right, then the Rightist also is. For it follows from *T* that, if John was forced to contract as he did, then he was free so to contract; that when he contracted, he exercised a freedom to contract, and, therefore, his market freedom. The right-wing claim is, accordingly, entailed by the left-wing claim it is supposed to contradict, and it—the right-wing claim—therefore lacks political significance.

I now temporarily leave Left and Right, in order to defend thesis *T*, that one is free to do whatever one is forced to do. The most direct argument for it is as follows: If you are forced to do *A*, you do *A*. But, if you do *A*, you are free to do *A*: you cannot do what you are not free to do. So, if you are forced to do *A*, you are free to do *A*.

I am not, in that first argument, equating being free to do something with being able to do it. The argument requires that being free to do something is a necessary condition of being able to do it, but not that it is also a sufficient one.[6] The argument does not equate being free with being able, since it is consistent with the view that I may be unable to do something I am free to do because I lack

[4] See the Hastings Center document on *Occupational Health*.

[5] Or, perhaps, short-run health, since it doesn't do your health much good in the long run if you don't have a job.

[6] Where 'being able to do *A*' is taken in its narrow sense of 'having the capacity to do *A*' being free to do *A* is not a necessary condition of being able to do *A*, but I intend 'being able to do *A*' in a perfectly ordinary but broader sense.

the capacity to do it. I am, in a clear sense, free to swim the English Channel, but I am nevertheless unable to. If I were a much better swimmer than I am, but forbidden by well-enforced law to swim the Channel, then, again, I would be unable to swim it, but because of unfreedom rather than incapacity.

Someone might object to the argument's premiss that whatever you do is something you are free to do. He might say that not any old doing (including, for example, doing something by fluke) proves freedom to do what is done. I think that this objection is wrong,[7] but I can afford to grant that it is right, for I can replace the premiss it contests by a weaker and less controvertible one which still delivers the desired conclusion, namely, that you are free to do what you are forced to do. The sufficiently powerful weaker premiss is that a person who, knowing what he is doing, intentionally does *A*, exercises a freedom to do *A*. Since, when you are forced to do *A*, you standardly do it knowing what you are doing, and so on, the desired conclusion may be obtained even if not *all* doings require freedom to do what is done.

A second argument for the claim that I am free to do what I am forced to do is that one way of frustrating someone who would force me to do something is by rendering myself not free to do it: it follows, by contraposition, that if I am forced to do it, I am free to do it. To illustrate: I commit a crime, thereby causing myself to be gaoled, so that I cannot be forced by you to do something I abhor. If you still hope to force me to do it you will have to make me free to do it (by springing me from gaol).

The fact that being unfree to do *A* renders it impossible for anyone to force you to do it constitutes a non-paternalistic justification for certain legislative restriction on freedom. Some people might be forced to sell themselves into slavery, or to work for very low wages, if their freedom to do so were not removed by legislation. Freedom-removing legislation, by making certain forcings impossible, can serve the interests of freedom itself, since, whenever someone is forced to do something, he is *pro tanto* less free than he otherwise would be.

Here, finally, is a third argument for the claim that you are free to do what you are forced to do: Before you are forced to do *A*, you are, at least in standard cases, free to do *A* and free not to do *A*. It is

---

[7] For it seems to me that, if you do something by fluke, then you were free to do it by fluke. I am free to hit the bull's-eye by fluke, but I would not be if you prevented me from picking up the dart.

natural to suppose that the force removes the second freedom,[8] but why suppose that it removes the first? It puts no obstacle in the path of your doing *A*, and you therefore remain free to do it.

The conclusion that being forced to do *A* entails being free to do *A* will no doubt be resisted, but it is demonstrably true, and I think resistance to it reflects failure to distinguish the idea of *being free to do something* from other ideas, such as the idea of *doing something freely*. I am free to do what I am forced to do even if, as is usually true, I do not do it freely.

I say that it is usually, not always, true that when I am forced to do something I do it unfreely, because I am inclined to accept something like Gerald Dworkin's claim that '*A* does *X* freely if and only if *A* does *X* for reasons he doesn't mind acting from',[9] and on that view some forced action is freely performed: if, for example, I am forced to do something which I want to do and had fully intended to do, then, unless I resent the supervenient coercion, I do it freely. But that is an unusual case. In the standard case forced action is performed unfreely, even though the agent was, because he must have been, free to perform the action he performed unfreely. What a person is free to do is a matter of his situation. Whether or not he does what he does freely is a (complex) matter of his mental state. Inferences from the first kind of freedom to the second are dangerous, and whereas it is demonstrable that John was free to contract as he did, it is extremely unlikely that he did so freely.

I labour the truth that one is free to do what one is forced to do because of its manifest bearing on the disagreement about John. But the truth also helps to explain the character and persistence of the analogous but more general disagreement whether wage-workers in a capitalist society are, as Marxists say they are, forced to sell their labour power. In oppositon to Marxists, bourgeois thinkers celebrate the freedom of contract manifest not only in the capitalist's purchase of labour power but also in the worker's sale of it. If Marxists are right, then workers, being forced to sell their labour power, are in an important way unfree. But it remains true that (unlike chattel slaves) they are free to sell it. The unfreedom asserted by Marxists is compatible with the freedom asserted by

---

[8] Though see sect. 4 below, where I argue against this natural supposition.

[9] 'Acting Freely', 381. I say 'something like' since, to cater for a point made by Lawrence Davis, it would be better to say '*A* does *X* freely if and only if *A* does *X* and does not do *X* for reasons he minds acting from'. See *The Philosophy of Action*, 123.

bourgeois thinkers. Indeed: if the Marxists are right the bourgeois thinkers are right, unless they also think, as characteristically they do, that the truth they emphasize refutes the Marxist claim. The bourgeois thinkers go wrong not when they say that the worker is free to sell his labour power, but when they infer that the Marxist cannot therefore be right in his claim that the worker is forced to. And Marxists[10] share the bourgeois thinkers' error when they think it necessary to deny what the bourgeois thinkers say. If the worker is not free to sell his labour power, of what freedom is a foreigner whose work permit is removed deprived? Would not the Marxists who wrongly deny that workers are free to sell their labour power nevertheless protest, inconsistently, that such disfranchised foreigners have been deprived of a freedom?

4. The disputants in section 3 failed to see that if a person is forced to do *A*, then he is free to do it (thesis *T*). They tended, indeed, to assert the opposite implication, that if he is forced to do *A*, then he is *not* free to do it. The Left, affirming as it did the antecedent of that implication, wrongly therefore affirmed its consequent; while the Right, being certain of the falsehood of the consequent, wrongly inferred that the antecedent is false too. In the present section we shall find once again that a shared mistake structures the Left/Right disagreement.

A Leftist convinced by the argument of section 3 might say that, although John was free to take a hazardous job, he was not free not to: he was not free to do something else instead. The response rests on the plausible principle that if a person is forced to do *A*, then there is no *B* which he is free to do instead. But that principle, though plausible, is questionable, and, if it were sound, then Right could exploit it against Left, as follows.

The Right could point out that someone like John can, after all, go on the dole, or beg, or make no provision for himself and trust to fortune, or, perhaps, take a less hazardous job which pays him

---

[10] Such as Ziyad Husami, if he is a Marxist, who says of the wage-worker: 'Deprived of the ownership of means of production and means of livelihood he is forced (not free) to sell his labour power to the capitalist' ('Marx on Distributive Justice', 51–2). I contend that the phrase in parentheses introduces a falsehood into Husami's sentence, a falsehood which Karl Marx avoided when he said of the worker that 'the period of time for which he is free to sell his labour power is the period of time for which he is forced to sell it' (*Capital*, i. 415; cf. p. 932: 'the wage-labourer . . . is compelled to sell himself of his own free will').

rather less money. No one would have prevented John from taking these courses. Therefore he was free to take them. Therefore, on the plausible principle the Left advanced, he was not forced to contract as he did.

But the principle is incorrect, and the Right's inference is therefore fallacious. To infer from the fact that John was free to do other things that he was therefore not forced to take a hazardous job is to employ a false account of what it is to be forced to do something. When a person is forced to do something he has no *reasonable* or *acceptable* alternative course. He need not have no alternative at all.

I think, moreover, that, if not always, then almost always, *when someone is forced to do something there is an alternative to what he is forced to do which he is free to do* (thesis T'). Consider two ways in which Smith, who wants Jones out of the room, might contrive to achieve his aim. Smith might drag Jones over to the door and push him out, thereby, as we say, *forcing* him out of the room. Or he might get Jones to leave by credibly threatening to shoot him unless he does. Now in the second case, but not the first, it is natural to say that Jones is forced *to leave* the room. Only in the second case is there something which Jones is forced to *do*, since in the first case he does nothing, or nothing relevant: he is just pushed out. And I suggest that the contrast is connected with the fact that in the second case Jones has an alternative: he is free to stand fast and be shot. And I think that generalizes: whenever a person is forced to do something there is something else which he is free to do instead. Or, if that is not always so, then the exceptions are of a special kind. One kind of exception might be where a threat so paralyses someone's will that choosing otherwise is in some strong sense impossible for him. But I am not sure that he is even then *unfree* to choose otherwise, as opposed to *incapable* of choosing otherwise.

Those who do not agree that Jones is free to stand fast *may* be persuaded by the following argument, which departs from the premiss that Jones might, after all, though credibly threatened, stand fast, out of, say, irrationality or defiance. Now if Jones stands fast, he was free to stand fast: it is impossible to do what one is not free to do.[11] But his being free to stand fast could not depend on his

---

[11] The objection to this premiss which was raised on p. 242 above could also be raised here, but it can be dealt with as I dealt with it there.

actually standing fast, since there is nothing one is free to do only if one actually does it. If, before standing fast, he is, as he must be, free to stand fast, then that is a feature of his situation whether or not he proceeds to stand fast. So if, in particular, he is forced to leave, and does not stand fast, then standing fast was nevertheless an alternative he was free to perform.[12]

If I am right, to be forced to do *A* is, at least standardly, to be forced to *choose* to do *A*. Thus, when someone says, 'I was forced to do *A*: I had no other choice', the second part of his statement is, in the standard case, an ellipsis for something like 'I had no other choice worth considering'. Now when Leftists claim that John was forced to take a hazardous job, they are not using 'forced to' in a special, unstandard way, and they certainly do not mean that John's situation paralysed his will.[13] Hence the fact that John was free to do other things, so far from refuting the Leftist claim, is an entailment of it: the Leftist claim entails that there were other things John was free to do, but that none of them were acceptable alternatives.

5. Sometimes people respond to my defence of the strange but (as they seem to me) true theses *T* and *T'* by complaining that my arguments dull the distinction between force and freedom, which

---

[12] It would, I concede, be natural for him to say: 'I was not free to stand fast, since I would have been shot had I done so.' And it is in general natural to say of the unacceptable alternatives available when one is forced to do something that one is not free to take them, because of their costs. That is certainly a reason for denying *T'*, but I think that it is outweighed by the main reason for affirming it, which is the argument just given, and, in particular, its premiss that one cannot do what one is not free to do. (How might one who affirms *T'* contrive to explain the recalcitrant linguistic data? He might suggest that the person who says he was not free to stand fast is engaging in harmless hyperbole. The unhyberbolical truth is that he was much less than *entirely* free to stand fast. His freedom to stand fast was very restricted, and we understand him to mean that, and not that he was not at all free to stand fast, when he says what he does.)

[13] Leftists are not, that is, questioning John's capacity to make decisions but emphasizing the limited scope he has for using that capacity. A tendency to confuse these importantly distinct issues is revealed in the following passage: 'The very setting of a prison adds a coercive element which raises questions about the autonomous decision-making capacity of the prisoner. It is reasonable to assume that economic stress and the need for employment also represent a severe restriction of free choice.' (Hastings Center, *Occupational Health*, 3). Economically stringent circumstances restrict freedom regardless of the effect they have on agents' powers of decision. They can, indeed, have that further effect, but the Leftist claim about John does not entail that they do, and the claim is therefore not false if they do not.

lovers of freedom should keep sharp. But I do not say that since people who are forced to do things are really free anyway, it does not matter that they are forced to do them. On the contrary: I emphasize that constrained people are, necessarily, free in certain ways in order to prevent those who notice the freedoms (disadvantaged) workers have from concluding that they are therefore not forced to take (hazardous) jobs.

If we contemplate the abstract nouns 'force' and 'freedom' and never pick at the nits and grit of what we ordinarily say when we use the verbs and adjectives which give those nouns their semantic substance, we shall be apt to think that those who enjoy market freedom cannot, in the very course of exercising it, be suffering from appalling constraint. Yet many of them do suffer immense constraint, and immense lack of freedom. Note that I never said that he who is forced has freedom *and does not lack it*. I said that he who is forced to do *A* is free to do *A*, and is free to do some *B* different from *A*, but, and this is why he counts as forced to do *A*, is free to do no *C* which is an acceptable alternative to *A*. If that tripartite truth cannot be restated as a simple relationship between force (as such) and freedom (as such), that is not my fault, or the fault of ordinary language. Fault lies with those who expect the truth about complicated matters to be both simple and immediately available.

6. If I am right, the Rightist has to show not that John exercised a freedom when he took the hazardous job, nor even that he had alternatives, but that he had an *acceptable* or *reasonable* alternative.

Now the Rightist might grasp that nettle, by claiming that John *did* have an acceptable alternative. He might point out that workers whose situation was not better than John's managed nevertheless to escape it, by setting up for themselves in (initially) small business, or by leaving places like Hazelton for less toxic employment elsewhere. Whoever escapes from a situation like John's is free to escape it, and what makes him free is the existence of an opportunity which he seizes. It is not credible that in John's case *no* such opportunities existed. He was therefore as free to escape as similarly placed people who did escape manifestly were. So he had an acceptable alternative, and was not forced to take a hazardous job. Note that the conclusion is not merely that he was free to try to escape, for that might have been true even if there had been no actual opportunity to escape. The conclusion is that there existed opportunities for self-betterment which John was free to seize.

I now describe three Leftist replies to this argument, which render it moot. None of the replies refutes the Rightist argument.

(*a*) The Leftist might claim that there are fewer escapes from situations like John's than there are people in such situations, so that necessarily most like John will be unable to escape.

But even if that is so, the Leftist is wrong to infer that persons like John are therefore not free to escape. From the fact that not all people like John, taken collectively, are free to escape it does not follow that each such person is not free to escape. And as long as the number of others who are actually seeking escape is relatively small, so that there exist exits unclogged by would-be escapees, then all, taken distributively, are free to escape, since there is at least one unexploited opportunity for each to exploit.[14]

(*b*) The second Leftist reply is to say that it is unrealistic to expect most people in John's situation to escape it through self-employment or emigration since most of them lack appropriate inner resources, skills of self-presentation, and so on. They are consequently unable to seize whatever opportunities to escape there may be.

But the Rightist will answer: precisely so. Some people are not intelligent enough or enterprising enough to exploit opportunities, but that does not mean that they are constrained by their situation. They lack what ungoaled mediocre swimmers (see page 242 above) lack: capacity, not freedom. Accordingly, what the Leftist says here about John does not show that he was *forced* to take a hazardous job.

It is hard to evaluate this Rightist response. Return to the case of the swimmer. If Jimmy is a non-swimmer because he was deliberately denied swimming instruction normally granted to others, is he then, perhaps, not only incapable of swimming, but also unfree to? If the answer is Yes, then poor provision of education to disadvantaged people might make them count as unfree to do what their educational deprivation makes them incapable of doing.[15]

---

[14] There is much more to be said about the relationship between individual freedom and collective unfreedom, and I try to say some of it in the next chapter.

[15] *Occupational Health* (p. 3) mentions working-class preoccupation with the present at the expense of the future, the cause of which is the greater urgency of

(c) The Leftist of (b) rejects the principle that one is forced to do A only if one has no acceptable alternative, on the ground that one may be unable to seize an alternative which undoubtedly exists. A different Leftist accepts the stated principle but insists on a more careful way of describing alternatives, with a view to showing that there existed no acceptable alternative for John. This Leftist says that one must consider (as the Rightist did not) the costs and risks attaching to attempts to seize opportunities before judging that they constitute acceptable alternatives. It is dangerous to embark upon self-employment, since fledgeling enterprises often fail, and the costs of failure can be very severe: a worker who has tried and failed to establish a small business may be worse off than if he had not tried at all. Similar remarks apply to the drastic and chancy course of leaving family, friends, and community for possible employment elsewhere. Good exits may exist but, so the objection goes, it is difficult to know where they are, and the price of fruitless search for them is considerable. Accordingly, the expected utility[16] of attempting an alternative is normally too low to justify the statement that workers like John are not forced to take hazardous jobs.

Now, this objection raises complex issues, which are discussed in section 16 of the chapter which follows. If that discussion is sound, then John has no acceptable alternative to taking a hazardous job if and only if it is true *both* that the expected utility of trying another course is less than that of taking the hazardous job *and* that working at a hazardous job is a thoroughly bad thing to do. We may take it that hazardous employment is indeed thoroughly bad. Hence the risk objection succeeds if and only if disadvantaged workers in hazardous employment lack superior alternatives (in expected utility terms).

It is extremely difficult to tell whether or not they lack such alternatives. The relevant facts are too hard to get at, and hard to organize in an informative way; and they will, of course, vary with

present constraints, and one effect of which is a greater likelihood of remaining within those constraints. Since the situation of urgency which causes the psychological deficiency is imposed not by nature but by society, one might argue that this particular deficiency is an unfreedom. (See ch. 13, sect. 15 below for further discussion of the difference between unfreedom and incapacity.)

[16] The expected utility of a course of action is the sum of the products of the utility and probability of each of its possible outcomes.

the varying situations of workers. It follows that there is almost certainly no general answer to the question which forms the title of this chapter, and that there is probably no definite answer to it in a large number of individual cases either, since so many of the assessments required to settle the issue are contestable. I shall comment in a moment on the moral upshot of this indeterminacy.

7. But first I must remark on an important simplification which was implicit in the foregoing discussion. I took for granted that John *knew* what the hazards were of the job he accepted. This was a simplification, since in fact much hazard is revealed only after the contract has been signed, and a certain amount of managerial effort is directed at preventing its revelation.[17] (If workers controlled industry there might be less headlong rush into new products and processes with attention to hazard only after it has begun to display itself vividly.)

When workers are unaware of hazards inherent in jobs they take, that has implications, which I shall not try to trace here, for whether they take them freely, for how free they are when they take them, and so on. The following is no doubt a valid argument, at any rate on one reading of its conclusion, but only a fool would try to make ideological capital out of its conclusion—which is not to say that there exist no fools:

> John chose to work in factory F.
>
> Factory F is hazardous.

Therefore,

> John chose to work in a hazardous factory.

8. Whereas it is extremely unlikely that John contracted freely (see page 243 above, it is hard to say whether or not he was forced to contract as he did, since it is hard to say whether or not he had an acceptable alternative (see section 6 above). Philosophy cannot resolve the dispute between someone who says that John was not forced to take a hazardous job since he had the acceptable alternative of leaving Hazelton and seeking unhazardous employ-

[17] See Nicholas Ashford, *Crisis in the Workplace*, 16, 19, 28–9.

ment elsewhere, and someone who says that the stated alternative was not acceptable, since John would have had to break cherished ties of family, friendship, and community to take it, and he could not have been sure what he would have got elsewhere. But philosophy can display the conceptual background to disputes of that kind, and that is what I have tried to do.

Now participants in the seminar for which these remarks were originally prepared were asked 'what if anything follows ethically from our understanding of the facts about worker freedom and unfreedom?'[18] Since there is some obscurity as to what those facts are, one might think that it is also obscure what follows ethically from them. And one might then think that the answer to the normative question, question (iii) (is it morally acceptable that people like John are situated as they are?), must remain uncertain. But that reasoning embodies two mistakes.

The first mistake is to suppose that the *precise* truth about John's freedom and lack of it is morally significant. John has no asset except labour power, and unskilled labour power at that. The *broad* truth of the matter is that this severely restricts his freedom, and that broad truth has moral implications. But I do not think that we gain in morally relevant understanding by achieving a *precisely* correct description of John's situation from the point of view of freedom and constraint. A refined description of his condition in the language of force and freedom is irrelevant to the crucial moral question, which is whether it is *fair* that he is placed in his manifestly adverse circumstances.

And the second mistake in the reasoning described two paragraphs back is to suppose that the broad, and normatively *relevant*, truth about John and his freedom is normatively *decisive*. To think so is to misconstrue the relationship between freedom and justice. Questions of freedom do bear on questions of justice, but sometimes the bearing is highly indirect, and the particular question whether John is suffering from injustice would not be settled by a demonstration that he contracts unfreely and that he is forced to contract as he does.

The broad truth about John is that he is so placed that taking a job which ruins or threatens his health might be his best bet, while

---

[18] This chapter was originally presented at a seminar held at the Hastings Center in 1982. The quoted question comes from a letter to its prospective participants by Thomas Murray.

others are so placed that they can make money out of John's relative lack of freedom. That seems to be an injustice, but what if those others are morally legitimate owners of what they own? If capitalists are morally legitimate owners of means of production, then they have no obligation to offer workers jobs, and, *a fortiori*, no obligation to offer them salubrious jobs, whether or not those who take the unsalubrious ones actually offered to them are forced to do so. As far as I can see, the only relevant obligation of capitalists would be to abstain from the fraud so many of them in fact practise when they fail to advise workers of the dangers of the jobs on offer. (Someone might object that even if capitalists are not morally obliged to offer jobs, they are obliged to offer unhazardous ones *if* they offer jobs. But while there is no conceptual incoherence in that view, I cannot see any reason for adopting it, once it has been provided that jobs known to be hazardous are labelled as . such.)

Someone who believes in the moral rights of capitalists could acknowledge that John was forced to take a hazardous job and add that while his position was indeed unenviable, it is inevitable that some people's entitlements impose restrictions on other people's freedom. That is a thoroughly consistent position, though the most prominent philosophical defender of capitalists' rights, Robert Nozick, seems not to think so. For he argues, absurdly, that a person's freedom is impaired only when his choices are restricted by actions of others which are unjust. According to Nozick, as long as people do only what they are entitled to do, no one can be unfree as a result.[20]

But you cannot *both* deny that justice restricts freedom *and* claim that private property is just, since the institution of private property, like any other set of rules for holding and using things, both grants freedom *and* restricts it: owners of private property are only free to do as they wish with what they own because non-owners are unfree to. A more consistent Nozickian would acknowledge the unfreedom inherent in private property and defend the justice of particular holdings of private property on the basis of their moral pedigree. Private property, he would say, is

---

[20] See *Anarchy, State and Utopia*, 262. For criticism of Nozick's views on this matter see my 'Robert Nozick and Wilt Chamberlain', 151, and 'Illusions about Private Property and Freedom', 228–9. See also ch. 13, sect. 3 and ch. 14 p. 292 ff. below.

justly held, whatever may be its effect on non-owners' freedom, if it came into being justly and was transferred justly from person to person until it reached its present owner. That is what people like Nozick are really saying, when the rhetoric of freedom, to which they are not entitled, is removed.

Let us focus on the claim that private property is justly held if (among other things) it came into being justly. Two questions must be answered about the initial formation of private property if a Nozick-like defence of existing private property is to stand and if, therefore, the currently dominant philosophical rationale for capitalism is to display John's adverse situation as free of moral taint. The first question is, by what means, if any, *could* private property be legitimately formed? And the second is, was *actual* private property formed by any such means?[21]

We can be pretty confident that the answer to the second question will be No. Imagine a typical property owner in confrontation with a trespasser who challenges the owner's property right, and imagine too, rather unrealistically, that the property owner is both thoroughly honest and exceptionally well informed. Then the dialogue between him and the trespasser might go as follows:

OWNER. Get off my land!
TRESPASSER. What makes it yours?
O. I bought it from Smith.
T. How did Smith get it?
O. His father willed it to him.
T. And how did Smith senior come to have it?
O. It belonged to Alley Oop, who gave it to Smith senior in payment for services rendered.
T. How did Alley Oop get it?
O. He seized it and successfully fought off all comers.
T. Well, I wasn't born soon enough to be one of those comers, so I'll fight you for it now.

To this Owner's only possible response is to apply, if he can, the same superior force which made the thing private property in the first place. Only readers with more intellectual restraint than I am

---

[21] I ignore here the (surely unactualized) possibility that initial malformation in the generation of private property was rectified later: see Nozick, *Anarchy, State and Utopia*, 152–3, 230–1 on principles of rectification.

able to muster will dissent from the view that, if it was morally all right then for sheer force to make the land Oop's, it is morally all right now for sheer force to make it Trespasser's, so that, even if the land is now legitimately Owner's, that does Owner limited good, since it may also be legitimately taken from him. If, on the other hand, Oop's original seizing was not morally all right, then Owner's claim collapses. So either way Owner's claim is insecure, if it is historically based, given what the history was probably like.

Now Nozick does not say that sheer force, regardless of circumstances, legitimately makes public property private. His answer to the first question (see page 253 above) is, roughly, that private property is formed legitimately if and when someone appropriates what no one privately owns without thereby making anyone else worse off than he would have been had the thing remained not privately owned.[22] But this condition is too weak, for reasons I am unable to develop here: it ignores what would have happened had the thing been privately appropriated by some other person, and also what would have happened had socialist rules been imposed on the use of the thing. The only different possibility Nozick considers is that in which the thing remains in unstructured common use, and there are other relevant possibilities to be considered.[23]

Philosophers of the political Right used to defend unrestricted private property against Left and liberal criticism in debate governed by a shared acceptance of principles of need, merit, and desert. Nozick's rejection of such 'patterned' principles[24] in favour of a focus on the history of holdings was supposed to make the philosophical defence of private property easier. I do not think that it does.

[22] See ibid. 178 ff. If this is not Nozick's answer to that question, he has not, remarkably enough, publicly answered it.

[23] For an extended development of this point, see my 'Self-Ownership, World-Ownership, and Equality'.

[24] *Anarchy, State and Utopia*, 155 ff.

13

THE STRUCTURE OF PROLETARIAN
UNFREEDOM

1. According to Karl Marx, a member of a social class belongs to it by virtue of his position within social relations of production. In keeping with this formula, Marx defined the proletarian as the producer who has (literally or in effect) nothing to sell but his own labour power.[1] He inferred that the worker is *forced* to sell his labour power (on pain of starvation).

In this chapter I am not concerned with the adequacy of Marx's definition of working-class membership. I propose instead to assess the truth of the consequence he rightly or wrongly inferred from that definition. Is it true that workers are forced to sell their labour power?

This question is debated in the real world, by non-academic people. Supporters and opponents of the capitalist system tend to disagree about the answer to it. There is a familiar right-wing answer to it which I think has a lot of power. In this chapter I argue against Leftists who do not see the answer's power and against Rightists who do not see the answer's limitations.

2. Some would deny that workers are forced to sell their labour power, on the ground that they have other choices: the worker can go on the dole, or beg, or simply make no provision for himself and trust to fortune.

It is true that the worker is free to do these other things. The acknowledgment that he is free to starve to death gets its sarcastic power from the fact that he *is* free to starve to death: no one threatens to *make* him stay alive by, for example, force-feeding him. But to infer that he is therefore not forced to sell his labour power is to employ a false account of what it is to be forced to do something. When I am forced to do something I have no *reasonable* or *acceptable* alternative course. It need not be true that I have no alternative whatsoever. At least usually, when a person says, 'I was

---

[1] For elaboration of this definition and a defence of its attribution to Marx, see *KMTH*, 63–77, 222–3, 333–6.

forced to do it. I had no other choice,' the second part of the statement is elliptical for something like 'I had no other choice worth considering.' For in the most familiar sense of '*X* is forced to do *A*,' it is entailed that *X* is forced to *choose* to do *A*, and the claim that the worker is forced to sell his labour power is intended in that familiar sense. Hence the fact that he is free to starve or beg instead is not a refutation of the mooted claim: the claim entails that there are other (unacceptable) things he is free to do.[2]

3. Robert Nozick might grant that many workers have no acceptable alternative to selling their labour power, and he recognizes that they need not have no alternative at all in order to count as forced to do so. But he denies that having no acceptable alternative but to do *A* entails being forced to do *A*, no matter how bad *A* is, and no matter how much worse the alternatives are, since he thinks that to have no acceptable alternative means to be forced only when unjust actions help to explain the absence of acceptable alternatives. Property distributions reflecting a history of acquisition and exchange may leave the worker with no other acceptable option, but he is nevertheless not forced to sell his labour power, if the acquiring and exchanging were free of injustice.

Nozick's objection to the thesis under examination rests upon a moralized account of what it is to be forced to do something. It is a false account, because it has the absurd upshot that if a criminal's imprisonment is morally justified, he is then not forced to be in prison. We may therefore set Nozick's objection aside.[3]

4. There is, however, an objection to the claim that workers are forced to sell their labour power which does not depend upon a moralized view of what being forced involves. But before we come to it in section 5, I must explain how I intend the predicate 'is forced to sell his labour power.' The claim in which it figures here comes from Karl Marx. Now I noted that Marx characterized classes by

---

[2] For further defence and elaboration of that claim, see ch. 14, sect. 4 above.

[3] For Nozick's view, see *Anarchy, State and Utopia*, 262–4, and, for further criticism of it, the refs. at ch. 12 n. 20 above, and ch. 14, pp. 292–6 below. A partly similar critique of moralized accounts of force and freedom is given by David Zimmerman at 'Coercive Wage offers', 121–31.

reference to social relations of production, and the claim that workers are forced to sell their labour power is intended to satisfy that condition: it purports to say something about the proletarian's position in capitalist relations of production. But relations of production are, for Marxism, *objective*: what relations of production a person is in does not turn on his consciousness. It follows that if the proletarian is forced to sell his labour power in the relevant Marxist sense, then this must be because of his objective situation, and not merely because of his attitude to himself, his level of self-confidence, his cultural attainment, and so on. It is in any case doubtful that limitations in those subjective endowments can be sources of what interests us: unfreedom, as opposed to something similar to it but also rather different: incapacity. But even if diffidence and the like could be said to force a person to sell his labour power, that would be an irrelevant case here (except, perhaps, where personal subjective limitations are caused by capitalist relations of production, a possibility considered in section 15 below).

To be forced to do *A* by one's objective situation is to do it because of factors other than the subjective ones just mentioned. Many would insist that the proper source of force, and *a fortiori* of objective force, is action by other people, what they have done, or are doing, or what they would do were one to try to do *A*. I agree with Harry Frankfurt[4] that this insistence is wrong, but I shall accede to it in the present chapter, for two reasons. The first is that the mooted restriction makes it harder, and therefore more interesting, to show that workers are forced to sell their labour power. The second is that, as I shall now argue, where relations of production force people to do things, people force people to do things, so the 'no force without a forcing agent' condition is satisfied here, even if it does not hold generally.

The relations of production of a society may be identified with the powers its differently situated persons have with respect to the society's productive forces, that is, the labour capacities of its producers and the means of production they use.[5] We can

---

[4] Frankfurt points out that natural things and processes operating independently of human action also force people to do things. See his 'Coercion and Moral Responsibility', 83–4. (Note that one can agree with Frankfurt while denying that lack of capacity restricts freedom: the question whether internal obstacles restrict it is distinct from the question which kinds of external obstacles do.)

[5] See *KMTH* 31–5, 63–5, 217–25; ch. 1, p. 5 ff.

distinguish between standard and deviant uses of the stated powers. Let me then propose that a worker is forced to sell his labour power in the presently required sense if and only if the constraint is a result of standard exercises of the powers constituting relations of production.

If a millionaire is forced by a blackmailer to sell his labour power, he is not forced to do so in the relevant Marxist sense, since the blackmailer does not use economic power to get him to do so. The relevant constraint must reflect use of economic power, and not, moreover, just any use of it, but a *standard* exercise of it. I do not know how to define 'standard', but it is not hard to sort out cases in an intuitive way. If, for example, a capitalist forces people to work for him by hiring gunmen to get them to do so, the resulting constraint is due to a non-standard exercise of economic power. And one can envisage similarly irrelevant cases of relaxation of constraint: a philanthropic capitalist might be willing to transfer large shares in the ownership of his enterprise to workers, on a 'first come first served' basis. That would not be a standard use of capitalist power.

Suppose, however, that economic structural constraint does not, as just proposed, operate through the regular exercise by persons of the powers constituting the economic structure, but in some more *im*personal way, as Althusserians seem to imagine. It might still be said, for a different reason, that if the structure of capitalism leaves the worker no choice but to sell his labour power, then he is forced to do so by actions of persons. For the structure of capitalism is not in all senses self-sustaining. It is sustained by a great deal of intentional human action, notably on the part of the functionaries of the state. Since the state deliberately protects the property of the capitalist class, the structural constraint by virtue of which the worker must sell his labour power has enough human will behind it to satisfy the stipulation that where there is force, there are forcing human beings.

The latter stipulation would be satisfied by doctrine weaker than that which presents the state as an *instrument* of the capitalist class. Suppose that the state upholds the capitalist order not because it is a *capitalist* order, but because it is the prevailing order, and the state is dedicated to upholding whatever order prevails. That relatively weak claim suffices to secure the contention that workers are forced to sell their labour power in face of the insistence that no one is forced unless somebody forces.[6]

5. Under the stated interpretation of 'is forced to sell his labour power', a serious problem arises for the thesis under examination. For if there are persons whose objective position is identical with that of proletarians but who are not forced to sell their labour power, then proletarians are not relevantly so forced, and the thesis is false. And there do seem to be such persons.

I have in mind those proletarians who, initially possessed of no greater resources than most, secure positions in the petty bourgeoisie and elsewhere, thereby rising above the proletariat. Striking cases in Britain are members of certain immigrant groups, who arrive penniless, and without good connections, but who propel themselves up the class hierarchy with effort, skill, and luck. One thinks—it is a contemporary example—of those who are willing to work very long hours in shops bought from native British petty bourgeois, shops which used to close early. Their initial capital is typically an amalgam of savings, which they accumulated, perhaps painfully, while still in the proletarian condition, and some form of external finance. *Objectively speaking*, most[7] British proletarians are in a position to obtain these. Therefore most British proletarians are not forced to sell their labour power.

6. I now refute two predictable objections to the above argument. The first says that the recently mentioned persons were, *while*

---

[6] For a more developed, and brilliant, account of structural force, which also satisfies the 'no force without a forcing agent' requirement see Jeffrey Reiman's 'Exploitation' 11–18. I disagree with Reiman's account of structural force with respect to only one of its claims: I do not think that he is right (see ibid. 15, 39) that a person can be forced to do A even when he has an acceptable alternative to doing A (though he can, of course, be forced to choose *between* A and such an alternative). I do not agree that Reiman's stage-coach passenger (ibid. 15) has an acceptable alternative to yielding his cash to the outlaw, since he has a 'decided preference' against all his alternatives to that course, each of which is thoroughly bad. (See the definition of 'acceptable alternative' offered in section 16 below.)

[7] At least most: it could be argued that *all* British proletarians are in such a position, but I stay with 'most' lest some ingenious person discover objective proletarian circumstances worse than the worst once suffered by now prospering immigrants. But see also n. 8 below.

they were proletarians, forced to sell their labour power. Their cases do not show that proletarians are not forced to sell their labour power. They show something different: that proletarians are not forced to remain proletarians.

This objection illegitimately contracts the scope of the Marxist claim that workers are forced to sell their labour power. But before I say what Marxists intend by that statement, I must defend this general claim about freedom and constraint: *fully explicit attributions of freedom and constraint contain two temporal indexes.* To illustrate: I may now be in a position truly to say that I am free to attend a concert tomorrow night, since nothing has occurred, up to now, to prevent my doing so. If so, I am *now* free to attend a concert *tomorrow night*. In similar fashion, the time when I am constrained to perform an action need not be identical with the time of the action: I might *already* be forced to attend a concert *tomorrow night* (since you might already have ensured that if I do not, I shall suffer some great loss).

Now when Marxists say that proletarians are forced to sell their labour power, they mean more than 'X is a proletarian at time t only if X is at t forced to sell his labour power at t'; for that would be compatible with his not being forced to at time $t + n$, no matter how small n is. X might be forced on Tuesday to sell his labour power on Tuesday, but if he is not forced on Tuesday to sell his labour power on Wednesday (if, for example, actions open to him on Tuesday would bring it about that on Wednesday he need not do so), then, though still a proletarian on Tuesday, he is not then someone who is forced to sell his labour power in the relevant Marxist sense. The manifest intent of the Marxist claim is that the proletarian is forced at t to *continue* to sell his labour power, throughout a period from t to $t + n$, for some considerable n. It follows that because there is a route out of the proletariat, which our counter-examples travelled, reaching their destination in, as I would argue, an amount of time less than n,[8] they were, though

---

[8] This might well be challenged, since the size of n is a matter of judgment. I would defend mine by reference to the naturalness of saying to a worker that he is not forced to (continue to) sell his labour power, since he can take steps to set himself up as a shopkeeper. Those who judge otherwise might be able, at a pinch, to deny that most proletarians are not forced to sell their labour power, but they cannot dispose of the counter-examples to the generalization that all are forced to. For our prospective petty bourgeois is a proletarian on the eve of his ascent when, unless, absurdly, we take n as O, he is not forced to sell his labour power.

proletarians, not forced to sell their labour power in the required Marxist sense.

Proletarians who have the option of class ascent are not forced to continue to sell their labour power, just because they do have that option. Most proletarians have it as much as our counter-examples did. Therefore most proletarians are not forced to sell their labour power.[9]

7. But now I face a second objection. It is that necessarily not more than a few proletarians can exercise the option of upward movement. For capitalism requires a substantial hired labour force, which would not exist if more than just a few workers rose.[10] Put differently, there are necessarily only enough petty bourgeois and other non-proletarian positions for a small number of the proletariat to leave their estate.

I agree with the premiss, but does it defeat the argument against which it is directed? Does it refute the claim that most proletarians are not forced to sell their labour power? I think not.

An analogy will indicate why I do not think so. Ten people are placed in a room, the only exit from which is a huge and heavy

---

[9] The foregoing section is reproduced from the article forming the basis of this chapter and the objection predicted in its first sentence occurs in more developed form in sect. 3 of Reiman's 'Exploitation', which I think substantially misguided. I disagree with Reiman's contention (p. 35) that 'the charge that capitalism is slavery of some sort can stand on the synchronic claim independent of the diachronic', where the synchronic claim says that the proletarian is forced to sell his labour power in order to get his next meal (see ibid. 32) and the diachronic one says that he is forced to continue to sell it in the sense that that is his enduring fate. *Pace* Reiman, the Marxian characterization of the proletarian condition is false if workers are not locked into their situations, if each can turn himself into a non-worker in, say, one week (which is consistent with the synchronic claim). What Reiman calls the 'permeability of the barriers around and between . . . classes' is partly constitutive of class positions themselves. (*KMTH* was rightly criticized on that score by Jon Elster at *Making Sense of Marx*, 343–4, and Elster's point also applies against Reiman's distinction between what it is to belong to a certain class and how easy it is to get out of it.) A complete description of pre-capitalist guild class structure must specify whether or not a journeyman can expect one day to be a master; and if proletarianhood were, in general, a kind of temporary apprenticeship, then the class structure of capitalism would not be what Marxists say it is.

[10] 'The truth is this, that in this bourgeois society every workman, if he is an exceedingly clever and shrewd fellow, and gifted with bourgeois instincts and favoured by an exceptional fortune, can possibly convert himself into an *exploiteur du travail d'autrui*. But if there were no *travail* to be *exploité*, there would be no capitalist nor capitalist production' (Karl Marx, 'Results of the Immediate Process of Production', 1079). For commentary on similar texts see *KMTH* 243.

locked door. At various distances from each lies a single heavy key. Whoever picks up this key—and each is physically able, with varying degrees of effort, to do so—and takes it to the door will find, after considerable self-application, a way to open the door and leave the room. But if he does so he alone will be able to leave it. Photoelectric devices installed by a gaoler ensure that it will open only just enough to permit one exit. Then it will close, and no one inside the room will be able to open it again.

It follows that, whatever happens, at least nine people will remain in the room.

Now suppose that not one of the people is inclined to try to obtain the key and leave the room. Perhaps the room is no bad place, and they do not want to leave it. Or perhaps it is pretty bad, but they are too lazy to undertake the effort needed to escape. Or perhaps no one believes he would be able to secure the key in face of the capacity of the others to intervene (though no one would in fact intervene, since, being so diffident, each also believes that he would be unable to remove the key from anyone else). Suppose that, whatever may be their reasons, they are all so indisposed to leave the room that if, counterfactually, one of them were to try to leave, the rest would not interfere. The universal inaction is relevant to my argument, but the explanation of it is not.

Then whomever we select, it is true of the other nine that not one of them is going to try to get the key. Therefore it is true of the selected person that he is free to obtain the key, and to use it.[11] He is therefore not forced to remain in the room. But all this is true of whomever we select. Therefore it is true of each person that he is not forced to remain in the room, even though necessarily at least nine will remain in the room, and in fact all will.

Consider now a slightly different example, a modified version of the situation just described. In the new case there are two doors and two keys. Again, there are ten people, but this time one of them does try to get out, and succeeds, while the rest behave as before. Now necessarily eight will remain in the room, but it is true of each

---

[11] For whatever may be the correct analysis of 'X is free to do A', it is clear that X is free to do A if X would do A if he tried to do A, and that sufficient condition of freedom is all that we need here. (Some have objected that the stated condition is not sufficient: a person, they say, may do something he is not free to do, since he may do something he is not legally, or morally, free to do. Those who agree with that unhelpful remark can take it that I am interested in the non-normative use of 'free', which is distinguished by the sufficient condition just stated.)

of the nine who do stay that he or she is free to leave it. The pertinent general feature, present in both cases, is that there is at least one means of egress which none will attempt to use, and which each is free to use, since, *ex hypothesi*, no one would block his way.

By now the application of the analogy may be obvious. The number of exits from the proletariat is, as a matter of objective circumstance, small. But most proletarians are not trying to escape, and, as a result, *it is false that each exit is being actively attempted by some proletarian*. Therefore for most[12] proletarians there exists a means of escape. So even though necessarily most proletarians will remain proletarians, and will sell their labour power, perhaps none, and at most a minority, are forced to do so.

In reaching this conclusion, which is about the proletariat's *objective* position, I used some facts of consciousness, regarding workers' aspirations and intentions. That is legitimate. For if workers are objectively forced to sell their labour power, then they are forced to do so whatever their subjective situation may be. But their actual subjective situation brings it about that they are not forced to sell their labour power. Hence they are not objectively forced to sell their labour power.

8. One could say, speaking rather broadly, that we have found more freedom in the proletariat's situation than classical Marxism asserts. But if we return to the basis on which we affirmed that most proletarians are not forced to sell their labour power, we shall arrive at a more refined description of the objective position with respect to force and freedom. What was said will not be withdrawn, but we shall add significantly to it.

That basis was the reasoning originally applied to the case of the people in the locked room. Each is free to seize the key and leave. But note the conditional nature of his freedom. He is free not only *because* none of the others tries to get the key, but *on condition* that they do not (a condition which, in the story, is fulfilled). Then *each is free only on condition that the others do not exercise their similarly conditional freedom*. Not more than one can exercise the liberty they all have. If, moreover, any one were to exercise it, then, because of the structure of the situation, all the others would lose it.

---

[12] See nn. 7, 8 above.

Since the freedom of each is contingent on the others not exercising their similarly contingent freedom, we can say that there is a great deal of unfreedom in their situation. Though each is individually free to leave, he suffers with the rest from what I shall call *collective unfreedom*.

In defence of that description, let us reconsider the question why the people do not try to leave. None of the reasons suggested earlier—lack of desire, laziness, diffidence—go beyond what a person wants and fears for himself alone. But sometimes people care about the fate of others, and they sometimes have that concern when they share a common oppression. Suppose, then, not so wildly, that there is a sentiment of solidarity in that room. A fourth possible explanation of the absence of attempt to leave now suggests itself. It is that no one will be satisfied with a personal escape which is not part of a general liberation.[13]

The new supposition does not upset the claim that each is free to leave, for we may assume that it remains true of each person that he would suffer no interference if, counterfactually, he sought to use the key (assume that the others would have contempt for him, but not try to stop him). So each remains free to leave. Yet we can envisage members of the group communicating to their gaoler a demand for freedom, to which he could hardly reply that they are free already (even though, individually, they are). The hypothesis of solidarity makes the collective unfreedom evident. But unless we say, absurdly, that the solidarity creates the unfreedom to which it is a response, we must say that there is collective unfreedom whether or not solidarity obtains.

Returning to the proletariat, we can conclude, by parity of reasoning, that although most proletarians are free to escape the proletariat, and, indeed, even if every one is, the proletariat is collectively unfree, an imprisoned class.

[13] In a stimulating commentary on the argument of sects. 7 and 8, Jon Elster notes that it involves avoidance of two fallacies, that of composition ('What is true of each must be true of all') and that of division ('What is true of all must be true of each'): 'It is true of any individual worker that he is free to leave the class, but not of all workers simultaneously. And the reason why the individual worker is free to leave the class is that the others do not want to leave it; and the reason why the others do not want to leave it is that whatever is desirable if it happens to all members simultaneously is not necessarily desirable if it happens to one member separately and exclusively' (first draft of paper on 'Freedom and Power', 63). Elster shows that such structures pervade social life.

Marx often maintained that the worker is forced to sell his labour power not to any particular capitalist, but just to some capitalist or other, and he emphasized the ideological value of that distinction.[14] The present point is that although, in a collective sense, workers are forced to sell their labour power, scarcely any particular proletarian is forced to sell himself even to some capitalist or other. And this too has ideological value. It is part of the genius of capitalist exploitation that, by contrast with exploitation which proceeds by 'extra-economic compulsion',[15] it does not require the unfreedom of specified individuals. There is an ideologically valuable anonymity on *both* sides of the relationship of exploitation.

9. It was part of the argument for affirming the freedom to escape of proletarians, taken individually, that not every exit from the proletariat is crowded with would-be escapees. Why should this be so? Here are some of the reasons:

1. It is possible to escape, but it is not easy, and often people do not attempt what is possible but hard.

2. There is also the fact that long occupancy, for example from birth, of a subordinate class position nurtures the illusion, which is as important for the stability of the system as the myth of easy escape, that one's class position is natural and inescapable.

3. Finally, there is the fact that not all workers would like to be petty or trans-petty bourgeois. Eugene Debs said 'I do not want to rise above the working class, I want to rise with them', thereby evincing an attitude like the one lately attributed to the people in the locked room. It is sometimes true of the worker that, in Brecht's words,

> He wants no servants under him
> And no boss over his head.[16]

Those lines envisage a better liberation: not just from the working class, but from class society.

---

[14] See *KMTH* 223 for exposition and references.
[15] The phrase comes from Marx, *Capital*, iii. 926. See *KMTH* 82–4 for a discussion of different modes of exploitation.
[16] From his 'Song of the United Front'.

10. In the rest of this chapter I consider objections to the arguments of sections 7 and 8, which I shall henceforth call argument 7 and argument 8, after the numbers of the sections in which they were presented. Shorn of expository detail, the arguments are as follows:

> 7. There are more exits from the British proletariat than there are workers trying to leave it. Therefore, British workers are individually free to leave the proletariat.

> 8. There are very few exits from the British proletariat and there are very many workers in it. Therefore, British workers are collectively unfree to leave the proletariat.

In the useful language of the medieval schoolmen, the workers are not forced to sell their labour power *in sensu diviso*, but they are forced to *in sensu composito*.

The arguments are consistent with one another. Hillel Steiner has pointed to a potential conflict between them, but it is unlikely to materialize. The potential conflict relates to my attribution to Marxism (see section 6) of the claim that the worker is forced to remain a worker for some considerable amount of time n, a claim which the conclusion of argument 7 is intended to deny. Now, the larger n is, the easier it is to refute the Marxist claim and affirm argument 7's conclusion. But as n grows larger, the number of exits from the proletariat increases, and the conclusion of argument 8 becomes correspondingly less secure. To sustain both arguments without equivocation one must choose an intuitively plausible n under these opposite pressures. But it is not hard to meet that requirement: five years, for example, will do.

Right-wing readers will applaud argument 7, but they will want to resist argument 8. Left-wing readers will have, in each case, the opposite reaction. In the remaining seven sections I deal first with four right-wing objections to argument 8, and then with three left-wing objections to argument 7.[17]

A one-premiss argument may be challenged in respect of its premiss, its inference, and, independently of the way it is drawn, its conclusion. Section 11 considers the inference of argument 8; sections 12 and 13 examine whether its conclusion is true, or, if

---

[17] Further left-wing objections to argument 7 have been pressed by George Brenkert in his 'Cohen on Proletarian Unfreedom'. I think they are misconceived, and I explain why in 'Are Workers Forced to Sell their Labour Power?'

true, interesting; and section 14 investigates its premiss. In sections 15 and 16 the inference of argument 7 is challenged, and in section 17 its premiss is scrutinized.

11. Someone who, unlike Frankfurt, believes that only human action can force people to do things, might object as follows to the derivation of the conclusion of argument 8, that British workers are collectively unfree. 'The prisoners in the room are collectively unfree, since the availability of only one exit is a result of a gaoler's action. If they had wandered into a cave from which, for peculiar reasons, only one could leave, then, though *unable*, collectively, to leave, they would not have been *unfree* to, since there would have been no one forcing them to stay. It is true that, *in sensu composito*, most proletarians must remain proletarians, but that is due to a numerical relationship which does not reflect human design. It is therefore not correct to speak of the proletariat as collectively *unfree* to leave, as opposed to collectively *unable*. In short, the restrictions on proletarian ascent are not caused by factors which would justify application of the concepts of force and unfreedom.'

I have four replies to this objection.

First, what was said about the cave, if it illustrates the thesis that people are forced only when people force them, also shows how unlikely a thesis that is. For it seems false that the hapless wanderers are forced to remain in the cave only if someone put them there, or keeps them there.

It is, moreover, arguable that the (anyhow questionable) requirement of a forcing human agency is met in the cave case. I say that there is collective unfreedom to leave in that as soon as one person left, the rest would be prevented from doing so. And just as there is individual unfreedom when a person's attempt to do A would be blocked by someone else doing it, so there is collective unfreedom when an attempt by more than n to do A would be blocked by that subset of n which succeeded in doing it. This applies to the proletariat, when the number of exits is limited. They are collectively unfree since, were more to try to escape than there are exits, the successful would ensure the imprisonment of those who failed.

But apart from the mutual constraint arising out of the surplus of persons over exits, there is the fact that the adverse numerical relationship reflects the structure of capitalism which, we saw in section 4, is sufficiently connected, in various ways, with human actions to satisfy the un-Frankfurtian scruples motivating the present objection. Proletarians suffer restricted access to means of liberation because the rights of private property are enforced by exercise of capitalist power.

Finally, even if we should have to abandon the claim that workers are collectively unfree to escape and embrace instead the idea that they are collectively unable to, the withdrawal would be only a tactical one. For anyone concerned about human freedom and the prospect of expanding it must also care about structurally induced disability (or whatever he chooses to call it), which he refuses to regard as absence of freedom. Even if he is right that the wanderers are not *forced* to stay in the cave, he surely cannot deny that whoever released them would be *liberating* them.

12. The objector of section 11 doubted that the situation of the proletariat could be described as one of collective unfreedom, but he did not challenge the very concept of a collective unfreedom distinct from individual unfreedom. I now deal with a differently inspired scepticism. Set aside the question of what causes the restriction on the number of non-proletarian positions. Does the resulting lack of access justify my description of the workers as lacking collective freedom? I argued that there is some sense in which they are not all free to escape, and, since they are free *in sensu diviso*, I called their unfreedom collective unfreedom.

Collective unfreedom can be defined as follows: a group suffers collective unfreedom with respect to a type of action A if and only if performance of A by all members of the group is impossible.[18] Collective unfreedom comes in varying amounts, and it is greater the smaller the ratio of the maximum that could perform A to the total number in the group. Collective unfreedom is particularly interesting when, as in our example, there is more freedom for a set of individuals taken individually than for the same individuals when they are taken as members of a group: collective unfreedom,

---

[18] That is, if and only if it is not possible that for all X, X performs A (even if for all X, it is possible that X performs A). One might also have to specify the kind of cause that makes it impossible, a complication discussed in sect. 11 above and here set aside.

we might say, is *irreducibly* collective when more can perform *A in sensu diviso* than can perform it *in sensu composito*. And collective unfreedom matters more the smaller the ratio mentioned above is, and the more important or desirable action *A* is.

A person shares in a collective unfreedom when, to put it roughly, he is among those who are so situated that if enough others exercise the corresponding individual freedom, then they lose their individual freedoms. More precisely: *X* shares in a collective unfreedom with respect to a type of action *A* if and only if *X* belongs to a set of *n* persons which is such that:

1. No more than *m* of them (where *m* < *n*) are free (*in sensu composito*) to perform *A*,

and

2. no matter which *m* members performed *A*, the remaining *n* − *m* would then be unfree (*in sensu diviso*) to perform *A*.[19]

Using both expressions as terms of art, one might distinguish between *collective* unfreedom and *group* unfreedom, and I am not here concerned with the latter. In the proffered definition of collective unfreedom the relevant agents are individuals, not a group as such. We are not discussing freedom and the lack of it which groups have *qua* groups, but which individuals have as members of groups. Thus, for example, the freedom or lack of it which the proletariat has to overthrow capitalism falls outside our scope,[20] since no individual proletarian could ever be free to overthrow capitalism, even when the proletariat is free to do so.

Another form of essentially interpersonal freedom is that canonically reported in sentences of the form '*X* is free to do *A* with *Y*,' where *Y* is another agent, and where if *X* does *A* with *Y*, then *Y* does *A* with *X* (the last condition is needed to exclude such actions as wiping the floor with *Y*: 'with' means 'together with' in sentences of the indicated form). This can be called *freedom-to-act-with*, or *relational freedom*.[21] Note that the relevant relation is neither symmetrical nor transitive. If I am free to do *A* with you, it does not

---

[19] The concept of sharing in a collective unfreedom might be used in an attempt to define the proletariat, for example, as the largest group in a society all members of which share a collective unfreedom with respect to the sale of labour power.

[20] See *KMTH* 243–5 for remarks on that issue.

[21] Robert Ware brought the important concept of relational freedom to my attention.

follow that you are free to do *A* with me, since, for example, doing *A* might be seeing a film which you would love to see with me but which I do not want to see. And if I am free to make love with you and you are free to make love with him, it does not follow that I am free to make love with him. Freedom-to-act-with figured implicitly in the argument of section 8, when I hypothesized a sentiment of solidarity which moved each person in the room to regret that (though free to leave) he was not free-to-leave-with the others. But freedom-to-act-with is different from what is here meant by collective freedom: in the case of the latter there need be no reference to another person in the description of the action people are free or unfree to perform.

Now someone might say: Since irreducibly collective unfreedom obtains only when individuals are free, why should it be a source of concern? Why should we care about anything other than the freedom of individuals?[22] The question forgets that it is a fact touching each individual in the group, namely, the mutually conditional nature of their freedom, which licenses the idea of collective unfreedom. As soon as enough people exercise the coexisting individual freedoms, collective unfreedom generates individual unfreedoms. If, though free to do *A*, I share in a collective unfreedom with respect to *A*, I am less free than I otherwise would be.

But it might be claimed that there are structures manifesting what I defined as collective unfreedom which would not normally be regarded as examples of lack of freedom. Suppose, for instance, that a hotel, at which one hundred tourists are staying, lays on a coach trip for the first forty who apply, since that is the number of seats in the coach. And suppose that only thirty want to go. Then, on my account, each of the hundred is free to go, but their situation displays a collective unfreedom. Yet it seems wrong, the objector says, to speak of unfreedom here.

I do not agree. For suppose that all of the tourists did want to go. Then it would seem appropriate to say that they are not all free to go. But in the case of individual freedom, while there is less reason

---

[22] One might reply: Because there are some things which we may hope groups are free to do which we would not expect, or would not want, individuals to be free to do. But that answer is out of place here, because of the distinction just drawn between group and collective freedom.

to regret an unfreedom to do what I have no desire to do,[23] I am not less unfree for lacking that desire.[24] Why should the position be different in the case of collective unfreedom? Thwarted desire throws unfreedom into relief, and sometimes thwarted desire is needed to make unfreedom deserving of note, but it is not a necessary condition of unfreedom.

The coach case is a rather special one. For we tend to suppose that the management lay on only one coach because they correctly anticipate that one will be enough to meet the demand. Accordingly, we also suppose that if more had wanted to go, there would have been an appropriately larger number of seats available. If all that is true, then the available amount of collective freedom non-accidentally accords with the tourists' desires, and though there still is a collective unfreedom, it is, as it were, a purely technical one. But if we assume that there is only one coach in town, and some such assumption is required for parity with the situation of proletarians, then the tourists' collective unfreedom is more than merely technical.

There are two significantly different variants of the merely technical version of the coach case. In the first the management decide how many coaches to order after first asking each tourist whether or not he wants to go. In that case there is a time at which all are free to go, even *in sensu composito*, though they cease to be after they have declared themselves.[25] But the management might order one coach without consulting the tourists, out of knowledge of the normal distribution of tourist desire. In that case there is no time at which all are free to go, *in sensu composito*, but the collective unfreedom is still purely technical and singularly unregrettable.

Now someone who accepts my concept of collective unfreedom might argue that it is not in general a lamentable thing, and that it

---

[23] Less reason, but not no reason, since the desire for freedom is not reducible to the desire to do what one would be free to do if one had it. I may resent my lack of freedom to do what I have no wish to do: Soviet citizens who dislike restrictions on foreign travel need not want to go abroad.

[24] See Isaiah Berlin, *For Essays on Liberty*, pp. xxxviii ff. 139–40; Hillel Steiner, 'Individual Liberty', 34. But see Elster, *Sour Grapes*, 127 ff. for a good challenge to the claim defended by those authors.

[25] That is, there is a time t at which they are all free to go at $t + n$, and a time $t + (n-m)$ at which they are not all free to go at $t + n$, where $m > m > 0$. See sect. 6 on the need to refer twice to time in fully explicit specifications of freedom.

need not be lamentable even when the amount of collective unfreedom is not, as above, directly or indirectly causally connected, in a benign way, with people's desires. There is at present (or was when I first wrote this) a shortage of bus conductors in London, so that there is a good deal of individual freedom to become one, but also a large amount of collective unfreedom, since not more than very few of us can be bus conductors. But so what?

The rhetorical question is apposite in this case, but it is out of place when there is unfreedom to abstain from selling one's labour power to another. As I remarked earlier, the extent to which collective unfreedom with respect to an action matters depends upon the nature of the action. I grant that collective unfreedom with respect to the sale of labour power is not lamentable merely because it is collective unfreedom, since some collective unfreedom, like some individual unfreedom, is not lamentable. It is what this particular collective unfreedom forces workers to do which makes it a proper object of regret and protest. They are forced to subordinate themselves to others who thereby gain control over their, the workers', productive existence. The contrast between them and those others is the subject of the next section.

13. In an argument which does not challenge the concept of collective unfreedom, Hillel Steiner and Jan Narveson[26] say that if there is a sense in which capitalism renders workers unfree, then it does the same to capitalists. For if having no choice but to sell his labour power makes the worker unfree, then the capitalist is similarly unfree, since he has no choice but to invest his capital. Sometimes authors sympathetic to Marx say similar things. Thus Gary Young argues that the 'same line of reasoning' which shows that 'the worker is compelled to sell his labour power to some capitalist . . . shows equally that the capitalist is compelled to obtain labour power from the worker'.[27]

I shall presently question the claim that capitalists are forced to invest their capital. But even if we suppose that they are, the disanalogy between them and the workers remains so great that the Steiner/Narveson challenge must be judged rather insensitive.

[26] In separate personal correspondence.
[27] From p. 448 of his valuable article on 'Justice and Capitalist Production'.

For the worker is more closely connected with his labour power than the capitalist is with his capital. When I sell my labour power, I put *myself* at the disposal of another, and that is not true when I invest my capital. I come with my labour power, I am part of the deal.[28] That is why some people call wage labour wage slavery, and that is why John Stuart Mill said that 'to work at the bidding and for the profit of another . . . is not . . . a satisfactory state to human beings of educated intelligence, who have ceased to think themselves naturally inferior to those whom they serve.'[29] I am sure that many will think it an irresponsible exaggeration to call wage labour wage slavery. But note that no one would say, even by way of exaggeration, that having to invest one's capital is a form of slavery.

But Steiner and Narveson are not, in any case, entitled to say that capitalists are forced to invest their capital. To begin with, some are so rich that they could devote the rest of their days to spending it on consumer goods. But let us focus on the more modestly situated remainder. When Marxists claim that workers are forced to sell their labour power, they mean that they have no acceptable alternative, if they want to stay alive. But capitalists, some might say, do have an acceptable alternative to investing their capital: they are free to sell their labour power instead.[30] Of course, Steiner and Narveson, in order to defend their thesis, might deny that that is an acceptable alternative, and I, for other reasons, might agree. But if they take that line, then they should not have proposed their analogy in the first place. So either the capitalist is not forced to invest his capital, since he could, after all, sell his labour power; or, if he is, then that is because of how bad selling one's labour power is, in comparison with investing one's capital.[31]

It might be said that the capitalist is, *qua* capitalist, forced to invest his capital: in so far as he acts in that capacity, he has no

---

[28] 'The fact that labour and the labourer are inseparable creates certain difficulties', David O'Mahoney declares, but he reassures us that 'analytically labour is no different from any other resource the owners of which contract with the entrepreneur to use it for his purposes' ('Labour Management and the Market Economy', 30).

[29] *Principles of Political Economy*, 766.

[30] We can set aside the special case of a wholly infirm capitalist. If capitalists were in general unable to live except by investing their capital, their bargaining position *vis-à-vis* workers would be rather different.

[31] And not only in comparison with investing capital, but also absolutely, if the account of acceptability in alternatives in sect. 16 below is right.

other choice. But even if that is so—and I am not sure that it is—it is irrelevant. For while it is sometimes appropriate to deal with individuals 'only in so far as they are the personifications of economic categories',[32] that form of abstraction is out of place here. We are not here interested in the freedom and bondage of abstract characters, such as the capitalist *qua* capitalist. We are interested in *human* freedom, and hence in the human being who is a capitalist; and if the capitalist *qua* capitalist is forced to invest his capital, it does not follow that the human being who is a capitalist is forced to. It is also irrelevant, if true, that the capitalist is forced to invest his capital as long as he wants to be a capitalist. Note that, in order to confer plausibility on the claim that the worker is forced to sell his labour power, it is not necessary to stick in such phrases as '*qua worker*' or 'as long as he wants to be a worker.'

Those capitalists who are not dizzily rich are forced to invest their capital or sell their labour power. So they have an alternative to selling their labour power which the worker lacks. But they are not gods. Like the worker, they 'enter into relations that are indispensable and independent of their will'.[33] Everyone has to take capitalism as it is. But people have different amounts of choice about where to enter the set of relations it imposes, and capitalists typically have vastly more such choice than workers do.

In the foregoing discussion I did not observe the distinction between the freedom of capitalists *in sensu diviso* and their freedom *in sensu composito*, since the Steiner/Narveson objection is presented without reference to that distinction. We can, however, imagine an objection of the same general style which does make use of it. 'The individual capitalist may have more freedom of choice than the individual worker, but your own emphasis is not on the unfreedom of the worker taken as an individual, but on the unfreedom he shares with other members of his class. And if we look at capitalists as a class, we find a similar collective unfreedom. They could not *all* become sellers of labour power, since for there to be sellers of it there have to be buyers of it. Capitalists consequently suffer from a collective unfreedom parallel to that of workers.'

I have three replies to this objection.

Recall, first, that collective unfreedom comes in varying amounts (see page 268 above). Then note that, even if the objection is

---

[32] Marx, *Capital*, i. 92.
[33] Marx, Preface to the *Critique of Political Economy*, 20.

otherwise sound, it demonstrates much less collective unfreedom for capitalists than can be attributed to workers, since the members of any group of all but any (say) two or three of the capitalists are not structurally prevented from giving their wealth to those two or three. Mass escape from the proletariat, leaving only two or three workers behind, is, by contrast, structurally impossible.

But one can go further. It is unlikely that capitalists suffer *any* collective unfreedom with respect to becoming wage-workers, since if literally all capitalists wanted to do so, so that none of their number was willing to play the role of hirer, it would probably be easy to find workers willing and able to fill it.

Finally, the objection ignores a way in which capitalists could stop being capitalists *without* becoming wage-workers: by yielding their wealth not, as above, to particular others, but to sociey at large. I do not propose this as a new road to socialism, since it is a practical certainty that capitalists will not travel it.[34] My point is that there is no structural barrier against complete self-extinction of the capitalist class, whereas there is a structural barrier to mass exit from the proletariat: the capitalists own the means of production.

14. The final challenge from the Right to be considered here concerns the premiss of the argument of section 8: that there are not very many exits from the proletariat. The objector I have in mind grants that there cannot be general escape in the direction of the petty (and more than petty) bourgeoisie: workers could not become, *en masse*, shopkeepers and employers of other workers, if only because there would then be too few left to produce what shopkeepers sell. But the objector draws attention to a way out which has not yet been mentioned in this chapter: proletarians can form workers' co-operatives. There is enormous scope for the creation of such entities, and therefore virtually unlimited exit prospects. If, then, exiting is not widespread, the reason must be the fecklessness of workers, their unwillingness to undertake risks, and so on[35]

Note that this objection is not intended to support the conclusion

---

[34] 'A proposition is a practical certainty if its probability is so high as to allow us to reason, in *any* decision problem, as if its probability were 1' (Richard Jeffrey, 'Statistical Explanation vs. Statistical Inference', 105).

[35] See Nozick, *Anarchy, State and Utopia*, 255–6.

of argument 7, that workers are individually free to escape, which is a thesis I not only grant but defend. Fresh support for it comes from the plausible claim that there exist unexploited opportunities to form co-operatives. But the opportunities have to be very extensive indeed for the premiss of argument 8 to be affected, and hence for collective proletarian unfreedom to be substantially smaller than I have maintained. So when, in due course, I reply to the objection, by describing obstacles to the formation of co-operatives (such as the hostility to them of the capitalist class, which has a lot of power), my aim is not to deny that there are a goodly number of unexploited exits of this kind, but to assert that there are not, and could not be, enough to permit *mass* escape from the proletariat through them.

The objector might develop his case as follows: 'The rules of capitalism do not prohibit the formation of co-operatives. They confer on everyone the right to contract with whomsoever he pleases howsoever he pleases; they therefore give workers the right to contract with one another instead of with bosses, and the great recommendation of capitalism is that it (and not a society of workers' co-operatives) is what results when free contracting is allowed to proceed. Workers in a capitalist society are free to transform it into a society without capitalists, within the rules of capitalism itself (as opposed to through political revolution), but they choose not to do so.'

The first thing to say in reply is that procedures permitted by the rules might be extremely difficult to carry out, for objective reasons. There is, for example, a serious problem of co-ordination affecting the initial formation of co-operatives. There might be many workers each of whom would be willing and able to prosper co-operatively with the rest, did he but know who they were and how to unite with them. The high costs of search and trial attending the formation of new enterprises create a need for initial capital which workers cannot easily supply. That is one reason why there is more tendency to convert existing firms into co-operatives than to found them from scratch. But the conversions are often ill-fated, since they are least resisted when commercial failure is actual or imminent.

Widespread exiting through co-operatives would require substantial external finance, but financiers are reluctant to back even commercially viable co-operative ventures, since dispensing with the capitalist owner sets a bad example: 'the capitalist economy reacts like an organism on which one grafts a foreign organ: it spontaneously rejects the graft.'[36] Towards commercially viable ventures that reaction is irrational, in the terms of bourgeois economics, but capitalists are less blinkered than economists about what is rational, all things considered. And there are also purely economic reasons for withholding finance, since special risks attach to investment in self-managed firms, such as the danger that the workers will 'plunder' it, that is, pay themselves such handsome wages that the co-operative will be unable to meet its obligations to investors. To forestall their anxieties investors might be offered a measure of control over the firm, but that would tend to turn the co-operators into sellers of labour power, in effect if not in form.[37]

There is a general reply to the position of the bourgeois ideologist expounded earlier in this section. It is that a capitalist society is not a set of rules, but a set of relations conforming to them, an economic structure. And transformations permitted by the rules might be blocked by the structure. Creation of workers' co-operatives on the extensive scale envisaged in the right-wing objection would, after all, mean the demise of great capitalist fortunes and institutions, whose agents are in an excellent position to frustrate transition to a co-operative market society. When the Labour government of 1974–79 denied support to workers' co-operatives of a kind routinely given to private industry,[38] the City of London did not rush in to fill the breach.

Recall that I do not deny that (despite the obstacles) there exist unexploited opportunities for exit through co-operation. My different point is that those opportunities are not, and could not be, extensive enough to constitute a means of extinguishing capitalism within the rules of the capitalist system. That is why the most

[36] Branko Horvat, 'Plan de socialisation progressive du capital', 183.

[37] See Jaroslav Vanek, *The General Theory of Labour-Managed Market Economies*, 291 ff. and 317–18 (on 'the dilemma of the collateral'); O'Mahoney, 'Labour Management', 33 ff.

[38] The first Minister of Industry in that government, Tony Benn, favoured co-operatives, which is one reason why he was replaced in the summer of 1975 by Eric Varley, who interpreted Labour's semi-socialist election manifesto commitments in an unsocialist way. See Ken Coates, *Work-ins, Sit-ins and Industrial Democracy*, 140 ff.; id. (ed.), *The New Worker Co-operatives*, 6, 95, 218. For a lucid presentation of the record of business and government hostility to co-operatives in my native Quebec, see the Vaillancourts' 'Government Aid to Worker Production Co-operatives'.

enthusiastic proponents of the co-operative market economy rely on the state to promote a transition to that form of society.[39]

15. One left-wing objection to the argument of section 7 does not question its premiss, that there are more exits from the proletariat than there are workers trying to leave it. The objection is that it is unrealistic to infer that the great majority of workers are individually free to leave. For most lack the requisite assets of character and personality: they have no commercial shrewdness, they do not know how to present themselves well, they are not good at perceiving opportunities, and so on.[40]

To assess this objection, we must distinguish between the freedom to do something and the capacity to do it.

Suppose that the world's best long-distance swimmer has just begun to serve a long prison sentence. Then he has the capacity to swim the English Channel, but he is not free to do so. My situation is the opposite of his. I am free to swim it, but I lack the capacity.

One might suggest, by way of generalization, that a person is unfree to do *A* if and only if, were he to try to do *A*, he would fail to do *A* as a result of the action(s) of one or more other persons; and that a person lacks the capacity to do *A* if and only if, were he to try to do *A*, then, even if circumstances were maximally favourable, he would fail to do *A*. If a person does *A*, then he has both the capacity to do it and the freedom to do it (at the time when he does it).[41]

The suggested analysis of '*X* if unfree to do *A*' is both controversial and difficult to interpret. Some would strengthen it by requiring that the freedom-removing action be *intended* to cause removal of freedom. I do not accept that. I think that if you get in my way you make me unfree even if you are there by accident.

[39] Vanek (*General Theory*, 165 ff.) says that there is not 'much real possibility ... in a liberal capitalist environment' for developing a co-operative market economy, and Horvat ('Plan de socialisation', 165 ff.) proposes what amounts to expropriation without compensation as a means of instituting it.

[40] See the requirements listed by Marx in the passage quoted at n. 10 above.

[41] One might say that one is *able* to do *A* if and only if one has both the capacity and the freedom to do *A*.

Some would reject the above definition of incapacity on the ground that it entails that someone who does *A* by fluke has the capacity to do *A*. I reply that if someone does *A* by fluke, then he shows a capacity to do *A*, to wit, by fluke, which other people might not have. Unlike a six-month-old child, I have the capacity to hit the bull's-eye by fluke. For the view I am opposing here see Anthony Kenny, *Will, Freedom, and Power*, 136.

Others, such as Harry Frankfurt, would defend a weaker *analysans*: for Frankfurt, natural obstacles restrict freedom. I think that he is right, but I have resolved (see section 4 above) to proceed as if he were not.

On the given definitions, the left-wing objection, as presented above, fails, since deficiencies of character and personality that make the worker incapable of leaving his class do not therefore make him unfree to leave it. But the definitions, when put together, possess an entailment which might enable the left-wing objection to be presented in a more persuasive form. It follows from the definitions that if one lacks the capacity to do *A* as a result of the action of others, then one is not only incapable of doing *A* but also unfree to do it. To see how this entailment might be used on behalf of the left-wing objection, let us first return to the case of the prisoners in the locked room.

Each is (conditionally) free to escape, and I stipulated that each has the capacity to seize and wield the key, so each, in addition, has the capacity to escape. The stipulation was not required to prove that they are free to escape, but it made the exhibition of their freedom more vivid. Suppose now that some or all lack the capacity to escape, because they cannot pick up the key; and that they cannot pick it up because they are too weak, since the gaoler gives them low-grade food, in order to make it difficult or impossible for anyone to escape. Then our definitions entail that those without the capacity to use the key are not free to escape.

Now if workers cannot escape the proletariat because of personal deficiency, then this need not, on the given definitions, detract from their freedom to escape, *but it does if the deficiency is appropriately attributable to human action* (if, for example, it is due to needlessly bad education?). If a worker suffers from an appropriately generated or maintained deficiency of a sufficiently severe kind, then he is not free to escape the proletariat, and he is forced to sell his labour power. Is he, in addition, forced to sell his labour power in the required Marxist sense? That depends on whether the causation of the deficiency is suitably connected with the prevailing relations of production (see section 4). Positive answers to these questions would upset the argument of section 7. If it is plausible to say that capitalism *makes* most workers incapable of being anything else, then it is false that most workers are free, *in sensu diviso*, not to be proletarians.

16. Argument 7 says that (most) British workers are not forced to sell their labour power, since they have the reasonable alternative of setting up as petty bourgeois instead, it being false that all petty-bourgeois positions are already occupied. The inference turns on the principle that *a person is not forced to do A if he has a reasonable or acceptable alternative course.* The objection of section 15 can be treated as a challenge to that principle. It says that even if an acceptable alternative lies before an agent, he is forced to do *A* if he is (or, in the improved version of the objection, if he has been made) incapable of seizing it.

A different left-wing objection to the inference of argument 7 is substantially due to Chaim Tannenbaum. Tannenbaum accepts the italicized principle. That is, he agrees that a person is not forced to do *A* if he has an acceptable alternative course; and he also does not deny that petty-bourgeois existence is relevantly superior to proletarian.[42] His objection is that for most workers the existence of petty-bourgeois exits does not, as I have supposed, generate an acceptable alternative course to remaining a worker. For one must consider, as I did not, the risk attached to the attempt to occupy a petty-bourgeois position, which, to judge by the rate at which fledgeling enterprises fail, is very high; and also the costs of failure, since often a worker who has tried and failed to become a petty bourgeois is worse off than if he had not tried at all. The Tannenbaum objecton does not challenge the premiss of argument 7. The exits may exist but, so the objection goes, it is difficult to know where they are, and the price of fruitless search for them is considerable. Accordingly, the expected utility of attempting the petty-bourgeois alternative is normally too low to justify the statement that most workers are not forced to sell their labour power.

Attention to expected utility also illuminates the case of the immigrant petty bourgeois (section 5), on whom argument 7 was founded. For their lot within the working class is usually worse than that of native proletarians, who are not victims of racism and

---

[42] Unlike some Leftists, who resist the inference of argument 7 by urging that petty-bourgeois life is no better than proletarian because of its long hours, short holidays, financial risk, and so on. I reply (1) that the petty bourgeois, being 'his own boss', has an autonomy Leftists are ill placed to disparage, since they so strongly emphasize the loss of it entailed by 'proletarianization'; and (2) that it is in any case possible to base the conclusion of argument 7 on the availability of higher-grade, not-so-petty, bourgeois positions, into which workers also from time to time rise.

who are consequently less prone to super-exploitation. Hence a smaller probability of success is required to make immigrant attempts at escape rational. The disproportionately high number of immigrants in the petty bourgeoisie is therefore less due to differences in expertise and attitude and more due to objective circumstances than seems at first to be the case.

To assess the soundness of the Tannenbaum objection, let us state the argument it proposes as it would apply to a typical worker, whom I shall call W:

1. The expected utility to W of trying the petty-bourgeois course is less than the expected utility of remaining a worker (even if the utility of becoming and remaining a petty bourgeois is greater than that of remaining a worker).

2. An alternative to a given course is acceptable in the relevant sense if and only if it has at least as much expected utility as the given course. (The relevant sense of acceptability is that in which a person is forced to do A if he has no acceptable alternative to doing A.)

Therefore,

3. The existence of petty bourgeois exits does not show that W has an acceptable alternative course.

Therefore,

4. The existence of petty bourgeois exits does not show that W is not forced to sell his labour power.

Therefore,

5. The conclusion of argument 7 does not follow from its premiss.

The first premiss is a (more or less) factual claim, and the second is conceptual. In assessing the truth of the factual premiss, we must discount that part of the probability of failure in attempts at petty-bourgeois enterprise which is due to *purely* personal deficiencies: see section 15. But, even if we could carry out the needed discounting, it would remain extremely difficult to tell whether the factual premiss is true, since the answer would involve many matters of judgment, and also information which is not a matter of judgment but which happens to be unavailable: the frequency with which enterprises founded by ex-workers succeed in the United

Kingdom is not given in the bankruptcy statistics, which do not distinguish those new enterprises from other ones. I shall, however, assume that the factual premiss is true, in order to focus on the conceptual claim embodied in premiss 2.

If a person (who does *A*) is forced to do *A* if he has no acceptable alternative, then what makes for acceptability in the required sense? Suppose that I am doing *A*, and doing *B* is an alternative to that. In order to see whether it is an acceptable one, do I consider only the utility of the best possible outcome of *B*, or do I take into account all its possible outcomes, summing the products of the utility and probability of each, so that I can compare the result with the expected utility of doing *A*, and thereby obtain an answer?

It seems clear that the best possible outcome of doing *B* cannot be all that counts, since, if it were, I would not be forced to hand over my money at gunpoint where there was a minute probability that the gun would misfire. People are regularly forced to do things to which there are alternatives with low probabilities of very high rewards.

It becomes plausible to conclude that expected utility must figure in the calculus of constraint. But I think it figures in a more complex way than premiss 2 of the Tannenbaum objection allows. An alternative to a given course can be acceptable even if it has less expected utility than the given course. Illustrations: 'You're not forced to holiday in Brighton, since you can also go to Margate, though you're less likely to have a good time there.'

Premiss 2 of the Tannenbaum objection is false, but something similar to it may be true. Reflection on the intuitive data leads me to propose the following characterization of acceptability, at any rate as a first approximation:

> *B* is an acceptable alternative to *A* *if and only if* *B* is not worse than *A* or *B* (though worse than *A*) is not thoroughly bad,

with expected utility being the standard for judging courses of action good or bad. Now, in order to apply the analysis, one has to make not only comparative judgments of courses of action but also ones which are absolute *in some sense* (I shall not try to specify it): that is how I intend 'thoroughly bad'. If we were allowed only comparative judgments, we would risk concluding that whenever someone does what is unambiguously the best thing for him to do, he is forced to do that thing. But unflaggingly rational people are not perpetually constrained.

Some consequences of the definition are worth mentioning.

First, even if A is an extremely desirable course, one might be forced to take it, since all the alternatives to it might be very bad. You could be forced to go to the superb and cheap restaurant because all the others are awful. It would then be unlikely that you are going to it (only) *because* you are forced to, but that is another matter. It is not true that you do everything you are forced to do *because* you are forced to do it.

Secondly, all the alternatives to A might be absolutely terrible, and no better than A, and yet one might still not be forced to do A, since some of the alternatives might be no worse than A. To be sure, there would be constraint in such a situation. One would be forced to do A or B or C . . ., but one would not be forced to do any given one of them. One would not, that is, be forced to do A or be forced to do B or be forced to do C . . . .

Thirdly, the extreme difficulty of assessing probabilities and utilities in real life means that it will often be intractably moot whether or not someone is forced to do something. But that is not an objection to this account, since the matter often is intractably moot.

We supposed that the expected utility of trying the petty-bourgeois course is less than that of remaining a worker. Then, if my account of acceptability in alternatives is correct, the substance of the Tannenbaum objection is saved if and only if trying the petty-bourgeois alternative is a particularly bad thing to do.

I cannot say whether or not it is, because the facts are hard to get at and hard to organize in an informative way, and also because of an indeterminacy in the ordinary concept of constraint, on which I have relied: when estimating the goodness and badness of courses of action with a view to judging whether or not an agent is forced to do something, should we consider his preferences only, or apply more objective criteria? The ordinary concept appears to let us judge either way. It seems to allow that neither party to the following exchange is misusing it:

'I'm forced to go to the Indian restaurant, since I hate Chinese food.'

'Since there's nothing wrong with Chinese food, you're not forced to go to the Indian restaurant.'

17. Tannenbaum accepted the premiss of argument 7—that there are exits from the proletariat through which no worker is trying to move—but denied that it showed that workers are (individually) free to leave the proletariat, on the ground that the escape routes from it are too dangerous. I now want to consider an objection to the premiss of the argument. I adduced in support of that premiss the remarkable growth in immigrant petty-bourgeois commerce in recent years. But I might be asked, 'How do you know that immigrants have taken places which would otherwise have been unfilled? Perhaps they prevented others from occupying them by getting there first.'

With respect to some instances of ascent this scepticism is justified. But not in all cases. Often enough the non-proletarian position occupied by an immigrant demands, initially, longer hours and stronger commitment than native British tend to find worth while, so that it would have gone unfilled had some non-native not filled it. And there must still be unoccupied places of that kind. (Note that an unoccupied place does not have to be describable in some such terms as 'the empty shop around the corner which someone could make a go of'. It suffices for the existence of an unoccupied place that there is a course of conduct such that if a worker engaged in it, he would become a non-proletarian, even though no one had ceased to be one.)

But I do concede that there are not as many vacancies as one might at first think. Much ascent into the petty bourgeoisie involves transfer of a secure place in the economic structure from one person to another, on the death, retirement, or collapse into the proletariat of the previous occupant. A good deal of immigrant ascent takes this form, and here it is plausible to say that the new occupant beat others to the place, and did not fill a place others would not have taken.

I argued the thesis of individual freedom to escape for the United Kingdom only. It could be that there is more crowding at the exits in other capitalist societies, and therefore less truth in the premiss of argument 7 when it is asserted of those societies. There is, after all, no 'British Dream', and in more pervasively capitalist cultures it might be only barely true that there is individual freedom to escape, and it might be, though false, nearly true that the overwhelming majority of the proletariat are forced to sell their labour power, even *in sensu diviso*, not for Tannenbaum-type reasons, but because there are virtually no exits available at any given time.

With respect to societies, what is nearly true (though false) may be more important than what is strictly true, since what is strictly true may be only barely true.[43] When considering such theses as that workers are individually free to escape the proletariat, we should beware of arguments which might at best show them to be barely true.

[43] To get an uncontroversial illustration of the sort of truth I have in mind, suppose that each year in the past over one hundred people came to my birthday party, and you ask me whether as many as one hundred came this year; I say 'No', since in fact ninety-nine came, though I do not tell you that. It is more important that it is nearly true (though false) that one hundred came than that it is strictly true that fewer than one hundred came.

14

FREEDOM, JUSTICE, AND CAPITALISM

Before I first went to university I had a belief, which I still have, and which is probably shared by the great majority of you. I mean the belief that the way to decide whether a given economic period is good or bad economically is by considering the welfare of people in general at the relevant time. If people are on the whole well off, then on the whole the times are good, and if they are not, then the times are bad.

Because I had that belief before I got to university, I was surprised by something I heard in one of the first lectures I attended, which was given by the late Frank Cyril James, who, as it happens, obtained his Bachelor of Commerce degree here at the London School of Economics in 1923.[1] When I heard him he was Principal and Vice-Chancellor of McGill University, where, in addition to occupying the Principalship, he gave lectures every year on the economic history of the world, from its semi-scrutable beginnings up to whatever year he was lecturing in. In my case the year was 1958, and in the lecture I want to tell you about James was describing a segment of modern history, some particular quarter-century or so: I am sorry to say that I cannot remember which one. But I do remember something of what he said about it. 'These', he said, referring to the years in question, 'were excellent times economically. Prices were high, wages were low . . .'—and he went on, but I did not hear the rest of his sentence.

I did not hear it because I was busy wondering whether he had meant what he said, or, perhaps, had put the words 'high' and 'low' in the wrong places. For although I had not studied economics, I was convinced that high prices and low wages made for hard times, not good ones. In due course I came to the conclusion that James was too careful to have transposed the two words. It followed that he meant what he said. And it also followed that what he meant when he said that times were good was that they were good for the employing classes, for the folk he was revealing himself to be a spokesman of, since when wages are low and prices are high you

[1] This chapter is a slightly amended version of the text of the 1980 Isaac Deutscher Memorial Lecture, which was delivered on 24 Nov. 1980 at the London School of Economics.

can make a lot of money out of wage-workers. Such candour about the properly purely instrumental position of the mass of human-kind was common in nineteenth-century economic writing, and James was a throw-back to, or a hold-over from, that age. For reasons to be stated in a moment, frank discourse of the Cyril James sort is now pretty rare, at any rate in public. It is discourse which, rather shockingly, treats human labour the way the capitalist system treats it in reality: as a resource for the enhancement of the wealth and power of those who do not have to labour, because they have so *much* wealth and power.

Last year's speaker in this series (Rudolf Bahro) is justly celebrated for his contribution to the understanding of actually existing socialism. My own theme this evening is actually existing capitalism, and I want to start with the capitalism of the United Kingdom. This capitalism is currently managed by a Conservative government which is engaged in a sustained attack on the living standards, and on the democratic powers, of two huge and overlapping groups of the population: working-class people and poor people. It is a government dedicated to the defence of private property, and to the restoration, as far as is thought politically possible, of property rights which Tories think have been eroded by decades of socialistic drift.

Like all very large human projects, present Conservative policy is variously inspired. It is, in part, motivated by the structural requirements of contemporary British capitalism. But it also satisfies, or is at least intended to satisfy, *revanchiste* aspirations rife among the middle and upper classes, many of whom feel that it is wrong for humbly situated people to be as comfortable and as powerful as they are thought now to be. It is wrong for a person who is only an industrial worker, or, worse, unemployed, and therefore not contributing to the national wealth, to pay low rent for commodious living accommodation, and to be freed of anxiety in respect of the education and health of his or her children. Members of the working class, and those below them, some of whom are not even white, expect too much and get too much, and have too much say in the workplace and elsewhere, to the detriment of the income and the authority of their class superiors. There is, as a result, in many Tory hearts, a deep desire for what Tony Benn has called a fundamental shift of wealth and power in favour of rich people and their families.

Now that desire is not the official justification of present government policy, partly because, as Cyril James may not have realized, we live in a democratic age, and policy must be defended before people in general, not just people of privilege; and partly, too, because human beings are so constituted that they need to believe, at least from time to time, that what they are doing is morally right. The disposition to generate ideology, and the disposition to consume it, are fundamental traits of human nature. As Isaac Deutscher said, in his book *The Unfinished Revolution*: 'Statesmen, leaders and ordinary people alike need to have the subjective feeling that what they stand for is morally right'.[2] Members of ruling classes need to feel that their rule is morally justified, and members of ruled classes need to feel that their acquiescence is morally appropriate.

That is why ideology plays such an important part in history, for otherwise encounters between classes would always be settled by brute force. And it was a feature of Isaac Deutscher's magnificent historical work that, while he was a materialist in the best Marxist sense, he was also a master at portraying the ideological atmosphere in which people breathe and think and live, in which, as Marx said, they become sensible of the structural conflicts between them, and fight them out.

I did not know Isaac Deutscher personally, but he entered my life with some force on two occasions. The first was when I was studying Soviet history and politics at McGill University. His book on *Stalin* was required reading, and many of us were excited by the contrast between it and the merely academic treatments of Soviet history we also had to read. Isaac Deutscher showed us that scrupulous scholarship was compatible with political engagement. The first and only time I saw him was in June of 1965, when he spoke at a teach-in on the Vietnam War at University College London. He did not speak about the war alone, but located it within a much wider pattern of events, and when he finished I felt, as I am sure many others did, that I had, at least for the moment, a deeper understanding of the nature of the world I lived in.

Arguments for Capitalism

The general need for ideology and the particular demands of a democratic age produce, when combined, a great body of justifying

[2] p. 103.

belief, which genuinely animates Conservative theory and practice. Whatever may be its ultimate and secret connection with more visceral springs of action, and with structural requirements of contemporary capitalism, there is a sincere conviction that the protection of private property, both on a petty scale and in its larger agglomerations, is a good thing, not because it benefits some and harms others, but for reasons which one need not be ashamed to state. Three such reasons are salient in the ideological discourse of members of the government and their supporters. The regime of private property is defended on the grounds that it enlivens production, safeguards freedom, and conforms to principles of justice. We can call these the *economic* argument, the *freedom* argument, and the *justice* argument.

The economic argument is that the capitalist market, in which, by definition, private property reigns supreme, has good economic consequences. It is splendidly productive, to the advantage of everyone. Even the poor in a market economy are less poor than the poor in other kinds of economy. The idea of incentives appears here. To interfere with the natural tendency for high rewards to accrue to those who enjoy wealth and high positions is to dampen their creativity as investors, entrepreneurs, and managers, to the general disadvantage. To practise policies of steeply progressive taxation, death duties, and the like, is to forgo the golden eggs the harried rich would otherwise lay. Widen the gap between rich and poor and both the rich *and* the poor will be richer than they otherwise would be.

But secondly, and distinctly, any deviation from the free market, apart from having the stated adverse effect on welfare, is a transgression against freedom. Economic freedom has good economic consequences, but it is also a good thing apart from its consequences, since freedom is a good thing, and economic freedom is a form of freedom.

And then there is the argument of justice. In the second week of the 1979 general election campaign Margaret Thatcher said that it was necessary to re-establish capitalism not only for economic reasons but also for moral ones. Private property, after all, belongs to those who own it. It is, consequently, a kind of theft to tax it on behalf of those who do not own it, which is why Ronald Reagan has reported that he can think of no moral justification for the progressive income tax (no matter how hard he tries). If this is *mine*, what right has anyone, even the state, to take part of it away from me? And if this is mine, what right has the state, through regulations and directives, to tell me what to do with it? The regime of fully free enterprise is good because it produces welfare and protects freedom. And it is also the form of economy demanded by principles of justice.

There is not time this evening to discuss all three arguments, and I shall say nothing about the economic one. The freedom argument I shall treat in some detail. And while I shall not be able to give the same attention to the justice argument itself, I shall spend a little time trying to satisfy you that the question whether or not capitalism is a just society is a very important one. To many that will seem obviously true, but there is a strong tendency on the Left to depreciate the idea of justice, and I want to combat that tendency in this lecture.

Ideology and Philosophy

In the course of my critique of ruling ideology I engage in philosophy, of the analytical kind. That is to say: I risk being pedantic in the interest of not overlooking a pertinent distinction, I try to clarify what we mean when we say or do not say this or that, and I am always on the look-out for specifically conceptual confusion. But an objection might be raised against the notion that analytical philosophy is an appropriate instrument to use in a critique of ideology. It might be said that its sophisticated conceptual techniques are irrelevant to the understanding and exposure of ruling-class doctrine, since that has its source in class interest, not conceptual error.

But the claim that the source of ideological illusion is class interest rather than conceptual error rests upon a false contrast. For the truth is that class interest generates ideology precisely by instilling a propensity to errors of reasoning about ideologically sensitive issues. Class interest could not in fact be the immediate source of the ideological illusions from which even reflective thinking suffers, for an illusion will not gain a grip on a reflective mind in the absence of some form of intellectual malfunctioning. And a common malfunction in the case of ideology is conceptual confusion. It is a striking feature of ideological disagreement that, in typical cases, not only does each side believe true what the other side believes false, but each side believes *obviously* true what the other side believes *obviously* false. It is likely, then, that (at least) one side is not just mistaken, but profoundly mistaken. Yet the mistake persists, and what makes it possible for it to endure is, I maintain, its conceptually complex substructure. Class interest, and not conceptual complexity, is the motivating principle of ideology, but conceptual complexity helps to explain why class interest is able to have the effect it does.

Consider, for example, the conflicting answers persons of different political persuasions will give to the question whether or not capitalism promotes freedom. For some it *evidently* does, and for others it *evidently* does not, and the dispute can take this extreme form, with honest advocacy on both sides, only because the concept of freedom lends itself, because of its complexity, to various kinds of misconstrual. And since philosophy of the analytical kind is particularly good at correcting misconstrual, at clarifying the structure of concepts which we know how to handle but are disposed to misdescribe, it follows that it can be a potent solvent of at least some ideological illusions. It can be used to expose conceptual misapprehensions which strengthen the *status quo*, since one thing which helps to consolidate the ruling order is confused belief about its nature and value, in the minds of members of *all* social classes, and also in the minds of those who have dedicated themselves against the ruling order.

Capitalism and Freedom

I turn now to the freedom argument. I think socialists should, and can, meet the freedom argument on its own ground, and I regret that it is their tendency not to do so. When partisans of capitalism describe interventions against private property as invasions of freedom, there are two needlessly ineffective responses which socialists often make. The first is made by mild and Marxist socialists alike. It is 'What price unrestricted freedom, when its consequence is poverty and insecurity for so many?' The second response, which is peculiar to more revolutionary socialists, runs as follows: 'The freedom dear to the supporter of capitalism is merely bourgeois freedom. Socialism will abolish bourgeois freedom but it will provide freedom of a better and higher kind.'

These responses are ineffective because it is not hard for the opponent to rebut or circumvent them. He can say, in reply to the first response, that poverty and insecurity are indeed bad, but that freedom is too important a value to sacrifice for the sake of their elimination. And since socialists, like everybody else, lack arguments which demonstrate what the real relative importance of various values is, there is little they can do to reinforce their objection at this point. As to the second objection, which describes freedom under capitalism as *merely bourgeois* freedom, here the advocate of capitalism can reply that he prefers freedom of the known variety to an unexemplified and unexplained rival. Most people will agree with him. And if the socialist protests that the freedom is exemplified, that it already exists in countries which call themselves socialist, then few who were not on his side at the outset will think that he has improved his case by this gesture in the direction of reality.

If, however, as I would recommend, the socialist argues that capitalism is, all things considered, inimical to freedom in the very sense of 'freedom' in which, as he should concede, a person's freedom is diminished when his private property is tampered with, then he offers a challenge which the advocate of capitalism, by virtue of his own commitment, cannot ignore.

In the following remarks I do not try to show that socialism offers more freedom than capitalism. Instead, more modestly, I prove that a widespread belief that capitalism *must* offer more rests on a series of conceptual confusions.

Libertarianism and Property

Two sets of thinkers agree that unfettered capitalism maximizes freedom: so-called libertarians, who, in addition, *favour* unfettered capitalism, and some (not all) liberals, who, sharing the libertarian belief in the identity of capitalism and freedom, part company with them on policy, since they hold that other values, such as equality, and welfare, justify restrictions on freedom, and they accuse libertarians of wrongly sacrificing too much of those other good things in too total pursuit of the one good of freedom. They agree with libertarians that pure capitalism is freedom pure and simple, or at any rate economic freedom pure and simple, but they think that economic freedom may rightly and reasonably be abridged. They believe that freedom must be balanced against other values, and that what is known as the Welfare State mixed economy achieves the right compromise.

I shall argue that libertarians, and liberals of the kind described, misuse the concept of freedom. They see the freedom which is intrinsic to capitalism, but they do not give proper notice to the constraint which necessarily accompanies it.

To expose this failure of perception, I shall criticize a definition of the libertarian position provided by one of their number, the philosopher Antony Flew, in his Fontana *Dictionary of Philosophy*.[3] It is there said to be 'wholehearted political and economic liberalism, opposed to any social and legal constraints on individual freedom'. Liberals of the kind just described would avow themselves unwholehearted in the sense of this definition, since they say that they support certain constraints on individual freedom.

Now a society in which there are *no* 'social and legal constraints on individual freedom' is perhaps imaginable, at any rate by people who have highly anarchic imaginations. But, be that as it may, the Flew definition misdescribes libertarians, since it does not apply to defenders of capitalism, which is what libertarians profess to be, and are.

For consider: if the state prevents me from doing something I want to do, it evidently places a constraint on my freedom. Suppose, then, that I want to perform an action which involves a legally prohibited use of your property. I want, let us say, to pitch a tent in your large back garden, perhaps just in order to annoy you, or perhaps for the more substantial reason that I have nowhere to live and no land of my own, but I have got hold of a tent, legitimately or otherwise. If I now try to do this thing I want to do, the chances are that the state will intervene on your behalf. If it does, I shall suffer a constraint on my freedom. The same goes for all unpermitted uses of a piece of private property by those who do not own it, and there are always those who do not own it, since 'private ownership by one person presupposes non-ownership on the part of other persons.'[4] But the free enterprise economy advocated by libertarians rests upon private property: you can sell and buy only what you respectively own and come to own. It follows that the Flew definition is untrue to its *definiendum*, and that the term 'libertarianism' is a gross misnomer for the position it now standardly denotes among philosophers and economists.

How could Flew have brought himself to publish the definition I have criticized? I do not think he was being dishonest. I would not accuse him of appreciating the truth of this particular matter and

[3] p. 188.
[4] Karl Marx, *Capital*, iii. 812.

deliberately falsifying it. Why then is it that Flew, and libertarians like him, and liberals of the kind I described, see the unfreedom in state interference with a person's use of his property, but fail to note the unfreedom in the standing intervention against anyone else's use of it entailed by the fact that it is that person's private property? What explains their monocular vision?

Part of the explanation will emerge if we remind ourselves that social and legal constraints on freedom are not the only source of restriction on human action. It restricts my possibilities of action that I lack wings, and therefore cannot fly without major mechanical assistance, but that is not a social or legal constraint on my freedom. Now I suggest that one explanation of our theorists' failure to note that private property constrains freedom is a tendency to take as part of the structure of human existence in general, and therefore as no social or legal constraint on freedom, any structure around which, *merely as things are*, much of our activity is organized. A structure which is not a permanent part of the human condition can be misperceived as being just that, and the institution of private property is a case in point. It is treated as so given that the obstacles it puts on freedom are not perceived, while any impingement on private property itself is immediately noticed. Yet private property pretty well *is* a particular way of distributing freedom *and unfreedom*. It is necessarily associated with the liberty of private owners to do as they wish with what they own, but it no less necessarily withdraws liberty from those who do not own it. To think of capitalism as a realm of freedom is to overlook half of its nature.

Inconsistent Definitions of Freedom

I should point out that I do not claim that anyone of sound mind will for long deny that private property places restrictions on freedom, once the point has been made.[5] The remarkable thing is that the point so often needs to be made, against what should be obvious absurdities, such as Flew's definition of 'libertarianism'.

---

[5] It was made very adroitly by Jeremy Bentham. 'All rights are made at the expense of liberty . . . . How is property given? By restraining liberty; that is, by taking it away so far as is necessary for the purpose. How is your house made yours? By debarring every one else from the liberty of entering it without your leave' ('Anarchical Fallacies', 57).

But there is a further and independent explanation of how libertarian absurdity is possible. You will notice that I have supposed that to prevent someone from doing something he wants to do is to make him, in that respect, unfree: I am unfree whenever someone interferes, *justifiably or otherwise*, with my actions. But there is a definition of freedom which is implicit in much libertarian writing,[6] and which entails that interference is not a sufficient condition of unfreedom. On that definition, which I shall call the *moralized* definition, I am unfree only when someone does or would *unjustifiably* interfere with me, when what he does or would do prevents me from doing what I have a right to do.

If one now combines this moralized definition of freedom with a moral endorsement of private property, with a claim that, in standard cases, people have a moral right to the property they legally own, then one reaches the result that the protection of legitimate private property cannot restrict anyone's freedom. It will follow from the moral endorsement of private property that you and the police are justified in preventing me from pitching my tent on your land, and, because of the moralized definition of freedom, it will then further follow that you and the police do not thereby restrict my freedom.

So here we have a further explanation of how intelligent philosophers are able to say what they do about capitalism, private property, and freedom. But the characterization of freedom which figures in the explanation is unacceptable. For it entails that a properly convicted murderer is not rendered unfree when he is justifiably imprisoned.

Even justified interference reduces freedom. But suppose for a moment that, as libertarians say or imply, it does not. On that supposition one cannot argue, without further ado, that interference with private property is wrong *because* it reduces freedom. For one can no longer take for granted, what is evident on a morally neutral account of freedom, that interference with private property does reduce freedom. Under a moralized account of freedom one must abstain from that assertion until one has shown that private property is morally inviolable. Yet libertarians tend *both* to use a moralized definition of freedom *and* to take it for granted that interference with private property diminishes the owner's freedom.

[6] And sometimes also explicit: see Robert Nozick, *Anarchy, State and Utopia*, 262.

But they can take that for granted only on the morally neutral account of freedom, on which, however, it is equally obvious that the protection of private property diminishes the freedom of *non-owners*, to avoid which consequence they retreated to a moralized definition of the concept. And so they go, back and forth, between inconsistent definitions of freedom, not because they cannot make up their minds which one they like better, but under the propulsion of their desire to occupy what is in fact an untenable position.

Yet libertarians who embrace the moralized definition of freedom need not occupy this inconsistent position. They can escape inconsistency by contriving to justify private property on grounds other than considerations of freedom. They can try, for example, to represent interference with rightfully held private property as unjust, and therefore, by virtue of the moralized definition, invasive of freedom. This is a consistent position. But it still incorporates an unacceptable definition of freedom, and the position is improved[7] if that is eliminated. We then have a defence of private property on grounds of justice. Freedom falls out of the picture.

Private Property and Justice

Private property is not straightforwardly defensible on grounds of freedom, but it might be an institution demanded by justice. Let us even suppose—to go beyond anything I can claim to have shown—that socializing the principal means of production would enhance freedom, because the extra freedom gained by the less well off would be greater than the amount lost by the rich. It might nevertheless be true that it would be unjust to expropriate and socialize any private property. If so, the case for maintaining private property would be very strong. For, at least at the intuitive level, considerations of justice tend to override considerations of freedom. That is because justice is a matter of rights, and rights are especially potent weapons in moral debate. An argument that a certain course or policy would expand *A*'s freedom tends to be defeated by the consideration that it would infringe *B*'s rights, and

---

[7] It is improved intellectually in that a certain objection to it no longer applies, but ideologically it is weakened, since there is more ideological power in a recommendation of private property on grounds of justice *and* freedom—however confused, in the recommendation, the relationship between them may be—than in a recommendation of private property on grounds of justice alone.

a defence of an action of *B*'s on the ground that he has the right to perform it tends not to be defeated by the reply that the action reduces *A*'s freedom.

The chief exponent within philosophy of the currently favoured justice argument for private property is Robert Nozick. He has put with clarity and fierceness the kind of case for private property we found Margaret Thatcher and Ronald Reagan gesturing at early in this lecture. His case is that to prevent people from acquiring private property, and, consequently, to deprive them of their legitimately acquired private property, is to violate their moral rights.

Moral rights are rights which are not merely legal ones. We say that we have them on moral, not legal, grounds. You may think that no such rights exist, that the whole idea is nonsense, but I do not agree. I do not think existing legal rights of private property have moral force, but I do think there are moral rights, and the following example will, I hope, induce some of the sceptics among you to relax your scepticism.

Suppose the government, using constitutional means, forbids protests against its nuclear defence policy on the ground that they endanger national security. Then we should lose the legal right to march as many did on the CND demonstration of 26 October 1980. And one way of expressing anger at the government's decision would be to say 'People have a right to protest against any part of government policy.' Since *ex hypothesi* that would not be true at the level of *legal* rights, we would be claiming to possess a right which is not a merely legal one. And that is what is meant, at any rate by Nozick and me, by a moral right. The language of moral rights is the language of justice, and whoever takes justice seriously must accept that there exist moral rights.

Now Marxists do not often talk about justice, and when they do they tend to deny its relevance, or they say that the idea of justice is an illusion. But I think justice occupies a central place in revolutionary Marxist belief. Its presence is betrayed by particular judgments Marxists make, and by the strength of feeling with which they make them.

Revolutionary Marxist belief often misdescribes itself, out of lack of clear awareness of its own nature, and Marxist disparagement of the idea of justice is a good example of that deficient self-understanding. I shall try to persuade you that Marxists, whatever they may say about themselves, do have strong beliefs about justice. I shall use an indirect method: I shall describe a characteristic social-democratic evasion on the issue of justice, and I shall invite you to agree that Marxists would make a strong judgment of justice at the point where social democrats evade the issue.

Now the most considerable *moral* objection[8] typical social democrats have to capitalist market economy, or, rather, to the unmixed capitalist market economy, is that it sends the weak to the wall. A capitalist society with no welfare structure would endanger the very lives of those who, from time to time, and sometimes for a long time, are unemployed; and, through absence of social provision, it would blight the lives of those who are fortunate enough regularly to find buyers for their labour power. In the unmixed market economy the condition of ordinary people is less good than it can and therefore should be made to be. For many social democrats this is the heart of their outlook. They are the contemporary exponents of a tradition of concern for and charity towards the badly off. They sometimes say that what they favour is a *caring* society.

Now to say that the free market harms the weak is not, on the face of it,[9] to make a judgment about its justice. What would be a claim of justice is that the free market deprives the majority of rights over what morally ought to be held in common. They are, as a result, weak, but that need not be part of the reason for saying that the institution which causes them to be so is unjust. Whether or not it is, *the socialist objection of justice to the market economy is that it allows private ownership of means of existence which no one has the right to own privately, and therefore rests upon an unjust foundation.* I am sure that revolutionaries believe this in their hearts, even those revolutionaries who deny that they believe it, because of ill-conceived philosophical commitments.

Social democrats who are unwilling to advance in the direction of the justice critique of capitalism will tend to lose in confrontation with libertarian Tories. For the Tory libertarian will acknowledge and regret that the free market harms many people. He may even, as Nozick does, encourage philanthropy as a remedy. What he

---

[8] Such objections are to be distinguished from ones based on the inefficiency or on the wastefulness of the capitalist system.

[9] I say 'not on the face of it', because the claim might properly figure in the course of an argument to the conclusion that capitalism is unjust, but it is not, as it stands, a thesis of justice.

condemns is *constrained* philanthropy, welfare payments sustained by taxation exacted by the might of the state. Such taxation, in his view, violates rights. If you care about badly off people, he says, then by all means help them, but don't force other people to do so: you have no right to force *them* to do so. And to this position it is not a principled reply to sketch forth vividly the inhuman effects of absence of coercive transfer payments. The principled reply is that the socializing state is not violating rights, or even overriding them in the interest of something more important, but righting wrongs: it is rectifying violations of rights, violations inherent in the structure of private property.

I said that libertarians can be in favour of philanthropy. They can even agree that the rich are morally obliged to help the poor. For it is false that whenever a person has a moral obligation the state has the right to force him to honour it. One might think that there is a strong moral obligation on healthy adults to donate blood in an emergency, when life is at stake, yet, in full consistency with that belief, regard as abominable a law requiring them to donate their blood, even if, without such a law, much avoidable death will occur. And if ownership of private property has a morally privileged status, akin to what most people think is my inviolable right to dispose over the parts of my own body—such as my own kidneys, one of which might be urgently needed by someone else— then it is an unacceptable invasion of the rights of the rich to tax them in favour of the poor, even if the rich lose less from such taxation than the poor gain (since the marginal utility of income is higher the lower you go down the income scale). That utilitarian argument begs a large question about justice. For if wealth belongs as of right to those who have it, then it is just too bad that others would benefit from some of what the rich have more than they do.

Social-Democratic Evasion

In the course of his *Critique of the Gotha Programme*, Karl Marx criticized socialists who 'put the principal stress on' the standard of living of the working class. He objected that 'any distribution whatever of the means of consumption is only a consequence of the distribution of the conditions of production themselves'.[10]

---

[10] *Critique of the Gotha Programme*, 25. Marx goes on to say: 'The capitalist mode of production . . . rests on the fact that the material conditions of property are in the hands of non-workers in the form of property in capital and land, while the

Now, it is usually thought that Marx emphasized the causal truth that the distribution of producer goods determines the distribution of consumer goods because of its policy significance: it is bad strategy to seek to alter the maldistribution of income without challenging the more fundamental maldistribution of what generates income. I have no doubt that Marx did believe that, but I think that he also intended to convey a distinct and independently defensible thesis, namely that it is a confusion to direct censure against the predictable and regular consequences of a cause which is not itself subjected to criticism. If you object to the consequences for welfare of a certain structure of property you must, at the very least, object to the cause—that structure—*because* of its consequences; and if the cause has been defended on grounds which prescind from consequences, then you must go beyond a discussion of consequences *considered merely as such*[11] and confront those grounds.

I suggest that social democrats tend to refrain from these necessary further moves, which raise issues more radical than they like to face. And I suggest that it lies in the nature of the revolutionary socialist attitude to proceed to those issues. That is why revolutionaries find confiscation a more appropriate response to severe inequality of ownership than perpetual rearguard action against the effects of that inequality. If I may be allowed to

masses are only owners of the personal condition of production, of labour power. If the elements of production are so distributed, then the present-day distribution of the means of consumption results automatically.' It follows that the capitalist mode of production 'rests on' a certain distribution of the elements of production. When, therefore, later in the same paragraph, Marx disparages attention of 'distribution' in favour of attention to 'the mode of production', he is there using 'distribution' as an abbreviation for 'distribution of the means of consumption'. He cannot be intending to say that the mode of production is more fundamental than distribution of any kind, since he has just said that the mode of production rests on one kind of distribution. Yet the standard Marxist view of the passage, which is a product of sloppy reading, is that Marx here says that production *and not distribution* is what matters. And that misreading is one source of Marxist hostility to the idea of justice.

I want, accordingly, to emphasize that Marx is not saying 'Give up your obsession with just distribution', but 'Prosecute your concern about distribution at the appropriately fundamental level.' Production relations are the fundamental thing, and they *are* modes of distribution of productive forces, as Marx unambiguously indicated in the *Grundrisse*: 'The worker's propertylessness, and the ownership of living labour by objectified labour, or the appropriation of alien labour by capital . . . are fundamental conditions of the bourgeois mode of production . . . These modes of distribution are the relations of production themselves, *but sub specie distributionis*' (p. 832).

[11] See n. 9 above.

oversimplify and exaggerate, it is as though social democrats are sensitive to the effects of exploitation on people, but not to the fact of exploitation itself. They want to succour the exploited while minimizing confrontation with those who exploit them.

I have insisted that the way to respond to Tory belief in the justice of capitalism is to enter the terrain of justice, and I say that revolutionaries, however much they may like to deny it, are already there, whereas most social democrats are not. But only most social democrats, and the present critique does not apply to that minority of them who do regard capitalism as fundamentally unjust but who think that for practical reasons policy should be inspired by other considerations, since they think that there is simply no prospect of eliminating capitalism at a tolerable cost. I disagree with those social democrats about policy, but they have not been my target. My target has been that majority of social democrats whose thinking is so unradical that they do not reach the point where they have to cite practical reasons for not attacking capitalism in a fundamental way.

Is Property Theft?

I have maintained that the view that capitalism is unjust is an elementary Marxist conviction, albeit one which is sometimes submerged. But I have not *argued* for the view that capitalism is unjust. The relevant argument is too long to be presented here, but I shall describe some of its stages.

It begins with the idea that capitalism is just if and only if capitalists have the right to own the means of production they do, for it is their ownership of means of production which enables them to make profit out of labour, and if that ownership is legitimate, then so too is making profit out of labour. The key question, then, is whether capitalist private property is morally defensible.

Now all, or virtually all, capitalist private property either is, or is made of, something which was once no one's private property, since (virtually) all physical private property comes immediately or ultimately from the land, which was there before any people, hence before any private owners of it, were. Some of what was once no one's remains substantially no one's even now, and therefore accessible to everyone: the air people breathe is still public property. The rest has been removed from the public domain and turned into private property. If, then, someone claims a moral entitlement to something he legally owns, we may ask, apart from how he in particular came to have it, how the thing came to be (anyone's) private property in the first place, and we may then examine the justice of that transformation. I believe we shall find that the original privatization was unjust, that, in a sense which I hope to make clear on another occasion,[12] property is theft, theft of what morally speaking belongs to us all in common.

Some may think it strange that someone who is more or less a Marxist should propose to himself the project of demonstrating that the capitalist system is unjust. That does not seem a very Marxist thing to get involved in. It sounds like moral philosophy, not Marxism. But whoever thinks that should ask himself why Karl Marx wrote the last part of volume i of *Capital*, the part on primitive accumulation, in which he contended that a propertyless proletariat was created in Great Britain as a result of violent expropriation of small-scale private property and property held in common. Part of his aim was to refute the idea that capitalists became monopoly owners of means of production as a result of their own industry and frugality, or that of their forebears. He was trying to show that British capitalism rests upon an unjust foundation.

To the extent that Marx's historical allegations are true, they tell against the pretension to legitimacy of British capital. But however successful he is on that score, his success from a broader point of view is limited. For he does not say, and it is not true, that primitive accumulation is always a savage affair. Capital does not always 'come into the world dripping from head to foot, from every pore, with blood and dirt'.[13] Sometimes it emerges more discreetly. And anyway, Marxists do not believe merely that this or that capitalist society, or even every capitalist society, is unjust because of its particular origin. Marxists believe that capitalism as such is unjust, that, therefore, there could not be a just formation of capitalist private property, and that thesis requires moral rather than historical argument.

[12] See now my 'Nozick on Appropriation', 'Self-Ownership, World-Ownership and Equality', 'Self-Ownership, World-Ownership, and Equality: Part II', and 'Are Freedom and Equality Compatible?' (the first article in that list is a slightly abbreviated version of the second, and the fourth is a compendious presentation of the claims of the other three).

[13] *Capital*, i. 926.

Justice and Historical Materialism

In my book on Marx I affirmed and defended an orthodox conception of historical materialism, in which history is the growth of human productive power, and forms of society rise and fall according as they enable and promote, or frustrate and impede, that growth. In the phase in which it promotes productive progress, a given form of society, because it promotes productive progress, contributes to the ultimate liberation of humanity, to the achievement of a condition in which the creative capacities of people in general can be developed, instead of just the creative capacities of an élite whom people in general serve. Capitalism was an indispensable means of raising human productive power from a rather low to a very high level, and it did just that in what Marxists allow was its progressive phase. But if it had that progressive phase, then, some will say, it is surely not unjust as such, but at most unjust in its reactionary phase, when it is no longer needed as a means of increasing productive power, and is, moreover, no longer good at doing it. Is there not, then, an inconsistency between the idea that capitalism is an inherently unjust society and some of the principal theses of my book on *Karl Marx's Theory of History?*

That is a difficult question, and the difficulty is not mine alone. Karl Marx said that 'development of the productive forces of social labour is the historical task and justification of capital(ism)'[14] but it is nevertheless clear whose side he would have been on in the class struggle at *every* stage of capitalist development. For if the working conditions of the industrial revolution were necessary for productive progress, it remains true that the workers suffering those conditions were victims of injustice, and that their bosses were exploiters.

There is a tension between the Marxist commitment to advancement of productive power and the Marxist commitment to those at whose expense that advancement occurs. I cannot fully relieve the tension here, but I shall state four logically independent propositions which, brought into proper relationship with one another,[15] would, I think, do so: i. All exploitation, including that which contributes to liberation, is unjust. ii. Liberation requires productive progress, and productive progress requires exploitation.

[14] Ibid. iii. 368.
[15] For an attempt to bring them into that relationship see sect. 5 of my 'Peter Mew on Justice and Capitalism'.

iii. Whether or not productive progress was inevitable, exploitation was. That is, exploitation was not only unavoidable for productive progress, but unavoidable *tout court*. Justice without productive progress was not an historically feasible option, because justice was not an historically feasible option. And finally: iv. Ruling classes always exploit subordinate classes to a greater extent than productive progress would require.

For some years right-wing ideas have flourished in Western society, in highly refined and also in crude forms. And while the recent virulence of reactionary thought is in good measure explained by factors which lie outside the domain of thought and theory, the impact in practice of the right-wing victory in consciousness has been tremendous. In this lecture I have sought to reaffirm some fundamental socialist convictions. I shall end with a quotation from *The Communist Manifesto*: 'The theory of the Communists may be summed up in a single phrase: Abolition of private property.'

Works Cited

By Marx and Engels

CW is an abbreviation for the *Collected Works* of Karl Marx and Frederick Engels, published in London by Lawrence and Wishart from 1975. *MESW* is an abbreviation for *Marx–Engels Selected Works*, a two-volume selection from their writings published in Moscow in 1958. Apart from Marx's 'Fragment' of 1858, all cited works of Marx and Engels are editions in English.

MARX, Introduction to *A Contribution to the Critique of Hegel's Philosophy of Law* (1844), CW iii (1975).

—— 'Comments on James Mill, *Élémens d'économie politique*' (1844), CW iii (1975).

—— *Economic and Philosophic Manuscripts* (1844), CW iii (1975).

—— and Engels, *The Holy Family* (1845), CW iv (1975).

MARX, Draft of an article on Friedrich List's book *Das Nationale System der Politischen Oekonomie* (1845), CW iv (1975).

ENGELS, *The Condition of the Working Class in England in 1844* (1845), London, 1892.

MARX and ENGELS, *The German Ideology* (1846), CW v (1976).

MARX, *Moralising Criticism and Critical Morality* (1847), CW vi (1976).

—— *The Poverty of Philosophy* (1847), CW vi (1976).

—— and Engels, *The Communist Manifesto* (1848), CW vi (1976).

MARX, 'Wage-Labour and Capital' (1849), CW ix (1977).

—— 'Address of the Central Authority to the Communist League' (1850), CW x (1978).

—— 'The Future Results of British Rule in India' (1853), CW xii (1979).

—— *The Grundrisse* (1857–8), Harmondsworth, 1973.

—— Fragment des Urtextes von *Zur Kritik des Poitischen Ökonomie* (1858), in Karl Marx, *Grundrisse der Kritik der Politischen Ökonomie* (Berlin, 1953).

—— *A Contribution to the Critique of Political Economy* (1859), London, 1971.

—— *Theories of Surplus Value* (1861–3); i (London, 1969), ii (London, 1969), iii (London, 1972).

—— 'Results of the Immediate Process of Production' (1863–6), in Karl Marx, *Capital*, i (Harmondsworth, 1976).

—— 'Wages, Price and Profit' (1865), *MESW* i.

—— *Capital* (1867 etc.); i (Harmondsworth, 1976), ii (Harmondsworth, 1978), iii (Harmondsworth, 1981).

ENGELS, *The Housing Question* (1872), *MESW* i.

MARX, *Critique of the Gotha Programme* (1875), *MESW* ii.

ENGELS, *Anti-Dühring* (1878), Moscow, 1954.

MARX, 'Notes on Adolph Wagner' (1879–80), in T. Carver (ed.), *Karl Marx: Texts on Method* (Oxford, 1975).

ENGELS, 'Speech at the Graveside of Karl Marx' (1883), *MESW* ii.

—— Introduction to the English edition of *Socialism, Utopian and Scientific* (1892), *MESW* ii.

MARX and ENGELS, *Selected Correspondence*, Moscow, 1975.

By Others

ARENDT, H., *The Human Condition*, Garden City, 1958.

ASHFORD, N., *Crisis in the Workplace*, Cambridge, Mass., 1976.

ARTHUR, J., and SHAW, W. (eds.), *Justice and Economic Distribution* Englewood Cliffs, 1978.

AVINERI, S., *Hegel's Theory of the Modern State*, Cambridge, 1972.

BALL, T. and FARR, J. (eds.), *After Marx*, New York, 1984.

BENTHAM, J., 'Anarchical Fallacies', in Waldron (ed.), 1987.

BERLIN, I., *Historical Inevitability*, Oxford, 1954.

—— *Four Essays on Liberty*, Oxford, 1969.

—— 'Herder and the Enlightenment', in Berlin, 1976.

—— *Vico and Herder*, London, 1976.

—— *Against the Current*, London, 1979.

—— 'Nationalism', in Berlin, 1979.

BERMAN, M., *All that is Solid Melts into Air*, New York, 1983.

BLANSHARD, B., 'The Case for Determinism', in Hook (ed.), 1961.

BLAUG, M., *Economic Theory in Retrospect*, London, 1968.

BONE, S. and ADSHEAD, M., *The Little Boy and his House*, London, 1936.

BRAVERMAN, H., *Monopoly Capital*, New York, 1974.

BRENKERT, G. G., 'Cohen on Proletarian Unfreedom', *Philosophy and Public Affairs*, 14.1 (1985).

CARLING, A., 'Rational Choice Marxism', *New Left Review*, 160 (1986).

COATES, K. (ed.), *The New Worker Co-operatives*, Nottingham, 1976.

—— *Work-ins, Sit-ins and Industrial Democracy*, Nottingham, 1981.

COHEN, G. A., 'On Some Criticisms of Historical Materialism', *Proceedings of the Aristotelian Society*, Suppl. Vol. 44 (1970).

—— 'Beliefs and Roles', in Glover (ed.), 1976.

—— *Karl Marx's Theory of History: A Defence*, Oxford and Princeton, 1978.

—— 'Robert Nozick and Wilt Chamberlain: How Patterns Preserve Liberty', in Arthur and Shaw (eds.), 1978.

—— 'Functional Explanation: Reply to Elster', *Political Studies*, 28.1 (1980).

—— 'Illusions about Private Property and Freedom', in Mepham and Ruben (eds.), 1981.

—— Review of Rader, *Clio*, 10.2 (1981).

—— 'Functional Explanation, Consequence Explanation, and Marxism', *Inquiry*, 25.1 (1982).

—— 'Marxism, Functionalism, and Game Theory', *Theory and Society*, 11.3 (1982).

—— 'More on Exploitation and the Labour Theory of Value', *Inquiry*, 26.3 (1983)

—— 'Reply to Four Critics', *Analyse und Kritik*, (1983).

—— 'Are Workers Forced to Sell their Labour Power?', *Philosophy and Public Affairs*, 14.1 (1985).

—— 'Nozick on Appropriation', *New Left Review*, 150 (1985).

—— 'Peter Mew on Justice and Capitalism', *Inquiry*, 29.3 (1986).

—— 'Self-Ownership, World-Ownership, and Equality', in Lucash (ed.), 1986.

—— 'Self-Ownership, World-Ownership, and Equality: Part II', in E. Paul *et al.* (eds.), 1986.

—— 'Walt on Historical Materialism and Functional Explanation', *Ethics*, 97.1 (1986).

—— 'Are Freedom and Equality Compatible?', in Elster and Moene (eds.), forthcoming.

—— 'Collins on Base and Superstructure', *Oxford Journal of Legal Studies*, forthcoming.

COHEN, J., review of Cohen, KMTH, *Journal of Philosophy*, 79.5 (1982).

COLLINS, H., *Marxism and Law*, Oxford, 1982

DAVIS, L., *The Philosophy of Action*, Englewood Cliffs, NJ, 1979.

DEUTSCHER, I., *Stalin*, Oxford, 1949.

—— *The Unfinished Revolution*, Oxford, 1967.

DRAPER, H., 'The Death of the State in Marx and Engels', in Miliband and Saville (eds.), 1970.

DUNN, J., review of Miller and Siedentop (eds.), *Times Literary Supplement*, 27 May 1983.

DWORKIN, G., 'Acting Freely', *Nous*, 4.4 (1970).

ELSTER, J., 'Exploring Exploitation', *Journal of Peace Research*, 15.1 (1978).

—— 'Freedom and Power', unpublished draft, 1979.

—— 'Cohen on Marx's Theory of History', *Political Studies*, 28.1 (1980).

—— 'Marxism, Functionalism and Game Theory', *Theory and Society*, 11.3 (1982).

—— *Explaining Technical Change*, Cambridge, 1983.

—— *Sour Grapes*, Cambridge, 1983.

—— 'Historical Materialism and Economic Backwardness', in Ball and Farr (eds.), 1984.

—— *Making Sense of Marx*, Cambridge, 1985.

—— 'Weakness of Will and the Free-Rider Problem', *Economics and Philosophy*, 1.1 (1985).

—— and MOENE, K. (eds.), *Alternatives to Capitalism*, Cambridge, forthcoming.

FISK, M., 'The Concept of Primacy in Historical Explanation', *Analyse und Kritik*, 4.2 (1982).

FLEW, A., *A Dictionary of Philosophy*, London, 1979.

FRANK, A. G., *Capitalism and Underdevelopment in Latin America*, New York, 1967.

FRANKFURT, H., 'Coercion and Moral Responsibility', in Honderich (ed.), 1973.

FROMM, E. (ed.), *Socialist Humanism*, Garden City, 1966.

GELLNER, E., (ed.), *Soviet and Western Anthropology*, London, 1980.

—— 'A Russian Marxist Philosophy of History', in Gellner (ed.), 1980.

GLOVER, J., (ed.), *The Philosophy of Mind*, Oxford, 1976.

GOLDMANN, L., 'Socialism and Humanism', in Fromm (ed.), 1966.

HARRIS, M., *Cultural Materialism*, New York, 1979.

Hastings Center, *Occupational Health and the Concept of Responsibility*, Hastings, N.Y., 1980.

HAWORTH, L., 'Leisure, Work and Profession', *Leisure Studies*, 3.2 (1984)

HEGEL, G. W. F., *Early Theological Writings*, Chicago, 1948.

—— 'On Love', in Hegel, 1948.

—— *The Philosophy of Right*, Oxford, 1958.

—— *The Phenomenology of Mind*, London, 1961.

HOLSTROM, N., 'Marx and Cohen on Exploitation and the Labour Theory of Value', *Inquiry*, 26.3 (1983).

HONDERICH, T. (ed.), *Essays on Freedom of Action*, London, 1973.

HOOK, S. (ed., *Determinism and Freedom*, New York, 1961.

HORVAT, B., 'Plan de socialisation progressive du capital', in Kolm (ed.). 1978.

HUSAMI, Z., 'Marx on Distributive Justice', *Philosophy and Public Affairs*, 8.1 (1978).

JEFFREY, R. C., 'Statistical Explanation vs. Statistical Inference', in Rescher *et al.*, 1970.

KENNY, A., *Will, Freedom, and Power*, Oxford, 1975.

KLAGGE, J., 'Marx's Realms of "Freedom" and "Necessity"', *Canadian Journal of Philosophy*, 16.4 (1986).

KOLM, S.–C. (ed.), *Solutions socialistes*, Paris, 1978.

LENIN, V. I., 'What "The Friends of the People" Are and How they Fight the Social Democrats', in Lenin, *Selected Works*, xi (New York, n.d.).

LEVINE, A. and WRIGHT, E., 'Rationality and Class Struggle', *New Left Review*, 123 (1980).

LUCASH, F. (ed.), *Justice and Equality Here and Now*, Ithaca, N.Y, 1986.

LUKES, S., 'Can the Base be Distinguished from the Superstructure?', in Miller and Siedentop (eds.), 1983.

MACKIE, J. L., *Persons and Values*, Oxford, 1985.

—— 'Norms and Dilemmas', in Mackie, 1985.

McLELLAN, D., *Karl Marx*, London, 1973.

McMURTRY, J., *The Structure of Marx's World-View*, Princeton, 1978.

MARSHALL, G., *In Search of the Spirit of Capitalism*, London, 1982.

MEEK, R., *Smith, Ricardo and Marx*, London, 1977.

MEPHAM, J. and RUBEN, D.–H. (eds.), *Issues in Marxist Philosophy*, iv (Hassocks, Sussex, 1981).

MILIBAND, R. and SAVILLE, J. (eds.), *The Socialist Register: 1970*, London, 1970.

MILL, J. S., *Principles of Political Economy*, Toronto, 1965.

MILLER, D. and SIEDENTOP, L. (eds.), *The Nature of Political Theory*, Oxford, 1983.

MILLER, R., 'Productive Forces and the Forces of Change', *Philosophical Review*, 90.1 (1981).

—— *Analysing Marx*, Princeton, 1984.

—— 'Producing Change', in Ball and Farr (eds.), 1984.

MUMFORD, L., *Technics and Civilization*, London, 1934.

NAGEL, T., *The View from Nowhere*, New York, 1986.

NIELSEN, K., 'On Taking Historical Materialism Seriously', *Dialogue*, 22.2 (1983).

NORMAN, R., review of Cohen, *KMTH, London Review of Books*, 21 Feb. 1980.

NOZICK, R., *Anarchy, State and Utopia*, New York, 1974.

O'MAHONEY, D., 'Labour Management and the Market Economy', *Irish Journal of Business and Administrative Research*, 1.1 (1979).

PARFIT, D., *Reasons and Persons*, Oxford, 1984.

PARKIN, F., *Marxism and Class Theory*, London, 1979.

PAUL, E. F. *et al.* (eds.), *Marxism and Liberalism*, Oxford, 1986.

PERSSON, G., *Pre-Industrial Economic Growth in Europe*, Oxford, forthcoming.

PLAMENATZ, J., *German Marxism and Russian Communism*, London, 1954.

—— *Man and Society*, ii (London, 1963).

—— *Ideology*, London, 1970.

PRZEWORSKI, A., *Capitalism and Social Democracy*, Cambridge, 1985.

RADER, M., *Marx's Interpretation of History*, New York, 1979.

REIMAN, J., 'Exploitation, Force and the Moral Assessment of Capitalism', *Philosophy and Public Affairs*, 16.1 (1987).

RESCHER, N. *et al.*, *Essays in Honor of Carl G. Hempel*, Dordrecht, 1970.

RICARDO, D., *Principles of Political Economy and Taxation*, Harmondsworth, 1971.

ROBERTSON, H. M., *Aspects of the Rise of Economic Individualism*, Cambridge, 1933.

SCHUMPETER, J., *Capitalism, Socialism, and Democracy*, New York, 1942.

SEMENOV, Y. I., 'The Theory of Socio-Economic Formations and World History', in Gellner (ed.), 1980.

SHAW, W., *Marx's Theory of History*, Stanford, 1978.

—— 'Historical Materialism and the Development Thesis', *Philosophy of the Social Sciences*, 16.2 (1986).

SRAFFA, P., *Production of Commodities by Means of Commodities*, Cambridge, 1960.

STEEDMAN, I., *Marx After Sraffa*, London, 1977.

STEINER, H., 'Individual Liberty', *Proceedings of the Aristotelian Society*, (1974–5).

SUCHTING, W., ' "Productive Forces" and "Relations of Production" in Marx', *Analyse und Kritik*, 4.2 (1982).

TAWNEY, R. H., *Religion and the Rise of Capitalism*, London, 1926.

VAILLANCOURT, P. and J.–G., 'Government Aid to Worker Production Co-operatives', *Synthesis*, 11.3 (1978).

VANEK, J., *The General Theory of Labour-Managed Market Economies*, Ithaca, NY, 1970.

VAN INWAGEN, P., *An Essay on Free Will*, Oxford, 1983.

VAN PARIJS, P., *Evolutionary Explanation in the Social Sciences*, Totowa, NJ, 1981.

—— 'Marxism's Central Puzzle', in Ball and Farr (eds.), 1984.

WALDRON, J. (ed.), *Nonsense upon Stilts*, London, 1987.

WEBER, M., *The Protestant Ethic and the Spirit of Capitalism*, London, 1930.

WOOD, A., *Karl Marx*, London, 1981.

YOUNG, G., 'Justice and Capitalist Production', *Canadian Journal of Philosophy*, 8.3 (1978).

ZIMMERMAN, D., 'Coercive Wage Offers', *Philosophy and Public Affairs*, 10.2 (1981).

Name Index

Index

Subject Index[*]

[*] I am grateful to Claire Creffield for excellent advice and help—G.A.C.